I0459067

JOHN HINCKLEY JR.
WHO I REALLY AM

JOHN HINCKLEY JR.

WITH JASON NORMAN

WILD BLUE
P R E S S

WildBluePress.com

JOHN HINCKLEY JR. published by:
WILDBLUE PRESS
P.O. Box 102440
Denver, Colorado 80250

Publisher Disclaimer: Any opinions, statements of fact or fiction, descriptions, dialogue, and citations found in this book were provided by the author, and are solely those of the author. The publisher makes no claim as to their veracity or accuracy, and assumes no liability for the content.

Copyright 2025 by John Hinckley Jr., Jason Norman

All rights reserved. No part of this book may be reproduced in any form or by any means without the prior written consent of the Publisher, excepting brief quotes used in reviews.

WILDBLUE PRESS is registered at the U.S. Patent and Trademark Offices.

ISBN 978-1-964730-96-7 Hardcover
ISBN 978-1-964730-97-4 Trade Paperback
ISBN 978-1-964730-95-0 eBook
Cover design © 2025 WildBlue Press. All rights reserved.

Interior Formatting and Book Cover Design by Elijah Toten
www.totencreative.com

WHO I
REALLY AM

CONTENTS

"PRETEND"

Pretend you are a virgin on fire
An outcast in the midst of madness
The scion of something unthinkable
Satan's long-lost illegitimate son
A solitary weed among carnations
The last living shit on earth
Dracula on a crowded beach
A child without a home
The loser of a one-man race
Rare meat thrown to a hungry lion
A faded flag on a windy day
Welcome to the truth
Welcome to reality
Welcome to my world.

John Hinckley Jr.

INTRODUCTION

Years of planning were about to pay off. So many hopes and dreams were about to come true.

In seconds, I would finish a job I'd started years before. Not the college degree I would never get. Not the music stardom career I'd failed to start. This accomplishment would mean so much more.

I would take a human life.

As strong as that statement sounds, it doesn't even touch the magnitude of this act.

The life would be of one of the most powerful, most beloved men in America, perhaps even the world. Only two months before, tens of millions of people had chosen him to run a country that needed some direction. His face, his name, symbolized America itself.

I was going to take it away. And then, for maybe the first time in my life, I could say that I'd accomplished something.

Just one more act, one quick deed, and everything I'd been planning would finally happen.

I had a rush I'd hardly felt in my life. I'd been hoping for this moment for years. I'd tried and failed elsewhere, but it was going to work this time. It was the best chance I would ever get.

It was tough, and it was harmful, even murderous, but it was right. To get to heaven, sometimes you have to walk through hell. I felt I was due some just desserts that tasted great.

Millions of people would see what was about to happen. They would remember it forever. Nearly two decades before, a president had been shot dead in public, and no one, including me, would ever forget where they were at the moment they learned of it. Hell, I'd been in elementary school, and I could walk you through every minute of my day that November. Moments from now, I would create another such happening.

For so many, my name would join the ranks of the infamous. It might even go to the top. John Wilkes Booth had been dead for over a century, but his name would be written in pitch-black ink forever. Same with the darkened moniker of Lee Harvey Oswald.

Now it would be me, John Hinckley Jr. If nothing else, history would remember me long after anyone present, or even alive, on that afternoon of March 30, 1981.

I was strangely okay with that. For the first time in my life, people would know me. I'd spent much of the past quarter century without a shred of direction. Very little to show for it.

I'd never wanted to be hated. If it were up to me, I would be famous already, but for the right reasons. The music career that I'd tried to start would have propelled me through the entertainment world. I would become as famous as a certain British foursome whose legendary appearance on *The Ed Sullivan Show* in 1964 had become an official kickoff of my own foray into music.

But that had kept *not* happening. I'd tried and tried and tried, and I'd gotten nowhere in my lyrical career. Forget albums, TV show appearances, my name being called on the radio. I don't think I'd ever even played a gig. It was as if nature was cruelly taunting me, keeping my dream just out of reach. I'd felt almost forced. Fate was bullying me, saying that if I couldn't be famous and loved, I would damn well better be infamous and hated.

As long as I was known. As long as people, then and of the future, would hear my name and make an immediate association. They'd known Oswald and Booth for these reasons. They would make the same connection with Sirhan Sirhan and even Mark David Chapman, whom I despised, despite here, only a few months later, following in his bloody footsteps.

If my dreams wouldn't come true, I would have to create my own mark, and many, including the man in front of me and the millions who had voted him into the White House two months before, would see it as a nightmare. By taking down someone who was famous for all the right reasons, I would be equally known for the worst ones.

It was nothing personal. It never had been. I wasn't a political fellow myself, though my family certainly had been. One of my brothers was planning to have dinner with the vice president's son a few days from then.

I didn't dislike Ronald Reagan. I never had. I still don't today. That's what people would never understand.

Hell, I didn't understand it myself. How could I do this, for the reasons floating through the warped cavern that was my mind, and had been for so long?

Well, because at that time, they seemed plausible. They seemed personal. They were special.

I can't say I'd always been a huge movie fan, but one cinematic masterpiece had grabbed and occupied a piece of my mind and heart as large as any other memories I had. Five years before, I'd walked into a theater and never been the same since. I'd seen the story of a young woman and a man who'd done what was necessary for her. Now I would do the same, just as he had, for that very lady. His actions had given her the same happy ending Hollywood loves, and now I would create my own.

Not for me, or not just for me. For us. She and I. Two people who would live together forever in harmony, and maybe even in eternity afterward.

Few would understand. I didn't expect them to. They were thinking wrong and doing wrong. My world, my reality, was the place to live and prosper. My intellect and foreshadowing had placed me somewhere so much better than their environment. I'd spent decades in their existence, but I'd found something else. I didn't understand why more people didn't have my amazing rationale. I could never comprehend why people were so resistant to live in a land like my own. Why was I the only person I knew who could think so clearly?

My role model, whom I'd met on movie screens a few dozen times over back through 1976, had shown me a sense of direction that few had. Like myself, he'd been surrounded by people who didn't try hard enough to understand his plight, to care about him as a person. But he'd been enough of a man, enough of a person, to do what was right for people who needed a little help, even if they hadn't really earned it from him. To do right simply because it's right; that's what a role model does.

Even if the guy in question didn't actually exist. He was a creation of Hollywood, a character being played by someone. Someone who acted for a living. Someone who, the very next day, would win the second Academy Award of his career.

He was real enough for me. His actions were justified enough for me. He'd done it, or almost done it, and now I was going to follow in his footsteps, maybe take an extra one, and win the heart of a beautiful, talented, friendly young lady whom millions had watched right alongside of me on those same screens.

I was going to kill *the president*. The individual name of the man was irrelevant. I'd come close to killing the former president. I'd been planning this murder for some time. I didn't care if Jimmy Carter had been re-elected, or if someone else had beaten Reagan for the Republican nomination. Whoever the president was, he was going to die, and I was going to be proud to be the one who made it happen.

In a few seconds, President Reagan would be gone forever. My mission would be accomplished. I would be left behind as a human example of a guy who never quit on his dream and his true love.

Hated? Loved? Adored? Admired? Detested? Even killed right then and there? I'd prepared myself for all of these possibilities and so many more.

Earlier that day, I'd tried to explain to someone—the person who had been the object of my affection for so long.

Well, affection was my word. Others went with fixation. Still others called it an obsession to the levels of psychosis. All a matter of perspective. For me, this was an act of love, and I needed to let someone know.

I'd seen her for years. Talked to her. Had the honor of meeting this beautiful, intelligent lady, whose heart I always knew I could one day win. I just needed one more quick chance, one more act of proof that I would go further for her than any partner she would ever meet in her life. I was everything she would need and want, and she was about to see it.

It was time. No more failing. Nothing else to try and not make it. I had a dream, and it was coming true. The death I was about to cause was for the greater good, for me and her.

Just as he always had, President Reagan made whatever time he could for his public. An eternally optimistic, friendly man by nature, he always let America know that he appreciated the work they'd done to put him in office.

Just seconds away now. He stepped from a building he'd just been inside. I was but a few feet away, almost close enough to reach out and grab him.

But I would never have time for that. My hand, already in my jacket, closed around my RG-14. It's a small enough gun that I could pull it out, even point it at him, quickly enough to avoid anyone noticing. The little baby was full of Devastator bullets, which explode on impact. I was going to end him, but I still hoped it would be fast enough that he didn't feel much.

He raised his left arm and waved. His ever-present smile stretched across his face.

He'd done both so many times before. These would be the last.

I pulled the trigger. Everyone heard the shots.

As I changed the world, my final thought was one last hope that my true love would finally feel the same about me....

1. CHILDHOOD

From the moment I shoved myself into the media spotlight, from the absolute second that the name Hinckley began to live in infamy, the media, and so many others, tripped all over themselves to find the answer to the most obvious question.

Why?

What the hell makes a man shoot the president of the United States, particularly right in a crowd of people? Doing it is ridiculous; doing it right in front of a huge group of witnesses, many of whom are armed, knowing that you're going to get caught and maybe even killed right then and there? Just one more aspect of the insanity that had long enveloped me.

Many people assumed I had some sort of political grudge against Reagan. Maybe I was a Jimmy Carter devotee, furious that our new president had the gall to knock him out of office. Perhaps Reagan had done something while he was governor of California that I was angry about, now scared that he would carry it over into the White House. I could have been some kind of secret agent on a mission from some other world leader, taking out my president to impress my master.

That would have been the easy answer. Looking back at assassinations, or attempts, throughout history, most of the perpetrators have had personal issues with their targets, people who, always just in the mind of these crazy people, had done harm to them and theirs.

Well, that ended pretty quickly. There was nothing to find in that regard. I wasn't a political fellow any more than the average news reader and voter. Reagan hadn't done anything to me or anyone else.

The media wanted a huge scandal. They wanted some sort of explosive, sensationalistic background. They were looking for an atomic bomb-level reason behind my act.

And they were just as surprised by what they *didn't* find. They were shocked at how anticlimactic the answer truly was.

Once my justification came to public light, people were floored at its absolute pettiness. I'd attempted to murder the leader of America... because I thought it would impress a young actress.

If my actions had seemed incomprehensible before, now America was knocked right off its axis. How could *anyone* find any sort of rationale in this?

So they kept looking for a new reason. What in the holy hell could have addled my mind so much that I actually thought something like this was legitimate, that it would have the effect I'd so hoped for? Where did that come from? How did it begin?

The media was looking for a cause, a rationalized explanation for the inexplicable. "Hey, here's how he went bad. This is the specific individual thing that pushed him over the edge!"

Maybe I was a drug addict whose brain was fried (not even close). Perhaps a soldier from Vietnam with a post-traumatic-shattered mind (not quite—the draft ended when I turned 18, so I just missed it). Or the old reliable explanation for adults stigmatized as doing evil—child abuse!

Yeah, that must have been it. I must have been beaten, starved, and brainwashed by evil parents, right? Something must have happened to me early on that slanted me for good! That's where the search always starts when adults do acts of random evil, doesn't it?

Again, there was nothing to find there. My household, my upbringing, were as normal as most and more so than many. You could stretch the word "average" across about 90% of my life, especially my first two decades.

By the time I showed up to the Hinckley family in Southern Oklahoma in late May 1955, my family had been around. I'm pretty sure I was, as parents like to diplomatically say, a *surprise*. In other words, a nice way of expressing that they were ready to live out their lives with no more additions. I always like to console myself that, after naming my older brother Scott, they wanted another son just so they could have a John Jr. in the family.

It wasn't that things had been tough for them. Not in the family sense. Scott tore things up all the way through school, turning into the same businessman my dad saw himself as, and expected, or certainly wanted, me to become as well.

I always called my sister Diane "Miss Everything," and this actually wasn't an exaggeration. Diane was only two years older than me, but she was always on fast forward: straight "A"s in school, Homecoming Queen, everything else. She didn't necessarily rub all that in my face, no more so than most sisters like to torment their little brother, but I would spend a lot of my life feeling like I was in the darkness of her shadow.

Business-wise, though, it was another story, at least at first. My father was a human oil magnet. He could practically look at a map and tell people where to drill, and his bosses had been using his skills there for quite some time.

He'd struck out on his own a few times, but things hadn't really worked out. He could always find oil, could always predict the best places to look, but his name wasn't established enough for those with money to see him as credible. Oil can take some serious time to pull out, and simply getting started on a single operation costs some serious dough. The right people weren't willing to donate either.

If they'd given him a few more weeks and dollars, we might have flourished. But the oil industry was starting to die out by the late 1950s, and what little was left was being sucked up by the big corporations. One man, or even a handful of men, as was the case with my dad, couldn't topple the giants, and my father saw his first few attempts fail.

But he knew where to go, and it wouldn't be far.

I was out of Oklahoma before my fifth birthday, so my memories of it are few. But there's one major one that ended up affecting my mother a hell of a lot more than me.

One day, I'd wandered out the front door of my house. She might have been with me, or watching from somewhere close, or maybe preoccupied for a moment elsewhere. My mother was always very attentive, so if she was distracted, I'm sure it didn't last for long.

Lucky me.

Somehow, I managed to stroll across our front lawn, onto the curb… and into the street. Right there in the middle of the pavement, I sat down.

Suddenly came the screams, mixed with foot pounding. My mother had roared out there like an Olympic track star, snatched me up, and hauled back to the house in a few nanoseconds. She didn't get in my face about it, or if she did, I don't remember, but I'm pretty sure a car or truck was at least in the vicinity. Damn sure I never set more than a few feet away from her for the rest of our time in Oklahoma.

But again, that didn't last. Just a state south, Texas had been booming in oil for decades, and the black liquid was powering up the entire state. My dad packed us up and headed south to Dallas.

This time, his skills paid off in every sense. Oil production, and the finances it provided, had tapered off a bit since the 1940s, but there was more than enough there for John Sr. to establish the Hinckley moniker in the community. Dallas was the new place for us to be.

While my father went off to work in the petroleum industry every day, I looked for my own spot in University Park. We were living in one of the area's most affluent areas. Big houses, more than one TV in the house, a large boat to take out in one of the nearby waters.

But I couldn't help but feel like looks were a bit deceiving. My father kept trying to make it on his own, but his work didn't come to profit; he kept having to do consulting work for others to make money. We were just scraping by, but you would never know that from our huge house and all the bells and whistles everywhere. He seemed to feel as if he could create a successful image to come home to and for our neighbors to see, it would eventually become reality.

That took time, but it did happen, if more due to his bosses than to him. His consulting firm hit things big and hard, and we would be on the move again.

But not yet.

As I always would, I'd established my own local roots in the sports world. Football, baseball—I did it all. Like about every boy in my neighborhood, I bounced back and forth between the Dallas Cowboys and the Texas Rangers, who had arrived in the area just after I did. We would stomp all over the Houston teams in typical intra-state fashion, and I would be the Most Valuable Player of both the Super Bowl and World Series, maybe even in the same year.

I never could have dreamed that I would actually become more famous than most guys who had won both of those honors.

I was trying to throw strikes and touchdown passes. I was doing what I could to make a few friends. I was doing just enough to make it in my new school. Just typical kid stuff.

Until that Friday in November 1963. A day, an afternoon, an hour that changed the world forever. A moment that the Hinckleys would experience right up close, even if nowhere near the levels of nearly two decades later.

2. THE SAD NOVEMBER DAY

Like most elementary schoolers on November 22, 1963, I was looking forward to the weekend. Report cards had come out, and I'd obtained my typical list of B's. The local football season was in swing, but winding down, and basketball would be around soon.

Honestly, I was even looking forward to the next week; with Thanksgiving coming, we would only have to show up for one or two days of school!

Walking down the hall after gym class that day, everyone looked excited. People were in large groups, talking at high speed and volume. Others were slumped against the wall, staring off into space. I figured that, like me, everyone was both tired from a full school week and excited about the shortened one coming up.

As I stepped into my classroom, I was shocked. My teacher was sitting there, crying.

I didn't know how to feel. This was almost brand new to me. My mother got upset sometimes, but I don't think I'd ever really seen her burst into tears. Grownups didn't do that sort of thing. Crying was for bratty kids, not adults. God knows my father would have hammered me if I'd shed a tear, just because I was a guy.

Another teacher showed up and told us what had happened. A few miles away, President John F. Kennedy had just been shot. They didn't have the full story yet, but it didn't look good.

Again, I had no clue what to say or do, as if any eight-year-old would. My family and I had visited, or at least passed by, Dealey Plaza tons of times. Now it would be forever burned into the nation's memory. My father had watched the Kennedy motorcade pass by that afternoon, just minutes before the murder.

The teachers, the staff, and especially the students could only stare, hoping that someone, anyone, would find enough poise to say, "Okay, here's what we're going to do now, and here's why it's going to work." But no one could, not for a while. As schoolkids do, I'd always assumed that teachers and principals knew how to handle every situation, but not even they could function. I'm sure having it happen so close by made it even tougher.

Finally, they told us we were going home early. It was the saddest early dismissal in American history. Not sure if she was aware, I raced home to tell my mother what had happened. But when I stepped through the house and saw her staring at the television, I knew she knew.

I kept hearing this weird new word: "assassin." I thought maybe my teacher had mentioned it when we talked about John Wilkes Booth, but I wasn't sure. I just knew that it sounded strange to hear, and certainly to say. It made me a little nervous, even when I would see it in the newspapers and eventually textbooks for the next few years. What did it mean? I kept envisioning some sniper-looking fellow dressed all in black, maybe in military fatigues. He didn't have a name, a past, even a present. He was just there to kill. It was all he'd ever done or would do. He was an enigma, a character, a persona you would see in a movie or on a TV show. It was hard to equate an assassin with a person.

I don't recall when exactly I found out that Kennedy had died. Like everyone else in America, I could only go about my day, not wanting to believe that something like this could occur. Our nation was either shocked to silence or too deep in tears to do too much.

How could this happen? How could someone assassinate the president of the United States? How could someone be so callous as to take out the man whom millions had elected to run the nation? Kennedy had been beloved by the nation over when he'd first taken office in 1961, although his numbers were dropping, particularly in our area. Those in the Deep South didn't always take to a Northerner whom many had seen as being born tasting the silver spoon, and the civil rights work he was doing didn't endear him to those in Texas. Even with a proud Texan as his vice president, people were starting to turn on Kennedy, and he'd noticed.

As he faced re-election the next year, many felt that the trip that would become his last was specifically to reassure the Lone Star State that he'd always been there for them. But he would never get a chance.

And then, two days later, we were shocked again when Lee Harvey Oswald was gunned down to his own eternity, right there on national television. He'd only been charged with the crime, and no one knew much as to why just yet, but that didn't matter to Jack Ruby, who meted out his own brand of justice right there in front of the cameras at the Dallas Police Department. No one would ever know why, or if, Oswald had killed Kennedy, or if he'd been the only one involved.

Once again, America didn't know how to react. Right outside the police station, people were already cheering the act. Many continued to do so later on.

As millions had seen him shoot an unarmed, handcuffed man, Ruby could hardly say he hadn't done it, nor would self-defense or an accident work. Instead, Ruby opted for something else, saying that his shock and sadness over the Kennedy murder had temporarily taken away his right to reason.

Not quite the insanity plea I would rather use, but not too far off.

It didn't work, and he was convicted of murder. In any case, up until his death in 1967, many still supported Ruby.

As was the case for millions of Americans, my family sleepwalked our way through Thanksgiving that year. We couldn't feel happy, certainly not thankful. We felt like there was no real direction to go.

I didn't think or care much about politics, but my parents certainly did. They'd been on the fence about Kennedy, but they despised his successor, Lyndon Johnson. My father admired Kennedy for going into combat in World War Two. After all, Kennedy at least had an excuse for being a liberal Democrat; he'd been born and raised in the North. Uber-conservatives like my parents saw the term "Southern Democrat" as an oxymoron, and they couldn't stand the new president.

Even as Barry Goldwater's chance dried up well before Johnson creamed him in the 1964 elections, my parents proudly posted the Republican's name on signs in our yard.

For the rest of that school year, I kept working—sports, classes, the typical ins and outs and ups and downs of elementary school. I kept dreaming of making it to the big leagues someday. No matter the sport, I was one of the standouts. I was one of the big men on Hyer Elementary's campus.

I liked music well enough, but no more so than most. I listened to the radio, mainly the country stations that were big in Texas. But by the end of 1963, I heard something new, and more and more often.

This wasn't country. It was snappier. Serious pop to it. More energy. Energy that I could feel. Energy that made me want to get up and dance, and eventually sing. These guys were on the radio enough that their lyrics started to become commonplace. My friends and I got more and more into it.

Over and over, a few guys, whose voices were accented in ways few of us in the Deep South had heard anywhere, were begging the ladies to let them hold their hands, to be their men. Judging from the way women were reacting, they didn't seem to need much persuading.

The next February, the voices in question showed their full human forms, landing at New York City's John F. Kennedy Airport, recently named after the fallen president. Thousands of people were there to greet a group that few in America had even glimpsed before.

Two days later, a man named Ed Sullivan introduced the Beatles. Hundreds in his Studio 50 and millions more watching all over the nation, more so than ever before to that point, danced, sang, and just generally felt a new sense of mania go rushing through them. Be it by "All My Loving," "She Loves You," or, of course, the finale of, "I Want to Hold Your Hand," these guys exploded onto our culture like the bombs Kennedy and Johnson had been dropping on Vietnam for years.

Staring at the TV, I could see my future. I knew exactly where I would end up. Sports, books, friends, family, everything else was secondary by miles.

Music was my life now. It always would be. Even if I wasn't double-digit age of yet, I knew exactly where I was going and that I would definitely end up right there.

People would forever know the name of John Hinckley Jr., the biggest star in the history of music.

That might be all they would ever know me for, but it would be more than enough.

3. MY FIRST STEPS TOWARD MUSIC

Like most young men who had seen the Beatles that wonderful night, and like many who would continue to see one boy band after another for the next few decades, I wasn't exactly open about my admiration for them. Hell, I was in grade school! I wasn't supposed to admit that I would have given everything but my left arm to be the one on that stage, hearing the screams from lovely young women across the studio, and many more watching from their homes! We boys liked to boast that we couldn't stand those Beatles, in all our juvenile pettiness, but I'd seen enough fellows rocking at the Sullivan show that I knew they were having a hell of a time, and I would have too, if I'd been there.

I didn't talk much about it at school or around my small circle of friends. Once I got home, however, it was a very different matter.

Actually, when you think about it, or at least when I remember it, this might have been my first mental episode back then. It's certainly a stretch to connect it to my later actions, but there was something there, and it had nothing to do with anything done to me. Not my parents, my friends or family, bullies at school, or anyone else.

I didn't see it as such back then—elementary and middle school boys don't think too hard about this—but it was basically an obsession. Not just an interest, lasting or passing. Not even a fixation. This was my first experience with a quality that would end up lasting for my entire life. It would be the way it would always be for me.

"Obsession" is considered a dirty word by many, but what those who don't go full-force into things the way I always have don't really consider is that we, the obsessed, don't always love it about ourselves. We just see it as getting into things and staying there. We have very few interests, but the ones we have will always be around.

Not because we like it. Not necessarily because we want it that way, but because it's the mental hand that we're dealt. Some of us handle it better than others.

But my life had changed, and I only had, needed, or even wanted one thing.

I was toiling away, putting pen to paper of my own lyrical creations as well. Songs sound so simple when you just hear them or read the lyrics alone. Think about it: "I'll tell you something, I think you'll understand. When I say that something, I wanna hold your hand!" How hard can it be to write something like that? Lennon and McCartney could have put that together in an afternoon, or so it sounded.

I could do that! I could put together more than enough tunes to fire off my own album. With a little time and effort, I would be the next big smash myself.

I was already dreaming of stardom. Many of us do at some point, especially after seeing something like the Beatles show. Who wouldn't want to be there? The world at your hands, loved across the globe, your ever-grinning face on TV, newspapers, and album covers everywhere? It would be a few years before Lennon made his infamous "more popular than Jesus" quote, but I would have believed it at that point.

And I wanted to be there as well. McCartney, Starr, Harrison, (of course) Lennon… and, someday in the very near future, Hinckley! Ed Sullivan would be clearing out his entire schedule for me! I would have women screaming my name and crowding around for kisses and autographs. All my friends at school would wish they could be me! My small circle of friends would expand at high speed. Amazing how cool you suddenly get when you're rich and famous!

So why couldn't I capture my own bottled lightning? One way to find out!

My parents had surprised me with a guitar for my 10th birthday, but they couldn't have guessed what I would do with it. I guess my dad thought I was interested in all sorts of music, not just what the Beatles had shown. He knew I sort of liked country, and he'd played in a jazz band in college, so I don't think he would have minded my picking up that habit.

At the very most, they thought I would probably strum away in my free time, between honor classes and sports practice. They didn't know, as I certainly didn't, that this would be the beginning of a focus that would last, to one degree or another, for decades.

Behind a locked door in my room, which, for me, was everything but another world to my home life, I sat there with my guitar, a pad and paper, and worked. Seclusion was everything but a necessity for me. I didn't have much of an attention span back then, as few hormone-crazed boys do, so any distraction could cause some catastrophic pause in my creative process. I didn't see any deep need to share my passion with my family. My brother and sister were too busy with their own lives to care much about what their little brother was doing, and my father would have liked nothing more than to reach up and yank my head out of the clouds. His first son was already showing the kind of academic work my father wanted, on the way to—he was certain—following him into the family business, or at least something more formal than a musical career.

My mother didn't exactly love my hopes to be the next Beatle, but she didn't step in front of them like he did. I think she figured that I was caught up in the wave of Beatlemania that had swept the country, and, like so many others, I would go full-force into it, lose interest, and move on to something else by the end of the year. Like a tidal wave crashing onto the beach or a firework exploding in the sky, it would be a huge deal, maybe even a nice sight, but it would be gone quickly, and I would be heading and thinking elsewhere. Something certainly more stable than performing.

But this was my new life, my first experience with literally being obsessed with something. I only wish it had been the last.

4. MORE ON MUSIC

From then on, it was all about the tunes. I stuck to sports and paid enough attention in class to maintain my typical B+ average, but I was hardly considering anything but making music.

When my family up and moved three hours south from University Park to College Park just before I started middle school, my parents thought I was staying in my room so much because I was depressed about it, my puberty-induced hormones going wild.

That wasn't entirely wrong. Even today, I still don't adapt well to major changes, which is part of the reason that, before I was fully released from being institutionalized, I was slowly worked back into society over a period of several years, rather than simply being shoved out the door. If that had been the case, I can almost guarantee I would have done something to get thrown right back in jail, as much as the world had changed.

I think that's part of the reason why so many prisoners or even residents, especially those who have been away as long as I was, spend so little time on the outside. The new world can scare and intimidate the hell out of you, and, being locked up for so long, you don't have much calmness or patience, so you respond with emotion and force to cover up your fear and anger. Then you get locked right back up. That's something that prisons, not just mental hospitals, should think more about—when a prisoner gets within a period, like a year, of his release date, it might be better to let him move in and out a few times, for a little longer each time, so he knows what to expect when he's out and how to handle it. Simply taking someone who has been locked in the same building for years, even decades, and expecting him to automatically be able to walk right back out into a productive lifestyle is unreasonable to the point of absurdity.

But getting back to what I was saying, isolating myself wasn't all about the fear of my new environment. Much of it was so I could keep focusing on my music. Hearing it, writing it, playing it, me and the music world were becoming one.

I started to work my way out of sports. Rather than playing, I started managing more. I kept stats and everything else in line for both the basketball and football teams, and I still pitched once in a while in baseball, but my focus was off the diamonds.

I'm still not entirely sure how this happened, but I was elected president of my seventh-grade homeroom class. I'm not sure if that was a welcoming gift to the new guy on campus, or maybe my classmates saw more in me than I did in myself, but I was pretty proud of that.

My normal, average life continued up through Highland Park High. I kept getting my B grades. Kept managing the football team. Joined the Spanish and Rodeo Clubs, and, ironically, the Student Government Club, although I've blocked out the memories of that. If we were in Deep Texas in the early 1970s, I'm pretty sure our political mindset was set in its way, and I don't feel the need to relive them now.

I had a small but solid circle of friends, and having a pool at my house certainly helped my social standing, especially in the summer.

The one thing I never did was date. I saw all of my friends leering after pretty girls, and some of the girls leering right back, but I never did much of that. I didn't have women exactly chasing me around, so I didn't feel the need to pursue them much. I was always pretty self-conscious about my looks, but not to the extent that I had a negative opinion of them. Girls weren't at my house, even to swim. My friends would go out on dates, maybe even trying to hook me up here or there, but I was never very receptive, other than a one-shot deal every once in a while. Women tended to see how few interests I had, how realistic my dreams of being a famous rock star truly were, and find a reason to date elsewhere.

In hindsight, some of my male friends probably thought I wanted to be more than friends with them. That's funny. That's really funny now. I can imagine how they felt when they learned that I'd tried to kill the president to impress a pretty girl.

And then the music kept coming. While my friends would be out living it up on the weekends, I was still up in my room, listening to the same Beatles albums again and again. My parents didn't like it much, or at least know how to handle it, especially after raising two extroverts in my siblings, but I think they were glad I was doing that instead of out boozing or drugging, which I was never a part of.

My friends and I would go to movies once in a while, but I was more about the concert life. The Beatles had already played their last American show together at San Francisco's Candlestick Park in August of 1966, and I'd been too young and too far away to make it up to New York for Woodstock in 1969, and if I could make a list of historical events I would have died to have attended live, those two would be at the top. But I got some pretty decent consolations.

My first concert was Iron Butterfly when I was about 16. I saw Bob Dylan do his thing live, along with the Who. Then, right after my junior year of high school ended in the summer of 1972, I saw a big chance.

Three and a half hours north in Fort Worth, the Rolling Stones were coming to town. Still trying to repair the damage from the Altamont disaster of 1969, the group had just kicked off the *Stones Touring Party* tour, and we were lucky enough to be their next stop.

I wasn't just going to watch them. I was going to meet them. Maybe inform them of my own musical dreams. Hell, maybe Keith Richards would let me show a couple of my personally created tunes on his guitar, and they would hire me right then and there as an opening act!

Dreams were starting to overtake me. Reality was becoming more created. I was building my own new world and getting ready to live in it.

Hours before the show was scheduled to begin, a friend and I pulled into the near-empty parking lot of the Tarrant County Convention Center. With lots of time and short lines to wait in, we got inside pretty fast.

Now what? We hadn't exactly walked in with a plan, other than getting there before the rush. We were going to sneak backstage to meet the band. Of course, they would be certain to welcome people who did that, right?

We got into the backstage area and found a small bathroom to hide in.

Then we waited. Minute by minute, hour by hour, we waited for them to show up. We couldn't wait to hear Mick Jagger's voice outside, describing his plans for the show. We knew Bill Wyman and Charlie Watts would be there soon, warming up. They would love to meet their new and two of their biggest fans!

Then the door opened. We stopped breathing.

But it wasn't Mick or Keith or Bill or anyone else from the band. Just a couple of roadies. Then security showed up. We could only stammer out why we were there.

Today, we would probably be arrested and banned from the arena, if not from ever seeing the Stones again. But these guys were surprisingly sympathetic. They took our tickets away and escorted us around the front.

But we still didn't leave. The show was sold out, but we managed to find scalpers eager to make a few bucks, and we paid, got back in, and rocked out to "Honky Tonk Woman" and "(I Can't Get No) Satisfaction." It's still one of the best concerts I've ever attended.

Okay, so I didn't walk away with new band membership. But just as when I'd seen the Beatles the previous decade, watching the Stones do their thing inspired me that I could be up on that stage too.

And maybe it was more than inspiration. It was feeding my obsession, my new reality. I was still forming the persona that I dreamed of becoming, maybe convincing myself that it was already here, or would be tomorrow.

I finished up at Highland Park. Now it was off to Texas Tech for college. My father was hoping that I would leave my musical pipe dreams at home and come back from my freshman year with some business classes and some new direction, hopefully toward a spot beside my brother in the family oil business.

But that's when I took the first steps out of my mind.

5. I START TO SLIP

Mental illness usually doesn't hit a person all at once. I've heard stories about basically normal people having a sudden, unexplainable psychotic break and ending up in a white coat with my arms confined behind my back, surrounded by padded walls for the rest of their short lives, but those are more made for drama, to scare people.

My insanity, at least the levels that would push me to nationwide infamy, came in small bits. One small step, one tiny section at a time. That's how a mind becomes destroyed. It's how you fall under your own spell. Little things happen, small changes come about, so miniscule that you don't really mind them, if you notice them at all.

Then more and more occur, and you just chalk them up to normalcy. You think that these are typical occurrences that everyone goes through. Part of growing up. Part of maturing. You keep changing, usually for the worse.

You're typically the last to notice these things, because, again, you believe that those around you are having the same things happen to them. But the people near you start to notice. Your family, your friends, they realize that you're not the same person you were. Not yesterday, but maybe a year ago. They notice certain changes in you, different habits.

While they do notice these alterations, many people don't feel the need to point them out. There's quite a few reasons there as well. They might not think it's any big deal; you're just not who you were a few years ago. No one is.

Maybe you're in a bad mood, one that's lasting a little longer than usual. Maybe you've found something new to worry about.

The worst that people usually do when they see these changes in you is to separate. They distance themselves from you. If they don't like what they see, they start avoiding you. They go out of their way to find other things to do, to worry about. Reasons to stay away.

My reasons for choosing Texas Tech to further my education weren't really special or even my own. My father kept looking for a way to kick my ass into gear, and he knew a college education could do that. He figured that if I just got a taste for the business world, I would take to it like he and Scott had.

I hoped they were right. Maybe I would change and be better for it. But I was still more of a follower. Many people from my high school went to Texas Tech, in part because it was pretty close to home, and that was good enough for me.

And then everyone left—me off to Tech, and my parents to Denver. My father hated the sweltering Texas weather and saw some good business opportunities in Colorado. My mother had grown into the Dallas community, and, though far less enthused to pick up and head so far west, she went along with it.

It didn't take long for things to go wrong for me in college. Maybe not *wrong*, per se, but certainly not in the direction my family had hoped. Just as I had in grade school, I kept going through the motions of one business class after another, just waiting for it to get done so I could work on my pseudo-music career. I did just enough not to fail in the classroom—after all, I was going to be the biggest thing to hit the music world since the Fab Four.

Those were my first big steps into my own created reality. I was slowly becoming not John Hinckley the student, not even the person. I was John Hinckley, the musician. That quickly became my entire persona. When I was working through the foreign language of an accounting class or watching a teacher work off a computer that took up three-fourths of the room, all I could think about was getting on stage. Jamming it up and hearing the crowds go wild for me. The person I dreamed of becoming started to take over. The character I longed to portray on stage bled into my personal life.

I never considered the possibility that the people I watched on stage were just normal folk off it. That Lennon, Jagger, Dylan, and everyone else were up there putting on a show, and that once the show ended, the lights went down, and the crowds went home, they went about their normal daily lives as much as anyone. Their lifestyles were certainly more hectic, probably more enjoyable than my own—I couldn't see how anyone could ever get tired of seeing legions of lovely women swooning over you—but they were regular people with unusual lines of work.

I didn't consider that. Didn't want to think about it. Pushed it out of my mind. Who they were on the stage was who they were off it, and someday, someday very soon, that would be me.

Armed with my trusty guitar, I traded study time for one jam session after another throughout my freshman year. I was friends with a lot of guys who also dreamed of making it in music, and we would pool our resources together in the dorms. I'm not sure how great we sounded or how much progress we made, but it sure was fun.

So much fun that I *happened* to neglect signing up for the spring term in time to grab my most important classes. So much that I *happened* to have to drop a class early in the term.

And so much that I decided to take the fall term off when my sophomore year began. I filled my parents' head with some lies about honing my work ethic and being a busboy at a local Italian restaurant, the first job I'd had since supermarket cashier-ship in high school.

Not really. I just needed more time to devote to finding my last key to success in the music business. Fulfilling my true calling.

I got an apartment in Dallas with a buddy I'd met in my freshman year, and we spent days, nights, weekends, any time they would allow it, rocking in a church rec room. We asked all over the place, but no one could ever squeeze us a gig. Our personal highlight during that period was hitchhiking a few hundred miles south to Austin for a music festival, which was so great that I can't recall a single band that played there. It was certainly no one on the levels I'd seen at some previous performances.

The following semester, it was back to Texas Tech. My father could never understand why everyone in the world didn't have a work ethic as strong as his. He'd zoomed through his own college years, so the thought of taking any time off, let alone an entire semester, for any reason short of a terminal illness was unfathomable to him. I didn't tell him that I'd decided to switch my major to English, minoring in history. I figured a little creative exposition couldn't hurt my songwriting career. I still wanted to wring songs, and I was plying hell out of that trade during my hours of solitude, but I figured it was time to expand a bit. Maybe I would write a bestselling novel. Maybe I would win some Pulitzers as a journalist. Of course, if those didn't work out, I could always go somewhere and teach history. I had enough personal passion for that subject that I could have turned it into a success.

All, of course, to have something to fall back on during lulls in my music career. Every artist has those from time to time, right?

That ended up being a pretty solid change for me. Everyone else thought so, at least. As far as they could see, I was putting more and more time into my schooling. I was turning in my work. I even made the Dean's List one semester. Here were the focus and enthusiasm that my parents had desperately hoped I would find for so long.

But I never really felt too different. It was more of the same. Go to class, do just enough to get by, then head back to my apartment and listen to records and music on my headphones. While I still wanted to charge out at the head of a band, like the Beatles or the Stones, I was getting more and more into Bob Dylan at that point. I really admired how hard he'd worked to do music since his motorcycle accident, and how much he could do with a guitar and harmonica. I was getting seriously into folk music, and he was my tour guide.

More and more, I became Hinckley the performer, despite the fact that, after years of makeshift rehearsals, I'd never actually played a single gig, not even as a background performer or opening act. I kept seeing myself, visualizing a life I dreamed of, as the next famous musician, the guy who was one break, one ounce of good luck, away from being a one-in-a-trillion, later-that-day success!

I'd long convinced myself that this was only a day away. Maybe less. But I could think of little else. Even my improving marks didn't affect me too much. Not that I wasn't proud of my success; I just didn't see it as important. This was just something that I was using to kill time until my destiny finished kicking in.

My new reality was coming closer and closer, enveloping more of me than I realized. I would basically spend a few minutes in the morning glossing over my requirements for the day—a class, a quiz, maybe a paper. Nothing too important. I was going to get those things done and not worry much about whether the grade was an A+ or F-.

But I'd earmarked the rest of the time almost down to the second. I was going to work on this song. I was going to finish that song. I was going to practice for this long. I was going to peruse the local ads for bands looking for additions, or places looking for those ready to do their thing.

My studies? I did them and then they were over. My music? I obsessed over it, reworking a lyric again and again until it sounded right, aligned with the melody. I would practice the same track again and again, reluctantly putting it away when I got too tired, and knowing I would spend twice as much time on it the very next day. I hated sleeping. It had the nerve to interfere with my trek to stardom.

More and more, I lived a lifestyle I was nowhere near. I knew that famous rock stars spent their days just like this. Well, except the inconvenience of schooling! They would go out and rehearse, dodge the media back home, and spend the rest of their time knocking out one outstanding song lyric after another.

I fully expected my phone to ring, a record dealer with an offer. I knew I would get something in the mail, an invitation to come open a major show, and then close with the main event. It would be nothing for Bob Dylan, Keith Richards—hell, even George Harrison—to show up at my door and say, "John, we heard you play, and we were wowed! We *wish* we had that kind of skill when we were starting out! Please, *please* come be a part of our act!" It was only a matter of time.

And, really, I don't think I minded it. I was living in a fantasy world, but hardly a nightmare. Other people saw it and still today, they label it as some sort of delusion, but I liked it, and I intended on staying there as long as I could. Others couldn't, wouldn't, didn't understand, but they didn't have to. Even if I was living alone, I was a happy, happy man.

But, as I figured out pretty quickly, I wouldn't stay that way. Those famous rock stars didn't live alone. They had millions of fans after them every day. They had people who loved them. They didn't have to live a life of solitude.

Sure, I didn't want that. But who would be good enough? Who might be a suitable love for the music world's newest sensation? Who would be there for me, no matter what? Who was worth giving up the adoration of millions of screamers to come home to, or at least to a hotel to, every night after the show?

It would take some time. But in about a year, I would venture into a Hollywood movie theater and come out with the perfect answer.

6. NOT HITTING IT BIG

As far as anyone else could see, things were going as well as ever for the Hinckleys in the fall of 1975. My parents had had some business troubles, but they never burdened us kids with them. My sister was getting married. My brother was looking to break into the oil business himself, and my father was praying to himself that at least one of his sons would carry on the family business.

And I'd finally found my own direction. My family wasn't happy with my switch in majors, but they let that go pretty fast when they saw how much my grades had fired up. I kept filling their heads with ridiculous stories about being the big man on campus, the professors' new favorite, talking to author agents, doing everything.

In the end, I could fool everyone except myself. Even with everything else going on, as much as I tried to be happy for everyone else—and I *was* happy for them, to a large degree—I was still down about college life. I wasn't learning what I wanted to know. I was good at it, did fine with the course material, but I didn't feel anything for Texas Tech in the academic sense. There was a ton of stuff I could do. I just couldn't find much that I wanted to do. It was all about biding time. I was still waiting, still knew, that my music career was going to come to fruition anytime now, and that those messages that Woody Guthrie was blasting through my headphones for hours every day were forms of subliminal communication that I would be up there next to him performing one day, and that he couldn't wait for it to happen.

The fall term ended and the winter one began. 1976 was going to be just as great. I was going to stay right there on the Dean's

List and then knock out a few more years, on the roll all the way to a diploma, maybe even with honors.

It was never going to happen. I knew that and had for a while. By this point, I was so used to dropping out of school and letting my family down in the bargain, that it would be only time before it happened again.

I made it about halfway through the first term of 1976, and things were still going fine.

But not for me. I wasn't thinking about my grades, my exams, nothing there. It was all about my music career, and I was going to throw everything else aside for that in a second.

My brother, like most of my family, had been there for me more than I deserved. Back in high school, he'd handed me down my first car, a 1965 Ford Mustang. Most guys would have waxed, polished, treated that vehicle better than their first girlfriends. Me? I hardly touched it and wouldn't have noticed if the back end fell off. More out of disgust than anything else, my dad had ditched it about a year later.

Why did my brother make the same mistake? Who knows? Scott was a hell of a lot nicer than I was. I just know that, come early 1976, I was behind the wheel of a sporty red Camaro that many of my classmates envied.

Then things went right back downhill. Rather, I shoved them downhill.

Giving my parents the same excuse about signing up late, I whined that I couldn't get the classes I'd hoped for. Then I *happened* to decide to drop a class. I guess I was piling one small disappointment on top of the next, building up to the big one.

That March, I dropped a bomb in the form of a letter home. No return address, not much to it. Just letting them know that I was leaving and didn't want to be found.

"I know you'll never understand," I wrote, as if anyone ever could or would fathom something so idiotic, "but I'm too miserable here to take it any longer. I'm sorry I'm doing this to you." I didn't even tell them where I was going or why.

They went into a panic. For all they knew, I'd found a nice cliff and jumped off. Those are pretty plentiful in Texas.

But there was nothing they could do. I was 21. I was an adult. I had every legal right to drop out of school, run away, and toss my future into the trash if I wanted to. Grownups are allowed to light their own lives on fire.

As it usually is, the truth ended up being very anticlimactic. It had been all about me not having the spine to be up front with them.

Per usual, I was thinking of me. Me and my music career. I was gonna go and find my success, even if I wasn't sure where the hell it was.

Well, I could narrow it down a bit. It was either Los Angeles or New York City. The Big Apple would eventually play a ton of roles in my life, but this time, I headed out west. To the land of famous people and agents so desperate to land the next headlining act that they would sign anyone with a tape.

That was what I kept telling myself. I'd put together a makeshift album of my tunes, and I just knew that the first representative I met would be jumping to put his name right below mine on a headline.

With a suitcase in one hand and a huge bag of tapes in the other, I stepped off the plane at LAX and jumped on a bus to Hollywood.

And then, where? Who the hell knew?

I walked. And walked. And kept walking. So much to choose from and no clue what to do or where to go.

For the first time that day, I did something sensible. As in, I found a little efficiency apartment, two blocks off Sunset Boulevard, right near the Sunset Strip.

Now I had a home base. A rally point to begin and end.

And that $100 a month spot would be my home for the next half year. When I should have been back in Texas banging out my sophomore degree, I was knocking on one agent's door after another. I went to Capital Records. I stopped by United Records. This, there, and everywhere else, just knowing every morning that *that day* would be the one where I found someone to reach out and yank my career over the finish line to stardom.

Sure. All I had was… no resume, no references, nothing but a tape that anyone with a guitar and a tape recorder could toss together in a day.

One secretary after another promised that their boss would get the material and be in touch soon. Agent after agent didn't call, even to politely let me know that I wasn't what they were looking for. I doubt I would need both hands to count the number of people who even listened to a single song of mine. They figured I was just some directionless dreamer with nothing going on.

Damned right.

Oh, and by the way, that car my brother had fixed up and gifted to me? Less than four months after picking up the keys for the first time, I'd sold it and used it for bus and plane fare and rent for my new place. I'm pretty sure that if my brother had been standing there when he found out I sold the car, he probably would have put me in intensive care.

Pretty soon, even all that money was gone. I wrote some letters home, first letting my folks know that I was, in fact, alive and not suffering, and then to implore them for some financial help.

My parents were shocked, saddened, depressed as hell. But not totally surprised. They felt that I was directionless, self-destructive, and determined to stay that way until I hit rock bottom. I'm sure they'd felt I'd landed there a few times already, only for me to hop on my personal backhoe and start digging again.

Then I changed my mind. Maybe this was some sort of rite of passage I had to get through before success. Maybe I was supposed to suffer for a while to appreciate the shit that we struggling artists have to go through to hit it big. Maybe if my journey was a little tougher, it would feel better when I actually did make it to the top.

Kicked out of my apartment, almost all of my tapes gone, it was me, the streets, and my guitar. The loneliest, most unwelcoming and unforgiving spots in the entire state, maybe even the country, were out there, reaching out their dark claws to pull me in. There wasn't a louder, faster place in America than Hollywood during the day; at night, it was like the world's biggest haunted house.

I was really into Woody Guthrie at that point. I really admired him, and not only for his music. He'd touched and inspired—and still does today—so many different genres of music. We're talking about everything from folk to kids' songs to "This Land Is Your Land." It's tough to imagine a more diverse career that has touched so many fellow artists and fans.

As late as 2012, this fellow was somehow still putting out new albums. Even though I'd been in middle school when he died, I sometimes felt ashamed that it had taken me so long to pick up on him.

Even his final round had been inspirational as hell. Huntington's disease, still one of the medical world's most prevalent enemies today, had tortured him for years before mercifully taking his life, just as it had his mother's life. Just as it would steal two of his daughters' lives. He'd had to fight that battle in front of millions, and I, like most of his heartbroken fans, respected the hell out of him for it.

In the midst of his epic-sized collection of songs, I kept stumbling onto "Hobo's Lullaby." More of a spoken-word solo, one man and his guitar, it was the sort of tune I'd put out in my personal demos.

"Go to sleep, you weary hobo," Guthrie implored. "Let the towns drift slowly by. Listen to the steel rails humming. That's the hobo's lullaby."

I figured he was sending me a message from beyond the grave. I didn't think it was a coincidence that I would land so deeply in his work, particularly *this* work, just as I lost everything.

Maybe I could put his words to life. I'd lived very comfortably for a long time, but it was the only lifestyle I'd ever known. Maybe the key to success, maybe a better life would be to simply lay my head wherever I happened to be. To not worry about the high-speed world I was living in. I had everything I wanted, but maybe not what I needed. I'd recently seen his biopic *Bound for Glory* and thought it was another sign that I had to heed his words.

Was having nothing the key to having everything? I was going to find out.

For weeks, I slept on roofs, park benches, on street corners, everywhere. I begged for food and ate every other day in a good week. I went days without bathing, and even then, I could only get as clean as a quick jaunt into a local restaurant bathroom could provide.

Oh, yeah, regular bathroom usage was a luxury itself. My body became conditioned to "release" maybe once a day, if that. It's not like I was putting much in there to digest anyway.

But my days weren't totally empty. I still had a few tapes to hand out, and I did so. I was still meeting friendly secretaries and other office folk, if not the agents themselves. I still hoped that one day I would get lucky.

Well, I did, although not in the way that I'd hoped.

Mid-1970s Hollywood was a place of extremes. I walked up Sunset Boulevard and saw the lap of the upper class, the people who were making money and showing it. Nice buildings, affluent cars, well-dressed preppies strolling quickly to their next eight-figure business venture.

Then I wandered farther, maybe had to turn down the block, and nothing but sleaze. X-rated film theaters everywhere. Dirt and grime and graffiti looming like the place had a psychotic decorator. Prostitutes who didn't even try to hide what they were doing.

In my growing insanity, I convinced myself that these ladies of the night actually gave a damn about me. They really saw me as something other than a dollar dispenser. They would remember me three minutes after our tryst.

Who cared? I took advantage. I didn't overindulge, but I had a few outings with these ladies. Once I was browsing a porn shop, and some gal slipped close and informed me what she wanted and what she was willing to offer.

Sounded acceptable to me. We snuck off to the back, had at it all over a couch, and went on about our business. As I left, I realized she was the cashier's girlfriend. I wondered if he'd been in on the matter all along. Maybe he'd set it all up. Maybe he'd watched us from a hole in the wall.

Perusing the porn industry? Diddling with prostitutes? I didn't know it, but I was already following in the footsteps of one of my future cinematic role models.

Yes, it's time to arrive there, the film that would become the reason people know and often despise the Hinckley name today.

***

Since before I'd even left Texas to venture out to Hollywood, I'd heard rumblings about some new film. Like just about the rest of the moviegoing public, I'd been as wowed by the second *Godfather* as by the first one. Robert De Niro had done just as great a job as Vito Corleone in the sequel as Marlon Brando in the original, and now he and Martin Scorsese were back together. I'd thought their *Mean Streets* flick from a few years before had been pretty cool, so when I heard about the new flick, I figured I would probably check it out.

Another upcomer would be trying to deepen her mark in the acting game as well. Like De Niro, she had some history with Scorsese. Their *Alice Doesn't Live Here Anymore* collaboration in 1974 was a hell of a ways away from *Mean Streets*, but this new one was much closer.

Since I'd arrived in Hollywood, the film had been everywhere. Back then, before the advent of home video, films stayed in theaters for a hell of a long time. I'm talking years sometimes, as long as the flicks were selling tickets. Again, without much at home aside from network television—cable had been around a while but was still looking for the match to light its powder keg—people usually had to leave their homes for entertainment, and if the movies were good enough, there was nothing wrong or even that unusual about seeing the same shows again and again.

I won't say I made it a priority to check out the film. I wasn't there on opening night, fistfighting with other patrons for a spot. It had been out since February, and now it was summer. But people kept seeing it, it kept making money, and it was getting good reviews. I figured I may as well go ahead and see it.

That woman from *Alice*? No, I'm not talking about Ellen Burstyn, who'd won an Oscar for it. This is about Audrey, a friend of Alice's son Tommy in the flick. Her role hadn't been especially prevalent, but I did notice her strumming a guitar in the flick, which I was, of course, impressed with, having spent so much time in that pastime myself. I'd seen some of her work in the past, and on the previews for this new film, so I figured she would do well.

But, again, I didn't only go in to see her. I figured that, just as with *Alice*, she might steal some scenes, but not really the show. I was also there for De Niro, for Scorsese, even for Harvey Keitel, who'd done great in *Mean Streets* himself.

My life as I knew it would be over soon. Much later, American history would change forever.

And it would be because of me. It would be because of a woman named Jodie.

Jodie Foster.

7. JODIE ARRIVES

Everyone always puts all the blame on 1976's *Taxi Driver* for forming and fueling my obsession with Jodie Foster. That's actually something of an oversimplification.

I'd actually been watching her do her acting thing for years before that, all over TV, like when she was Becky Thatcher in the *Tom Sawyer* movie three years before *Taxi Driver*, when she was an 11-year-old kid.

Now stop right there. I was a *fan*, and that's all. Like millions of people, I enjoyed watching her because she was a talented actress. Not because she was a kid. I'm not into that, and I never was. I have never in my life been attracted to the extremely underaged. It took years for me to see her as an attractive woman—again, a lovely, mature *woman*. I'm not about being into young girls. Personally, I think what those people do is a hell of a lot more obscene than anything I'm known for.

Taxi Driver didn't get me interested in Jodie, but it reached out and yanked me into her world, or at least the world I saw on the screen. No longer was I, like so many others, just a fan of hers, sitting there watching on screens small and big. I could become a part of the life she lived. I could be her hero. I could rescue her, have her swoon at my large-hearted masculinity, and take her off into a safe world, where we would dote on each other forever.

The film provided me an outlet to that. It didn't just make me fall further for her; it showed me who I could become, and why I should try so hard to do so.

Honestly, she wasn't even the first thing I noticed about the film. I was more taken with her protector. I saw more of a role model in him than anyone else I'd known.

I'm talking about Travis Bickle, the role which, even after half a century, a novel-length resume, and all his Academy Awards, many people still put first on their list of Robert De Niro's most recognizable works. I could relate to that lonely, directionless, dead-end job lifestyle he had. He had hopes and dreams, just like everyone else and me, but this cruel, oppressive society kept him from making them real.

How dare you, reality? How damn dare you?

He hung out in porn shops and theaters. He kept writing bullshit letters home to his family, bragging about how his life was going, how he was taking off with the Secret Service, he was doing everything.

All in his head. Yeah, I'd been there for a while.

My psychosis was really kicking my ass at this point. As I watched the film over and over again, it became almost subliminal. Someone had actually learned about me, then put my own life story on the big screen for me to see and for me to learn from. It was showing me who I'd been and who I still was—and, as the film went on, what I had to do.

Eventually, of course, I did start to fixate on Jodie, as much as on De Niro. On Iris more than Travis. Every time I saw it, I looked forward to the scene where Travis and Iris head out for breakfast. It's one of the first scenes where Travis (and, through him, me) sees Iris as person, not just a prostitute. No snazzy, sleazy clothes. No self-offering. Just a normal lady who today some waitress would probably report for playing hooky from school.

"You sell your little pussy for nothin', man?" Travis demands. "For some lowlife pimp? I don't go screwing and fuck with a bunch of killers and junkies the way you do." That's pretty tough to say to a woman, let alone a 14-year-old (talking about Jodie, not Iris). It was tough to watch, and I'm sure it was difficult for Jodie to play that scene, but she pulled it off amazingly.

Here was where I really identified with Travis. Here you had a guy who had hardly anything going on, who had no issue spending time with the dregs of society, who'd been shit on by so many, but still had a certain compassion for someone else, someone he hardly knew. Even a person with so little going for him had a sense of morality, someone he was willing to fight for simply because it was right. I would like to think that, if my back was against the wall and I saw someone in her time of need, whether she realized it, I would have the guts to step up for her.

That scene really sent home a connection to me through Jodie. Here you had a guy who had just won an Oscar two years before for that masterpiece *Godfather 2*, and she was holding her own right there with him. Many, including me, probably felt that she even came out ahead in this scene. How could someone with so little experience at life itself, let alone acting, absolutely tear it up against Robert De Niro?

I wasn't watching Jodie at that point because she didn't exist. I think most actors want their audiences to feel that way, but this was something new. Something bigger. I could hardly remember that once filming ended, she'd walked off the set, gone home, and lived her life just as she would if she were in any other profession. Jodie wasn't using Iris to play this person. She *was* this person, whether the cameras were on or not. Jodie didn't exist anymore. Iris did and always would.

"So what makes you so high and mighty?" Iris demands back. "Didn't you ever try lookin' through your own eyeballs in the mirror? I don't know who's weirder, you or me."

That was it. She was talking to me. It wasn't Jodie and Robert. It wasn't Iris and Travis.

Someone recognized my weirdness and didn't look down on it. She appreciated it! She was a true kindred spirit, someone who would want to know me. Someone who could inspire me, and I could have the same effect on her.

More and more, she was talking to me. Over and over, she was reaching out. Letting me know that she was here for the rescuing, that she just needed, and sure as hell desperately wanted, her hero to rush in and save her. If Travis couldn't do it, John sure as hell could and would.

Taxi Driver blew the hell out of my mind every time I saw it, and I'm talking about at least a dozen times. That's why, even with so many viewings, I never went with anyone. No dates, no friends, always solo outings. I tried to not even sit near anyone in the theater. This was my story, and I wasn't sharing it. As far as I was concerned, it was me and Iris there. Even Travis became almost irrelevant to the piece.

I figured one of the first steps was to look for a stronger way into Travis's world. One that didn't involve Iris, at least at first. I could create his persona and step into it, and eventually reach out and bring Iris in. I figured that if I could incorporate his entire lifestyle into my own, she would be as into me as she was to him.

To a point, I was already there, down to the reprehensible concept of paying for sex. I wasn't going to start driving taxis, although that actually would have been my kind of work at the time. Staying out late, spending so much time alone, getting paid with only enough human interaction to drive from Point A to Point B? Not a bad racket for a guy like me.

Also, again, Travis doesn't have a problem outright with women of the street. It's only when he sees one all but forced into it, living a life she only thinks she likes from being too young to know better, that he decides to finally take a moral stand.

And it works! In the type of happy ending that I was too insane to realize never happens outside of Hollywood, he kills the bad guys, gets heralded as a hero, and saves his young lady back to the same upbringing she left behind.

Now, he was the hero I wanted to be—and I wanted to be the one who saved the naive streetwise gal known as Iris. It worked for him, right? It would certainly work for me.

Before he goes to work, Travis writes a short self-ode to Iris, letting her know that she won't see him again and that what he has is hers. That writing would become my example for my lovelorn offering just before I shot the president.

Now it was about biding time. I was trying to figure out how to become more of Travis. I was partly there, but not all the way. To win Iris's heart, to carry out the deeds that saved both their lives, I needed to become him, or as close as I could.

One of my next major steps, I admit, was something of a cover-up. Travis's first lady was actually Cybill Shepherd's Betsy, who ditches him and runs after his idea that a great first date is an X-rated movie, followed by following her to work and shouting at her.

How could she *not* fall for such a guy? Hell, even I wouldn't have done that to my new lady. But, of course, it was all the fault of Betsy's boss, Leonard Harris's Charles Palantine, looking to move from Congress to the White House. Now Travis was going to make him pay.

Well, that hadn't quite entered my mind, at least not for my first few *Taxi* screenings, the concept of harming others to win a lady's heart. But finding my own Betsy? Hell, I could do that! I hadn't much in the past, but I could now.

If I wanted to become Travis, it was a necessity. It was time to take a stronger interest in the opposite sex than I ever had before. I could find my own Betsy, and I wouldn't even have to shoot or stab, let alone kill anyone for her!

Would I?

Fortunately, it didn't take me long. I couldn't stop calling my parents and boasting about this lovely young lass I'd just happened to run into in a local laundromat.

Her name was Lynn. Lynn Collins. Sounds like a pretty good name for an actress, doesn't it? Well, that was what she wanted, and what she was already moving toward—being right up there next to Jodie on the screen. It would be a package deal; I would rule the music world, she would be at the top of acting's A-list, and we would be entertainment's new and last power couple.

I couldn't believe how lucky I was. This beauty came from a well-off California family. We would take long walks everywhere, expanding each other's minds in ways that classrooms never had or could.

My parents couldn't wait to meet her. I promised they could soon, that Lynn wanted to drop in and see their place.

But if I wasn't really that into Lynn? Maybe I was using her as a way to become Travis long enough to get with Iris? Perhaps I was pulling her out as a façade, an excuse to keep hitting the theater long enough to fuel my growing Jodie interest.

Yes, for now, I'm not labeling it an obsession. Not just yet. She was still one of my favorite actors, and I loved watching her work. I thought she was the best thing about the film. But I still wasn't fixated on her in the love interest sense. Even through the dark caverns of my mind, I still knew that, while this character was shoved into adulthood, she herself was only 14 in real life and had been 12 or 13 during filming. I didn't feel paternal toward her or anything; more that I saw her as scared, vulnerable, in need of her pistol-waving knight in shining armor to rush her, save her from the bad guys, and live happily ever after.

I don't know if I felt I loved her at that point. Love was always a pretty foreign concept to me for my entire life, so I'm not sure I would have recognized it if I'd felt it at all. I wanted to do something for someone that would make her remember me forever, and such a grand gesture would more than suffice.

You know, it's weird. Eventually, as films always do, *Taxi Driver* went out of the public eye. If Jodie had never acted again after that film, I may not have done what I did. I could have forgotten her, forgotten Iris, found something else to obsess over.

Actually, that's probably not true. I would have done the same thing, or something similar to it. I would have done it for someone else. I would have found some other actress, developed the same nutjob psychotic complex toward her, and acted something out from her film, just knowing that *that* would win her love. It's just how deranged I was becoming at that time.

Anyway, as we all know, and as anyone would have, Jodie kept tearing it up in the acting game. My life had gone through yet another overhaul. Too broke to keep filling my parents' heads with lies about record deals that were *this close* and holdover jobs I was picking up along the way, I wrote them another letter detailing how my health was going to hell, how agents kept jerking me around, how things didn't work out with me and Lynn, and that I just *had* to come back home and drown my sadness in some solitude.

I got a tiny apartment and a busboy job in Denver. Mainly, I would wake up late in the afternoon, head to the disco tech, spend a few hours cleaning up spilled food and occasional vomit, then come home and play my guitar until I fell asleep, usually when the normal working class was leaving for the daily job.

All the while, Jodie continued to be my salvation, my guiding light pointing me toward a goal to work for, a reason to keep moving forward. I played hooky from work the night of November 27, 1976, when she hosted *Saturday Night Live*. I sang along with her and the rest of the young cast of *Bugsy Malone* and laughed my ass off at her antics in *Freaky Friday*. I was even a little scared of her in *The Little Girl Who Lives Down the Lane*; of course, I was supposed to be, as her character was a killer, albeit a pretty justified one. Hell, if this girl could personally take out the much older ones who were after her, maybe she didn't need rescuing after all. Maybe that's why I stopped watching that film very quickly.

The next year, Jodie was nominated for a Best Supporting Actress Oscar for her work as Iris, and I knew damn sure she was going to win. Holding her own up against that cast? Creating such a character and leaving such an impression on so many? It was a masterclass taught by a novice! Of course, the Academy Awards would be as wowed by her as I was. If I'd had a dime to my name, I would have bet it on her and given odds away!

And then she didn't. Ridiculous. They gave it to Beatrice Straight, who had been in *Network* for all of two scenes and less than six minutes! Absurd. I spent the entire week ready to explode after that one. What a bunch of garbage! Foster had shown one hell of a character arc, taking Iris from fake toughness all the way to vulnerability. Straight had had one major monologue. How dare they pass my Jodie over in favor of someone who had so little time to make any sort of impression?

By early 1977, I'd taken one more jaunt out to Los Angeles, sure than someone would help me hit it big in music. I'd fallen flat, crashing into one brick wall after another. I didn't make it a month in that spot.

Nothing to do now but return to school, making it look like I was moving forward with formal education when I knew music would always be my forte.

Then I met some new people. People who had direction. People who had goals, ideas to believe in. Ways to work together to make something big happen.

Even if they were all, in hindsight, completely ridiculous.

8. RACISM

I'd never thought of myself as racist. I don't think anyone ever had believed I was.

Of course, my upbringing didn't exactly make for a diverse environment. My high school and most of the surrounding areas were all White. Introverted extremist that I was, I didn't really get involved with the civil rights action of the 1960s and '70s.

It wasn't so much that my neighbors and I didn't like Black people. It was just that they weren't around much. I didn't go to school with them, didn't work with them, didn't see them often, rarely enough that I never really thought too much about them one way or another.

I heard racist ramblings across Lubbock quite often, but I didn't pay attention to it much. It was one more example of my obsession with my music career taking my focus off everything else.

I can't really hide behind the old reliable standby, "I can't be racist. I have Black friends!" that you hear so many White people use as a front to camouflage their bigotry. I didn't have Black friends, Black acquaintances, neighbors, anything like that. Then again, I didn't have much of those things in the White or any other color department either.

Well, maybe I did, in a way. During my sophomore year at Texas Tech, there was a Black student named Dwayne in my dorm. Literally no one wanted to room with him. I saw the looks people gave him in the hallways. I saw people rush into their rooms and slam the door as he walked by. Others literally morphed to the other side of the hallways or even the sidewalk to keep from getting near him.

Sadly, that was acceptable at that time. Even after Blacks had fought so hard for equality in the 1960s, even after racial discrimination had required the law to fight it, many decision-makers at the school were totally fine with him being treated the way he was. I don't know if any student ever said to them, "I won't room with Dwayne because he's Black," but any other excuse, legitimate or otherwise, would have been accepted in a moment. It looked like Dwayne would be left out in the cold.

Then they asked me if I would room with him. I said yes. I was no kind of civil rights activist. I didn't see myself as personally taking steps forward against racism. I wasn't any kind of role model, showing people that integration was no big deal, nothing wrong with it if you just gave it a chance.

I really didn't give a damn. I wasn't thinking about who I was rooming with or why. I didn't care if the guy's skin was purple. I was there to sharpen my guitar skills, form a band, grab huge gigs, and maybe study a little bit if there was time left over. I wasn't going to be friends with the guy. Like anyone I roomed with, I was going to finish the term and walk away forever.

That's not to say we were enemies. We got along fine, albeit on my typical superficial level. He never gave me grief about my music, and all I cared about was getting through the semester, unless a huge musical opportunity came up, like the one that would snatch me to Hollywood the next year. I didn't expect to think of Dwayne at all as soon as that year ended, and I don't think I have since, until I went about writing this book.

Back in college with little to do, trying to recover from the latest setback to my music career, I was lonely as hell. My self-esteem, fragile at the best of times, was just about gone altogether. I could still find some solace in my guitar, but less and less. Playing it didn't feel as good anymore, and I was scared that, in a fit of sudden extreme depression, I would smash it into the wall, then cry over it until I had a grief-caused heart attack. I almost wanted that to happen.

As our economy went slowly to shit in the 1970s, two letters appeared in the Texas Tech newspaper. The first was something of a warning. I was worried that if our economic crisis continued, we would throw the president out and put up a dictator. This democracy stuff wasn't working, and there were no signs it would change. Hadn't been for a while.

But if we were going to make a change, we would step behind a guy who would put the country on his back and have all the power. As in, a dictatorship. As in, Nazism.

I was worried that, with us still in the midst of the Cold War, we as a country were terrified of Communism. Not many Americans knew much about that form of government other than it was the Russians' way of thinking, and anything praised by the red-flagged herring of the Soviets would never get the chance to fly over here. Given the choice, we would support a guy like Hitler over fellows like Leonid Brezhnev (Mikhail Gorbachev, who would work with President Reagan to end the Cold War, was years away from power).

My name appeared at the end of that letter, and I was proud of it. I was thinking deeper, seeing more possibilities, having the guts to admit that our country might go a certain way if we couldn't heal ourselves.

The other letter, however, was a bit different. It came from a guy named Bob Smith or Steve Jones or some other obvious pseudonym. That's what people do when they don't want anyone to know that they're the ones speaking, or writing, their minds.

If the first piece was soothsaying, this one came across as almost pure evil.

Until now, no one really knew that I wrote that piece, at least as far as I'm aware. If they did, I wouldn't have had to drop out of Texas Tech, or try to kill the president, to not be allowed back on campus.

It took the same tactics that a certain rejected artist had used to take control of his country. It warned, but also reassured.

It told America that, for the most part, its problems weren't its fault. It fell at the feet of people who made up a single-digit part of the population. It discussed how Jews were there to screw over the good, common man, and had been for a long time. Anti-Semitism might just be the vaccine to cure our ails.

The fake name? The pseudo-anonymous author? If you couldn't guess by now, it was me. I had a certain admiration for Hitler back then. I respected that he'd gone from living on the streets of Vienna to ruling a country, to starting a world war, to coming within a few wins of conquering the planet. I'd written some top-level paper describing, if not publicly praising, his drive to success.

I think I was just looking to belong, to believe in something. Groups like the National Socialist Party of America are perfect for such people.

I really believe that most people who join these groups—the ones whose title is always a $10 way of saying, "We're racist, and you should be too!"—aren't racist themselves. At least, that's not the only reason they join. They enter these groups because such organizations almost always say yes to everyone, as long as they're the right race and religion. No tests to pass, no academic hurdles to jump, not even much of an application form to fill out.

Just dues to pay, of course. People are much more apt to like you, or pretend to, if you pay them to do so. You buy friends and acceptance and keep telling yourself that these people actually give a damn about you; that they wouldn't plant a machete in your back at the first provocation.

I would feel that, eventually. But when I first learned of the group in early 1977, I couldn't help but feel a little impressed, despite my extremely low standards of the time. Itself formerly known as the American Nazi Party, the group wanted to hold a huge march through Skokie, Illinois, an area heavy in Jews and other Holocaust survivors. Represented by a Jewish lawyer on behalf of the American Civil Liberties Union, the group had taken its First Amendment battles all the way to the Supreme Court, where it won the right to speak its mind—and then it pretty much all went for naught, as Chicago allowed the march to be held there instead.

Hell, it sounded courageous on the face of it. These people had a cause, something everyone was working so hard for. If that many people were willing to fight so hard, it must be worth believing in, right? Like I said, this was hardly my first experience with White supremacy, but it was the strongest, the most organized and unified group.

That, and they had really cool-looking uniforms. I dropped my information and a few dollars in the mail. I would eventually have to submit a photograph to prove I was White (those were much harder to fake back then!) but soon, I became a National Socialist.

At least, in name. I wanted to be a name, a face of the party. I even flew to Chicago, where the Socialist group had its personal headquarters.

But as soon as I stepped into O'Hare Airport, tragedy almost struck. I had the great-grandmother of all panic attacks. Shaking, sweating, almost crying, hardly coherent, I thought I was having a massive heart attack, or about to.

Almost unable to move, I could barely make my way to a small chair in the lobby that had a TV attached to it. O'Hare, per usual, was a jammed madhouse that afternoon. Normally, I can't stand that sort of environment, but it was a gift that day; people were too busy to notice me. If the medical staff had seen me or been alerted, I would certainly have wound up in the hospital.

For hours, I sat, staring at that TV without knowing or caring what was on the screen. I was concerned that my heart was about to overload and stop. I literally thought I would never walk out of that place.

But I did. Very slowly, and for no real reason I could see, my body did slow back down. I could think. I could breathe. I could move, but not much.

And I didn't have to. After flying halfway up the country, spending hours on a plane and several more in the airport, I got on another plane and headed right back down to Texas.

It might have been a divine intervention sign to get the hell out of the group! But I didn't leave right away.

Of course, once I shot the president, the group members couldn't wait to drag me through the muck. As much as they would love it if all the non-Christian and non-White folk were to suddenly disappear, they didn't want to be associated with someone who acted out such violence in public. These are the people who always claim they don't advocate physical action against others but rarely decry it when it does happen.

The group leaders blithered to the press about how my "membership" had only lasted a year, that I'd been gone as soon as 1979. That was garbage, as, even up to the assassination attempt, I'd never officially left the group.

The bigger lie, however, was created just to fit my agenda as a presidential assassin.

"He felt that we were not sufficiently militant for him," then-leader Harold Covington whined to any reporter who would listen. "He wanted us to go out and commit unlawful acts." Someone else with the party claimed that I "wanted to shoot people and blow things up."

Ridiculous. I'd never advocated for violence against any large group, let alone anything that malicious. How ironic that the group had never publicly accused me of wanting to shoot anyone until a few days after I'd done so.

Yes, I'd talked to Covington. But only a few times, and I never recommended any sort of violence. I simply opined that the party wasn't going to get anywhere by simply handing out leaflets. If they wanted to expand, they had to work harder.

But threats? Violence? The potential mass murder of a bombing? Nothing. Not even remotely close. But that's what people do when they need an excuse to throw you to the wolves.

But I had a bit of revenge, not that these guys needed to look any worse.

As pissed as Covington's statements made me, I had to respect something he'd done about two years before. Rifling through the desk of the organization's then-leader, Covington had just *happened* to stumble on some kiddie porn. The SOB in question not only got kicked out of the organization—some things are too low even for Nazis!—but went to jail for a few years. Not long enough, and he should be glad he wasn't housed alongside me at the time.

But Covington, who died in 2018, couldn't keep his organization going. It dissolved before I even went to trial for the Reagan shooting.

Was that because of the bad publicity I brought? I like to think so.

9. 1978

When you're obsessed with something, or someone, to the point of psychosis, it's all you have. All you think about. It becomes the only thing in your mind. You think it's even in your heart. Why? Because that's where love is, and you truly believe that what you're feeling is love. You think everyone in love feels this way. Loving someone means they're always on your mind.

Your mind gets so set on a person that everything else is secondary. Months become minutes. Years become hours. It's all you have, all you need, and all you want.

For years after I saw *Taxi Driver*, that's how I felt. From the moment I watched it, I knew I would be with Jodie, and I knew I would have to kill the president to do it. Of course, even as psychotic as I was, I knew I couldn't just grab a gun, drive to Washington, and fire away. Presidents didn't hang out on the White House lawn or walk alone down the street to get a newspaper and coffee in the morning.

But it was always on my mind. Every time I saw the president on TV or read about him in a newspaper, I vowed he was on borrowed time.

Life for me became one repeating cycle after another. I would go to college for a while, then drop out. I would get an apartment, survive for a few months on my father's dime, then move, get evicted, whatever. I would work one menial job after another, then quit, get fired, whatever.

More and more, though, my depression kept growing. I felt more and more alienated from my family, but God knows they had more than enough to worry about than their directionless son. My father was doing great in the oil business in Colorado, but he couldn't enjoy his wealth because he kept having to spend money, maybe even waste it on me, over and over.

The same two life forces that had pushed me along for over a year were still there. The first, of course, was my music career. Over and over, I would set up a tape recorder, introduce myself, talk about what I could offer and why I would be a good risk for any agent who would represent me, and then strum out a few of my songs. I was one or two good gigs and contracts from blasting straight through the music world. I could write the greatest lyrics ever and then sing them out, and music fans across the country would be shocked at how amazing they were and disappointed that it had taken me so long to hit it big.

Record, sing, send to a record company in New York or Los Angeles, repeat. I probably went through that maybe 40 times. Giving up wasn't an option.

And then, of course, there was Jodie. Hey, maybe I would get lucky twice at once. Perhaps one of my tapes would land in the office of her own representative, and he would inform her about me. Maybe he would be full-blown convinced that my song should be on the soundtrack of her next film. We could even do it as a duet! Maybe some sort of sequel to *Alice Doesn't Live Here Anymore*, except her Audrey is now the one chasing the musical dreams, and I would be the grownup version of Alice's son Tommy, rooting for her all the way.

I knew that would fix everything for me. If I could have a reunion with Jodie, have a life with her, everything would be okay. That wasn't wrong, was it? Just to want to be loved? To have a dream and want to see it come true, even willing to put down the work for it?

But at least I had Lynn as my salvation, right? An upcoming actress, she would have been as wowed by Jodie's work as I was, albeit in a different way. She always struck me as more like Betsy's character in *Taxi Driver*—in part because she was my age, slightly older than Iris!—and she, like most women, certainly didn't mind being compared to Cybill Shepherd.

I kept telling my parents all about Lynn. That she was flying in from Chicago to spend some holidays with me. How her resume from both there and Broadway was filling up, one quicky entry at a time. That she came from a well-off family, just like I did. That we could sit and interact for hours, even days at a time, mentally challenging each other. I kept promising to send them some photos of us and let them talk to her on the phone sometime very soon.

"This rendezvous has been in the works ever since she wrote to me back in November," I blubbered. "With her unlimited financial resources, she's decided to visit me here in balmy Lubbock... I was a bundle of nerves, until I finally set eyes on her, and then everything was perfect." I'd spent so much time getting my living quarters ready for Lynn's arrival, hoping she would like it, planning out each day together down to the detail.

Then I told them I was considering giving up everything to move to Hollywood with her, while she became the next big thing. That, they had a problem with.

"In my twenty-four years," I ranted at my folks, "there has been exactly one girl that has cared anything at all for me, and now you want me to tell her to just forget about it for a year, until I get a degree, which will be meaningless in my life as a songwriter.... It would be the greatest and most unnecessary risk of my life to stay here in Lubbock and leave her alone in Hollywood with all of the Casanovas and Don Juans running around out there. You think a piece of paper is more important than a potential lifetime relationship.... Lynn wants me in California. She couldn't care less whether or not I have a college diploma." Years later, those letters would be seen by people far from my intended audience.

I actually had a huge stroke of luck right around this time. Decked out in my Toyota, I was heading down Mockingbird Lane, one of Dallas's longest streets. I remember that I'd just stopped in the middle of the street, about to pull into a 7-Eleven.

Then I almost got killed. Some guy in a huge car ran right into me. My mind could hardly conceive what had happened. I didn't even hurt.

Maybe I was dead. Maybe, in a few seconds, I would float up and see my lifeless body there in the driver's seat, my head and neck oddly shaped, if not separated. I blinked a few times, almost pinching myself to see if I was still alive, let alone conscious.

I was. As hard as I'd been hit, I should have at least had serious whiplash. But I was fine. Even the other driver came through. He told me he didn't have insurance, but that he would help me out.

We exchanged information, and he hopped in the car and left. I was all but certain I would never hear from him again.

But I did. A few weeks later, I got a check for $500. He was a man of his word.

And if that weren't enough, not long after, it happened again. Right after hanging out with my sister and nephew in December 1978, I was driving back to Dallas. Suddenly, my car skidded, went hydroplaning off the road, and landed in a ditch. Right in the middle of a freezing night, I had to walk for almost an hour to find a working pay phone and call a tow truck, which itself was lucky as hell in that time and place. But again, my car was damaged but not totaled.

Nothing to do but chalk these experiences up to signs from elsewhere. Signs from above. I needed to keep trying. Trying to break through the glass ceiling (it seemed more like iron) to my music career and win Jodie's heart in the process. There was, of course, that these incidents were the dark hand of karma, warning me to change course or risk worse injuries the next time around. The third time might not be such a charm.

That never entered my mind at all. After all, who was I to question such fate?

10. MY WRITING "FUTURE"

I could have gone somewhere else. I had the skills to make it somewhere else. If I'd been able to take my mind off music and Jodie for a little while, things might have turned out differently. If I could have added one more focus to my mindset, who knows what might have happened for me in my academic career, professional life, otherwise.

I almost did. Not just the songs I was writing, which, if I do say and write so myself, showed some great creativity, and not just the letters I was sending home about Lynn, which gave me some great practice in detailing our lives, our love, her as a person, and so much else. She was moving up in the local stage area, had joined a choir, was doing everything.

But again, that's how obsession screws with your mind. When it gets so strong that it distorts everything else in your life—hell, everything else in the world!—you can't see anything else. You also can't really see, or don't want to see, what could happen for you a little ways down the road.

It's all about right now. Often, we're not even talking about this evening. We're talking about *this very second.*

There was another project that, if I'd stuck with it a little longer, could have carried me far too.

I'd already been wowing my college professors with my writing ability. Essay after research piece brought me one "A" after another. The ones who had seen me come to the brink of flunking out were probably shocked nearly to incoherence to see my name once again on the Dean's List.

Back in school in early 1979, I was probably within a year of graduating. I'd been on a roll since changing my major, and the way my grades were pouring in, my relationship with Lynn, my sailing seemed to have smoothed out enough all the way to the degree.

So much so that I actually started a deeper form of writing. Stepping away from being the next Lennon or McCartney (or fellow Texas Tech alumni John Denver), I was going to be the repeat of Arthur Conan Doyle. I banged out a few chapters of my debut mystery novel. It would be called *It's a Mystery to Me*, and it would be the first of many. So many.

I also banged out a few more stories whose impact would be felt later. One short piece was called "Son a Gun Collector," a piece about an abused son whose father assaults him for touching a gun. But the kid gets revenge with another piece, "and blood splatters all over the wall." Then there was "West of Denver," the sad tome of a young boy who starts shooting up cars, only to find himself in psychiatric care.

Years in the far future, a different audience would be reading those pieces for non-academic reasons.

I kept that up throughout the fall of 1979, still wining, dining, and wooing Lynn, herself now landmarked in Hollywood on the way to hitting it big. I was one great agent meeting away from doing it all in music; she was one big role away from being the hottest thing in acting.

That winter, we decided to jaunt over to New York. She was showing up on Broadway, and I was going to shop around both my novel and my music to a new round of agents.

I sat there in my car at the Lubbock airport, just waiting for her to arrive for us to join up for the flight over. I believe she'd told me which plane she would be arriving in, but I couldn't recall. I just sat there and stared at the airfield, waiting for her to emerge from the next plane, or maybe the one after that.

Minutes passed. Hours went by. One plane after another landed. Some people, usually those in hardcore business attire, almost ran off, probably on their way to a meeting. Fathers emerged holding their babies. Large groups, probably tourists back from a huge trip, exited at the same time, typically all dressed the same.

But no Lynn. Not on this plane, nor any other.

I tried to give her the benefit of the doubt. I told myself that she'd missed her flight. Maybe she'd gotten sick and forgot to call. Perhaps her agent had sprung a new offer on her, and she'd had to rush right into performing, planning to let me know as soon as she got home.

The sun started to go down. It was like it was mockingly waving goodbye to me as well.

I took a lonely drive back to my apartment. No phone calls. No letters or emergency telegrams. Nothing.

As far as my family knew, I was absolutely in New York. We were there, talking to agents, directors, everyone who couldn't wait to hear from us. But I spent that Christmas sadly staring between the wall and the TV, hearing my neighbors celebrate and talk about the year they'd had and how the next one would be better, as we always hope for.

Just as they always did, things had gone south and ground to a halt. I didn't go back to school, feeding my family some garbage about getting hired and fired from a newspaper in Dallas.

Then I came up with a new whopper.

I called my father, so full of enthusiasm that I seemed ready to reach through the phone. I was sure he could almost feel the smile across my face. I had an idea that was going to hit it big.

It was called LISTALOT. I'd registered a mail-order business to tear it up. I was going to send out notices for all the top country music fan clubs in America. I was going to give lessons on following in my footsteps, though I hadn't actually taken any, in setting up one's own such business. Magazines across the country would be carrying the LISTALOT name with the Hinckley one slightly smaller than it.

All I needed from him was a measly $100. A c-note could turn everything around, start a business as lucrative as his had been.

He went along with it. All spring and into the summer, I kept up with news about how LISTALOT was doing so well. Me selling information, more and more people wanting in on it, doing everything, and yet still managing to balance my studies in an educational journey that got closer to the end every single class.

But I was biding my time. All the way, my new objective was coming into focus.

I couldn't stop telling everyone how great Lynn was. How she and I were making our marks together, doing everything.

It was all part of my plan. It was one façade after another on the way to a truth full of love that would last forever.

Taking another "break" from college that summer, I was on my way home again. My family didn't even ask about LISTALOT; they knew how much my word meant on that. They didn't bring up Lynn either, figuring we were just going through the same difficulty that plagues every relationship.

Not long before, I'd found a local doctor to chat with about my anxiety, and he'd given me something called Surmontil. He and I had agreed that my depression was severe enough to get on some medication, but I think he was subtly trying to tell me that my mental state was getting a little too fragile, as the drug can also help those of us being nabbed by psychosis.

But I didn't agree. I thought I was just sad all the time. I certainly was, but that was obviously not the only issue. So I went back to him and convinced him that I needed something different. He added Valium to the equation.

The medical community had gone crazy (no pun intended) over the drug during the 1970s, spending billions of dollars on billions of dosages throughout. I think many wanted the purifyingly relaxing feeling it gave. Doctors didn't need much convincing to write someone a prescription for it, and I'm pretty sure many people were fudging their symptoms just to grab it.

I probably was. But I didn't have much left to try, and if this didn't improve things for me, maybe it could help me end them.

Yes, that happened again. One night, I *happened* to take a few too many Valium. My skin got all cold, clammy, and colorless. I could hardly walk without shaking.

Like a jerk, I scared the hell out of my mother on a jaunt to her place. Honestly, I don't remember if I wanted to die, get attention, or even just experiment. I was afraid to go to sleep, or maybe she was afraid for me to go to sleep, fearing that so many pills would cause my body to forget how to work.

I made it through, and I was actually very glad that I did. Because my life's work was actually starting to take more focus than before.

Back at home, my parents were unpleasantly shocked at how much my weight had gotten out of control. I'd never really been much of a fitness guy, but they were worried my health could be in danger. As they left the country for some business trips, I told them I would take care of myself and their house.

A crash diet reached out and yanked about 30 pounds off me that summer. I had a reason to slim down and spruce up, and I could feel it getting closer.

Shockingly, the fall enrollment deadline at Texas Tech came and went without me. But I had a new idea.

There was a short writing course being held at Yale University. Not *by* Yale itself—like someone with my academic history would be allowed anywhere near it!—but on its campus. It would rush students through the basics of scripts, music, novels, everything that could help me keep making my niche in a creative metropolitan. Maybe one of the professors would be a full-time Yale teacher and pick me up for a partnership or something, perhaps even an internship. Maybe there was a new agent in the local area who would find my book as enthralling as others!

But even my father wasn't falling for this one. Not all the way.

He'd given all his kids some stock in his company, and to fly across the country and enroll, all I needed was to sell mine off, which could net me a pretty significant $3600. Before he let me do that, however, he actually wrote up a contract for me.

I would pay the tuition and travel, but I would be sure to keep over a grand for myself. If things in New Haven didn't work out, I would dump the remaining dough into Texas Tech and finish up there. I signed at high speed.

The very next day, my father drove me to the airport and put me on a plane. I'm sure he thought I was looking for an excuse to go see Lynn, but that was okay if I'd been telling the truth. He and my mother were sure that, with both a Plan A and a Plan B, I was going to take those last few educational steps.

But there was no plan at all, not in that sense. There was no writing program because there was no school holding it, by Yale or even near it. The money would be gone soon. I would never be back at Texas Tech, or any other college, ever again. My days as a student were over. I'd even broken it off with Lynn. I had a reason.

I had something else in mind. Something so much more important. When I got on the plane that day, I wasn't running away. I did have a goal, a reason to suddenly jet across the nation. There was someone there who was worth it.

A few months before, I'd gotten an update on my eternal love. The entire country had learned it at the same time, but I was sure it was actually directed at me.

I finally had a chance to see her in person, in living color. To literally reach out and touch her. To have her hear my voice directly, and listen to hers in return.

For the first time, I could meet Jodie Foster, the person. Away from the cameras, away from the roles, away from everything. My new goal, my job in life, would be to protect Jodie, and, through her, Iris, from the evils of the world.

She was worth giving it all up. So much money, a degree I would never have, a career I didn't want, not for then. In the grandest gesture of love in history, I was spending four figures to fly from one coast to the other, all for her. Of course she would fall as deeply for me.

I knew what I was there to do. I had for a long time. Now it was time to have the guts and the warm heart to make it real for both of us, to reach out and lead her into our life together. We would be united. We would be together forever. The Hollywood films she'd made could never touch the love we would share that would live happily ever after and even longer.

11. FINDING JODIE

Jodie,

*I love you six trillion times. Don't you maybe like me
a little bit? (You must admit it. I am different.)*

It would make all the difference.

John Hinckley Jr.

**One of a few notes I slipped under Jodie's
door during her freshman term at Yale**

My beloved Jodie had always made sure to stay right in my
eye. I'd missed her for the last few years of the 1970s, but I still
thought about her all the time. Her absence made my fixation
grow stronger. When she came back in 1980, it was a whole new
woman before the camera.

As she reached adulthood, her characters did as well. A few
months after *Taxi Driver*, she'd scared the living hell out of
millions, me included, as the murderous title character in *The Little
Girl Who Lives Down the Lane*. Along with being so terrified,
though, those same people were just as taken by the power she
showed in carrying a film on her back, not the secondary character
Iris had been.

She became the impromptu leader, the gang mother, if you
will, for a group of her friends in 1980's *Foxes*. It was cool to see
her at the head of the line, rather than being forced into following,
like Iris had been.

Then, later that same year, came *Carny*. For the first time, I,
like so many others, saw Jodie as sexual. Seductive, even. Her

Donna became a stripper in a traveling show, racking up all sorts of power over the men who desperately wanted her. When she was in the background, mostly clothed, with near-naked women in front of her on the stage, all I could see was her. When Donna got caught in bed with another character, I was pissed. I felt betrayed. It should have been me. It was, of course, me she was dancing for in those lovely stripping scenes. Only me.

Any guilt I may have felt about swooning over a teenage girl was gone. Now she was an adult. Now she was legal. Now it was okay for me to imagine being with her, marrying her, falling in love with her, even making love to her. I'd met her as a kid, but now we were two consenting adults, and I couldn't wait for her to say yes to me. Maybe even, a little ways down the road, "I do."

Her work was as enthralling as ever. So much so that she inspired me to take the next step in my music career, even though I wouldn't be able to capitalize on it until it was too late. My musical muse came to visit right around then, and I managed to piece together the rhyming tune of "I Desire."

I Desire

I desire

I desire

I pledge allegiance to the thought

That your love is all that matters

And your gestures have the power

To bring the whole world to its knees

Don't let me torment you

Don't let me bring you down

Don't ever let me hurt you

Don't let me fail because

I desire your attention

I desire your perfect love

I desire nothing more than this

To give you happiness

Could become a lifetime goal

A smile I might bring you

Is more important than world peace

Don't let me torment you

Don't let me bring you down

Don't ever let me hurt you

Don't let me fail because

I desire your attention

I desire your perfect love

I desire nothing more

I pledge allegiance to the fact

That you're wise to walk away

For nothing is more dangerous

Than desire when it's wrong

Don't let me torment you

Don't let me bring you down

Don't ever let me hurt you

Don't let me fail because

I desire your attention

I desire your perfect love

Sounds like one hell of a love song, doesn't it? That's how I meant it. If anyone but me had written it, it would probably been seen as the most romantic of tunes. When people learned that it had come from my mind, however, their views changed.

But unlike most of my work, at least they would see it and hear it. Just not from me personally.

Not long after I was institutionalized after my acquittal in 1982, the band Devo came calling. My poem had shown up in the *Los Angeles Times,* and the guys who had jumped into the musical mainstream with "Whip It" wanted to convert it to music.

It didn't take me a nanosecond to say yes. We signed with Broadcast Music, Inc. to add it to the Devo album *Oh, No! It's DEVO*. By the end of 1982, I was finally receiving royalties for my music writing.

Well, for a while. I made a few hundred bucks off of it, and then it just stopped. Clearly, the American public was pissed that I was profiting from my notoriety, especially so soon after my trial, and the band had been forced to discuss with the FBI its decision to add the song at all. Right around 1985, they stopped sending me checks. Even today, the album still sells pretty well, in Europe and Asia, if not here. I haven't seen a dime in generations.

I never really found out why. I think certain people might have figured that they didn't want to pay me, that it was okay to duck out of a contract with an attempted murderer. They were pretty sure that my crimes would obliterate my right to compensation. Even after I was released, I never had the means to pursue the issue, even though I still feel I was robbed.

I was still all about saving Jodie, rescuing Iris. I was still going to be the guy who rescued the sweet, innocent lady from the dangerous streets and made her my lady. Seeing her on the cover of May 1980's *People* magazine, I snatched it up and started reading.

Then I received some outstanding news.

She was stepping away from the acting world and into the student one. She was trading Hollywood and the film world for the theaters of Yale University. The former valedictorian of her Los Angeles high school, she wouldn't be Jodie the movie star but, for a while, Jodie the class pupil.

And I was sure it was because of me. I was so proud of her academic accomplishments and couldn't wait to tell her so. I was sure she would be honored to hear it. She was making herself available, a new kind of public figure. Away from the glitzy world of cameras and reporters, Jodie was switching to a regular, normal lifestyle. Just as I hadn't been so successful myself over at Texas Tech, she would be right there on campus, strolling around between African-American literature classes and stage work.

That is, until I showed up. It didn't matter how many times I'd had to lie to others, or how much money I'd had to scam others out of. It was all a cover to make our love real, and it would be worth it. As soon as I, her knight in shining armor, strode onto campus and straight up to her, she, in awe of my passion and devotion to her, would leap to take my arm as we strolled off into the sunset.

Now there was the formality of getting there and doing a simple job. As the summer of 1980 ended, a new face appeared on the New Haven campus.

Well, two new ones. Hers and mine. It would be just a matter of time until we met.

"Yale actually invited me—little smog-ridden me—to sink my blond teeth into its dusty brick and ivy," Jodie had bragged to *Esquire Magazine* in October 1980. (In a sad, pitch-black foreshadowing, the cover depicted a frightened woman in a Yale T-shirt with a gun to her head.) "I suppose college life will be as close to death and dying as I, Woody Allen, or the Talking Heads shall ever come.... Here I come for knowledge, where pained and pimply youths growl and groan over steaming cups of viscous stuff! I mean, what a thrill it'll be to wake up to smokers' coughs, ink-stained teeth, and faces creased by last night's pizza."

Armed with a fake name and background, I stepped into the registrar's office. I told them that I was looking for a friend, but I wasn't quite sure where she was living.

Without hesitation, someone handed me an epic digest of everyone's name and address. Flipping through, I couldn't find her. I started to get a little frustrated.

Then I saw it: Alicia Christian Foster. Clearly, she'd hidden in plain sight for me. The world knew her as Jodie, but it took a bit of research to locate her real name. Obviously, she only wanted a certain few to find it, and I was in that group.

As it happened, her dorm was a short walk from the office itself. It was finally time. I was going to walk right up there, as gallant as if I were on the red carpet at her latest movie premiere.

Through the Welch Hall doors. Right up to her room. My fist up. Knocking on the door.

Nothing. No one was there.

What if she'd opened the door? What if she'd been there? In my warped mind, she would have leaped right into my arms and all but begged me to carry her away.

But what? I'm sure I wouldn't have been the first fan she would run into on campus. Maybe she would have thought I was there for an autograph or a photo. Maybe anything.

I'm sure she was very glad she happened to be elsewhere at that moment. For all I know, she could have been in the bathroom, taking a nap, anything that could have kept her from opening the door.

No matter. There would be more times and places.

I kept going back. I wrote poems. I scribbled notes to her, declaring my love and our destiny to be together. I took a greeting card and wrote "I Love You" all over it. I kept putting them under her door.

I always signed the letters. I didn't want her to think I was just some nutcase, tormenting her for the hell of it. People like that creeped the hell out of me. What I had—what I thought we had—was as real as my psychosis would allow. It was love. Never anything wrong with love. I was in the local bars, not really drinking, but showing off her picture and bragging to all the campus guys that this famous lady was mine, and would be soon and forever.

I never did get lucky with my door-knocking. A short while later, I almost did, elsewhere.

But then I decided to pick up the phone. Her number had been in the same book as her address. Dialing that number, I gulped, knowing I was as close to my dream as ever.

The first three times, I fell short. Busy signal after busy signal. Then her roommates informed me that she wasn't there. But the sixth time was a charm.

FOSTER: Hello?

HINCKLEY: Hello? Is, ah, Jodie Foster there?

FOSTER: This is.

HINCKLEY: What?

FOSTER: Who is this?

HINCKLEY: This is the person that's been leaving notes in your box for two days.

FOSTER: Whose box?

HINCKLEY: W.C. 31, I think, or C.W.

FOSTER: Uh-huh.

HINCKLEY: Is this Jodie?

FOSTER: Yes?

HINCKLEY: 'Cause, if you, are you the one that's been on the phone?

FOSTER: Yes, but I don't know you. No, but I haven't been on the phone.

HINCKLEY: Um....

FOSTER: Am I supposed to know you?

HINCKLEY: Well, no.

FOSTER: No. Oh, well, I don't, we have, we must not have much in common.

HINCKLEY: Jodie, listen.

FOSTER: Yes?

HINCKLEY: I just want to talk to you. OK?

FOSTER: I got to go out to dinner.

HINCKLEY: Um.

FOSTER: Seriously, this isn't fair. Do me a favor and don't call back, all right?

HINCKLEY: Jodie, please. Can I (unintelligible), listen I got to go back to New York City too, so...

FOSTER: Um....

HINCKLEY: Um. Are you going to be out all night tonight or what?

FOSTER: Yes.

HINCKLEY: Jodie, can we talk?

FOSTER: I don't think we can.

HINCKLEY: Jodie.

FOSTER: Look, it's nice meeting you but, I, I'm not supposed to talk to people I don't know, OK?

HINCKLEY: Well, I think you might know me.

FOSTER: Oh, I know you? From where?

HINCKLEY: I think you saw me today. What were you wearing?

FOSTER: I can't remember.

HINCKLEY: Were you wearing a sort-of, green pants?

FOSTER: I don't remember.

HINCKLEY: Greenish, greenish, greenish brown.

FOSTER: Maybe.

HINCKLEY: Okay, see, I can't remember now. Can I call tomorrow night?

FOSTER: That's fine.

HINCKLEY: Will you be in?

FOSTER: Um, maybe.

HINCKLEY: Will you talk?

FOSTER: Um, maybe.

HINCKLEY: Will you talk?

FOSTER: Sure.

HINCKLEY: Well, you just changed your mind, see?

FOSTER: I got to go, okay? Look, I can't be bothered with your noisome habits.

HINCKLEY: Jodie.

FOSTER: I got to go. Bye-bye.

HINCKLEY: Jodie ...

A few days later:

FOSTER: Hello?

HINCKLEY: Hello, is Jodie there?

FOSTER: Who is this?

HINCKLEY: Jodie?

FOSTER: Who is this?

HINCKLEY: Is this Jodie?

FOSTER: Oh, no! Who is this?

HINCKLEY: Is this Jodie?

FOSTER: Who is this?

HINCKLEY: This is John.

FOSTER: John who? Oh no! Not you again.

HINCKLEY: What's the matter?

FOSTER: Is this John Hendricks?

HINCKLEY: No.

FOSTER: John who? John Hinckley, I mean?

HINCKLEY: You are all having a party or something?

FOSTER: No, we're not, we're trying to get some sleep.

HINCKLEY: Oh, it's 12 o'clock.

FOSTER: Yeah, that's right. It's 12 o'clock.

HINCKLEY: We....

FOSTER: Past my bedtime.

HINCKLEY: What are you doing now?

FOSTER: And you keep calling me, and I don't know who you are.

HINCKLEY: I just told you.

FOSTER: You are always trying to bug me. I know you just told me.

HINCKLEY: Jodie.

FOSTER: Yes.

HINCKLEY: I saw you.

FOSTER: (To roommates) Yeah, I should tell him I am sitting here with a knife.

HINCKLEY: What did you say?

FOSTER: Nothing.

HINCKLEY: Listen, don't, don't hang up, please.

FOSTER: Why not?

HINCKLEY: Because.

FOSTER: Because what?

HINCKLEY: Why are you gonna go to bed so early?

FOSTER: Look, I really can't be bothered with this, and I don't want, I don't want to be mean, and do you know, it just, it upsets my roommates, and it upsets me, and I am serious, it upsets me to have people calling that I don't know who they are, and you know, it upsets everyone, and, and...

HINCKLEY: Oh, yeah, they said that. Do, do a lot of people do this?

FOSTER: Yeah, a lot of people do, and it's, I don't think it's fair. The reason that I came in here was not to have this.

HINCKLEY: I know it.

FOSTER: You understand that.

HINCKLEY: I know, I know you want to be anonymous and all that stuff.

FOSTER: No, then, then why are you calling me if you don't know who I am? See, I mean…

HINCKLEY: I don't know who you are?

FOSTER: If you, if I, I don't know you, then why, why do you call?

HINCKLEY: Because I want to talk to you. Listen, Jodie, Jodie….

FOSTER: Yes.

HINCKLEY: I just, I just got through reading this article in *Esquire*.

FOSTER: Uh-huh.

HINCKLEY: I thought it was great.

FOSTER: Thank you very much.

HINCKLEY: Did they ask you to write it, or did you just send it in?

FOSTER: They asked me.

HINCKLEY: Hmm?

FOSTER: Look, I really can't talk to you. OK? But did, do me a big favor. You understand why I can't, you know, carry on these conversations with people I don't know. You understand that it is dangerous, and it's just not done, and it's not fair, and it's rude.

HINCKLEY: Oh.

FOSTER: All right.

HINCKLEY: Well, I'm, not dangerous. I promise you that.

FOSTER: Well, I understand that, but it's, it's just that, it's the same thing, OK?

HINCKLEY: Well, so you just don't ever want me calling again?

FOSTER: No. It's been really nice talking to you, though.

HINCKLEY: Well, see, has it really?

FOSTER: Yes.

HINCKLEY: You sound thrilled.

FOSTER: I know. I am thrilled, believe me.

HINCKLEY: Why does it upset your roommates. Just tell me that.

FOSTER: Because you call at all, all the time, and, and they are studying. They're neurobiologists and genetic experts and American studies masters here, and it's not fair, and I don't think it's fair to their study habits, and it's not, it's not fair to bother me with somebody I don't know.

HINCKLEY: But see, I, ah...

FOSTER: That's basically what it is.

HINCKLEY: I don't live here, so I won't be calling you all the time.

FOSTER: Oh, you're leaving tomorrow, right?

HINCKLEY: No, Monday.

FOSTER: Monday, now it's Monday.

HINCKLEY: Now, when did I say I was leaving tomorrow?

FOSTER: You said you were leaving tomorrow for New York. That's....

HINCKLEY: No, I said I was leaving for New York City. I didn't say tomorrow. I've got a, what are they laughing at?

FOSTER: They're laughing at you.

HINCKLEY: Jodie.

FOSTER: Seriously, this isn't fair. Do me a favor and don't call back. All right.

HINCKLEY: How about just tomorrow?

FOSTER: Oh, God! Oh, seriously, this is really starting to bother me. Do you mind if I hang up?

HINCKLEY: Jodie, please.

FOSTER: No. Look, you understand the reason why I have to hang up, you know.

HINCKLEY: I, I'd, I'll, I'll, I'll end the conversation.

FOSTER: OK.

HINCKLEY: Let me, just call, can I just call back tomorrow.

FOSTER: No.

HINCKLEY: Why not?

FOSTER: Well, because I won't answer the phone. I'll put it off the hook. But if you do want to call me back tomorrow, that's fine.

HINCKLEY: But will you talk?

FOSTER: No.

HINCKLEY: Just one more time.

FOSTER: OK.

HINCKLEY: What, what time do you want me to call?

FOSTER: I don't care.

HINCKLEY: Well, when do you have to study?

FOSTER: I won't be here.

HINCKLEY: Well, where are you gonna be?

FOSTER: I'm going away for the weekend.

HINCKLEY: Oh, it's almost over, Jodie.

FOSTER: Yes, I know.

HINCKLEY: Can I call tomorrow night?

FOSTER: That's fine.

HINCKLEY: Will you be in?

FOSTER: Um, maybe.

HINCKLEY: Will you talk?

FOSTER: Sure.

HINCKLEY: Well, you just changed your mind, see?

FOSTER: Look, I can't be bothered with your noisome habits.

HINCKLEY: Ah, ah, are we, will you talk or not? I mean…

FOSTER: Yes, I will.

HINCKLEY: Well, then, thank….

FOSTER: All right. Good night.

HINCKLEY: Thank you, Jodie. Good night.

Eventually, millions of people would hear those tapes or read about them, and debate and discuss them until the end of time, conversations that continue today. They would be heard at my trial.

But I wasn't thinking about that; then came the biggest opportunity of my life. As close as I'd ever come, and, it turned out, ever would.

The night before, I'd gone out at a local bar. I wasn't a big drinker, and I didn't expect Jodie to be, but you never knew. Even if she was underage at the time, I could see her getting a little special treatment from the bartenders. Or maybe she would just stop by to hang out with some of her friends.

I threw back a few and got a little more social than normal. As I sat at the bar, some of her school colleagues ventured up to me to order some cold ones of their own. I made some small talk, pulling out a photo of her and bragging. I think I told some of them that I was already dating her. I may have just said that I wanted to.

Anyway, many of them looked like they just wanted to get the hell away from me. Some laughed, others smiled politely and stepped back. Nobody got into anything deep with me, so I'm sure none of them actually bought that this random guy they'd never seen before was the true love of one of America's most famous ladies.

When I got back to my room, I put together another note for her, and I was on my way to her dorm. As I turned the corner to the front door, I saw someone standing in front of the building, getting ready for the morning with some impromptu aerobics.

It was her. My Jodie was right there. Her hair was different, and she looked a little shorter than she had on the screens, but I knew it was her. I was mere feet away from the screen heroine of millions, destined to be my true love forever. Close enough to literally reach out and touch my dream.

I stepped forward. My whole life had been about this moment.

"Excuse m-me," I stammered in all my non-Casanova-ness.

She looked up and gave me a welcoming smile. Now was the time.

"Do you know where the library is?" Yes. That was the best I could do. The biggest chance in the world, and that popped out of my stricken mouth.

"Oh, yes," she said, as polite as she'd been on the phone. Appearing to not recognize the voice she'd heard shortly before, she pointed over.

Even I, as insane as I was, knew that if I stood there and stared at her for a few more seconds, she would get creeped out fast. I hurried away, convincing myself that I would get another chance to make an impression.

No matter what else I did—like, say, what happened the next March—that would be about the biggest regret of my life.

Drowning in embarrassment, I kept bouncing back and forth between New Haven and New York. I was holing up at one hotel after another, trying to find work in the local record stores. Still trying to capture the spirit of Travis Bickle, I became a fixture in Times Square, mainly in the X-rated areas. I picked up a few prostitutes and, unlike he and Iris, we closed the deals. I thought it was exciting to be in his environment.

Then I decided to step in a little further. I decided to emulate his work. If Iris had been enthralled by what Travis had done in the fictional sense, I knew Jodie would be even more captivated by me making it real.

Travis had almost shot a presidential candidate and gotten away. Then he'd killed for Iris and ended up a local hero, to her and others.

That was it. That could be me. That could be us. I vowed it would be. And I wouldn't stop until it was.

"I bought so many handguns because Travis bought so many handguns. Ask him, not me."

From my interview with *Newsweek*

12. CHASING CARTER

Okay, so my first attempts had fallen short. I would wow her with my persistence, my devotion. She would appreciate just how far I would go for her. Now it was time to do my part. I couldn't let her forget about me. I had to show her what type of man I truly was. How far I was willing to go for her love.

My resolve to take out the president had grown throughout the year. That very summer, I'd ventured by the White House. Noticing a group of people standing there gawking at it, I figured I would join in. Not because I was especially enamored with it, or with the guy that lived there, but because I figured it was simply the thing to do.

I leaned against the fence in front of it and had a friendly passerby snap a photo of me. Certain people would call this a glimpse straight into the mind of a psychopath.

The press loved this photo, though not as much as one I would take later. There I was, kneeling against the fence, looking for all the world like I was furious. Not happy because I was in front of a national landmark, not showing that this was a moment that I would always remember. I looked like I wanted to slug the guy taking it. I looked like I would rather be anywhere but there. Most people would take a photo in front of the House and have a smile across their face. I just looked royally pissed.

It was amazing how much mileage the media got out of a facial expression. Clearly, I was already over the edge. This was an obvious sign that my desire to kill the president had already solidified.

Okay, maybe there was some truth to that. But... well, offhand, I can't think of any "but"s on that statement.

Like millions of other Americans, I liked Jimmy Carter as a person. Always honest, pretty moral, good family man. As a president, well, that was another story. My family, big oil businesspeople that they were, couldn't stand him, holding him personally responsible for the energy crisis of 1979.

My father blamed the president for his own foray into oil falling short time and again. This had changed by the late 1970s, but Carter still got blamed for the economy going to hell and inflation jumping through the roof, among other issues.

Fair or otherwise, I didn't have much respect for Carter in the presidential sense. But I wasn't going to kill him because he was a bad president, or because he or his administration had done anything to me personally. He was just a man with the wrong job at the wrong time.

He was almost out of time to convince people to vote for him again. I came within a piece of hunting gear to cutting all of his time altogether.

At the beginning of October 1980, President Carter was scheduled to speak at the Dayton Convention Center in Ohio. Five floors up at a hotel across the street, I sat and waited.

Fortunately for him, I didn't have the rifle that I'd taken up to the roof at another hotel in DC the previous December. All I had was a couple of handguns. I'd made sure to snatch them up at a few different places. I'd bought one in Dallas, a few more in Lubbock, and a box of bullets somewhere else. Even in a state as gun-loving as Texas, such a large order all at once might have set off some red flags, and I didn't want that. I'd stayed within the bounds of the law.

The one in Dallas was a .22. I'd grabbed it at Rocky's Pawn Shop, paying less than $50. It was small enough that I could move it around without being seen. Small enough that I could keep it hidden until it was time for action.

That would come in handy later. Right then, I needed something else.

If I had a rifle scope, all I would have to do was wait until Carter and his entourage arrived, lean my gun out the window, and fire straight down on him and his. I could take him out, and maybe even a few more. How gutsy that would be.

I drove all over town, looking for the final piece of weaponry that could have spelled his doom and my stardom. But I couldn't find one, not one compatible with my weapons.

And as it turned out, it couldn't have worked anyway.

The next day, when Carter got out of his car to wave to the crowd before heading into the center, I was in the midst. Clips of me being there would be broadcast at my trial.

But unless I could get close enough to choke him out, I couldn't have done anything. I'd left my guns in a locker at the bus station I'd pulled into the day before. Quite an unwelcome surprise I'd encountered that morning.

Off to Tennessee he went, and I followed. But my trip to Nashville ended the same way, and it's as illogical as everything else I'd done, to and past that point.

A week later, I'd gotten word that the president was staying at the Opryland Hotel. Armed with my trusty .38, a pair of .22s, and enough high-velocity, explosive ammunition to blast him and everyone around him to tiny bits, I was gearing up like a solider going into battle. It was me against him for Jodie's heart and love, and I vowed I wouldn't mess up this time. I was locked, loaded, and lustful for bloodshed, all for the right cause.

But just as I was about to step out of my hotel room, a thought hit me, almost as hard as the bullets that I was carrying.

The Opryland Hotel, the very one I was about to ambush, had been built to house the Grand Ole Opry, a haven for upcoming country acts. When Carter was there, it had only been around for a few years. Since then, it has helped hundreds of singers and their bands break into the country music world.

I still didn't quit, not all the way. Not yet. I drove around Nashville, seeing the sights of country music. And deep inside, I felt a flicker of something I hadn't thought much about in years: my own music career.

Growing up in Dallas, I'd been quite familiar with country music. It hadn't been my favorite genre for a while, but this was the first time in a long time I'd been around such a haven for music in general. So many people had walked into this city and left with their name etched in the music world.

Maybe it was a sign. Maybe I should go back to where I'd wanted to go for so long. Maybe being around all this music was a subtle message from fate telling me that the music career I'd all but given up on was still out there for me.

I couldn't do this here. I couldn't kill anyone, let alone the president, in such an area, so devoted to music tribute. For a short while, I was filled with hope that I could go somewhere, be it to New York, home to Denver, or wherever else and try to get back into the music world. I couldn't deface such a place with such a violent act, no matter the justification.

I could still kill him. Still wanted to. I just couldn't do it there.

But if a few things had gone differently in the next few days, I might have gotten thrown too far off course.

By the time Carter was rallying his Tennessee supporters at the Opryland, I was heading out. His next stop would be New York, and I figured I would wait and take him out then and there. If that didn't work, I'd return to New Haven to make another direct play for my Hollywood lady.

I rushed into Nashville International Airport, later than I'd intended. If the plane took off without me, I knew I would have little shot at Carter.

I'd hoped that, since I was late, the airport people wouldn't bother with screening. Maybe they would grab my luggage and shove it in under the plane. But as I hurried through the terminal and up to the boarding area, I found that my gear would be X-rayed, just like everyone else's.

I went dead cold and started sweating. I could go to jail. I could stay there for a long time. I could go up on federal charges.

Honestly, it wasn't incarceration itself that had me so worried. It was that, if I was out of commission for a while, Jodie might move on, get married, leave the country, put herself too far out of my reach. Maybe we would elect a new president—like we would shortly thereafter—and he would be unreachable, impossible for me to prove my love.

That was on my mind more than spending a few years behind bars. But at that point, it wasn't only my guns that had me so terrified.

Shaking like crazy, I placed my suitcase on the checkpoint. Maybe the officers would turn their heads and miss it. Maybe they wouldn't recognize the three guns and box of bullets I was carrying.

Ridiculous. Of course they did. And I was right off to a holding cell, then to the jail downtown.

They left me there for a few hours. Then they pulled me out and had an interrogation.

Sort of. I don't recall how I explained that I just happened to be carrying a few large guns and heavy ammunition with the president in town, but apparently it was good enough for them. I do remember that I informed them that I was, in fact, a Yale student on my way up to New Haven for a writing class.

Sure. But the cops didn't check me out, not all the way. Remember, at this point, I didn't have a record, hadn't stolen the guns, and had just begun my presidential stalking, so there was nothing that stood out. I'm sure in hindsight, they probably wished they'd looked a little deeper.

Since then, they did. My guns stayed at the airport until the FBI came and got them after I tried to kill Reagan, and they were pissed that my situation had been all but glossed over. After my murder attempt, the FBI started taking extra precautions to be ready to show up if guns were found on a potential passenger.

They took me to a courtroom, actually a tiny room in the back of police headquarters, and a magistrate handed down a bond of $62.50. They took my guns and sent me on my way, telling me I needed to be back there for another hearing in five days, or my bond would be forfeited.

The hell with that. They could keep it. It was a small price to pay for moving on with my quest.

And when I finally got to New York, I looked into my bag and breathed a sigh of relief that almost sucked down the hotel walls.

The guns were gone. Fine. I could replace them. But in the midst of my clothes, toiletries, and everything else, was something that could have put me away for a while.

Something else that seemed logical at the time and ridiculous at that moment, I'd been keeping a diary of all my plans. I'd proudly talked about what I would do to win Jodie's heart. I'd outlined my goals to take out the president in all kinds of detail, preaching about how important it was, how devoted a man could be to his dream.

If someone had so much as opened my tome, I would have been gone. All kinds of charges. Stalking, threatening the president, everything. They would certainly have connected my guns to my writings, and I could have gone away for a hell of a long time. The next time I was in New York, it could have been to Attica!

After I tore the book apart and flushed it down the toilet, I sat on the bed and waited for my heart rate to slow. Then I smiled. Obviously, fate was on my side. Clearly, something strong wanted me to finish my job. I'd gotten lucky, and it must have been a message to continue. What I was doing was right, and I obviously wasn't the only one to believe in me. I had some help from above. No other explanation.

For a brief while, I was relieved enough to take a breather. If I had some extra help from karma in my goal to kill the president, maybe it wasn't so urgent. Maybe I could kick back for a while and return when I had a better opportunity. I'd been chasing Carter all over. Perhaps I could wait until he came to me.

So, I pulled a pause. Rather than scooting back to DC to bump him off, I headed down to Dallas for a while. My sister had just had a son, and I had a great time hanging out with my first nephew.

And, yes, I bought another gun. A bigger one. I had a new plan, but I didn't feel the need to go right out and act on it. Not yet.

Then I ran out of money and had to go back home. That caused the old fire to relight. I had something to get done, and I was tired of putting it off. I started to get upset again. I almost felt ashamed that I'd taken a break at all. The next time I went out, I wasn't coming back without a dead president.

But then came the first Tuesday of November 1980, and the guard changed in a big way. The guy who had been president for four years was almost immediately turned into an afterthought. He had the living hell beaten out of him on election night.

After I'd come within a scope's shot of killing Carter, now he wasn't the president anymore. Taking him out wouldn't make a difference. I lost all feeling for him one way or another. The same fate that had inspired me to continue my trek had now thrown a mountain-sized obstacle in my way.

13. ROOF SHOOTING

I could feel the president's clock ticking down. I was pissed at him. I was pissed at the world for interfering with my plans.

I was going to kill the president. I didn't care who he was, or she was, or whoever else. Whatever person who was holding the Oval Office was going to die at my triggering hand, and that was all I could think about. All I'd thought about for a very long time.

Like I said, it didn't matter *who*. The president of the United States was going out, and I would be the one who would proudly accompany him there.

But that November night had tossed me right the hell off course. My first attempt at taking out Jimmy Carter had fallen far short, and I wouldn't make that mistake again. The next time, I would be there sooner, get closer, be more prepared. He wasn't getting away. I was planning things out to the deepest detail. The next time he ventured out and I was close, he was going down.

And then America changed my plans for me. I'd been too focused on my killing goal to worry too much about the 1980 election, but even I was smart enough to know that Carter wouldn't be the president for too much longer. When I was in New York, back home in Colorado, even in DC, everyone had been badmouthing him for months. Our economy was shit, inflation was through the roof, there were crises all over the world, and he was getting blamed for everything. Whether or not he deserved it, I didn't give a damn. All I could think about was taking him down and moving up in Jodie's eyes.

That's a big reason why I didn't vote; I simply didn't care who won. Carter's work, or inaction, hadn't affected me much individually, or at least, I didn't think it had. It may have and I just wasn't worried. But quite a few people were, and that election night was thrilling.

Like, say, my family. My parents were absolutely thrilled that Reagan had become our new leader. They did everything but throw a party. This guy was out for business owners. This guy would fight for the common folk. This guy would clean up the messes that Carter had made and lead us straight to prosperity. Considering Reagan's landslide win, millions of people obviously felt the same way.

Back to Colorado for a quick jaunt, I watched my parents celebrate in their own special uber-conservative way.

I was left to put on an act.

"Maybe," I halfheartedly managed in the midst of my family's celebration, "there's hope for this country yet." Yeah, not if I had anything to do with it.

Well, maybe that was unfair. There was hope for this country, but our president wasn't it. With me around, he didn't have much hope. Maybe this George Bush guy, his vice president, would take this country to prosperity after I'd taken Reagan out.

Or maybe I would be there myself. Yes, that was it. That was the new message my mind was telling me. I would take out the president, and everyone would understand why. They would see me as a guy who had a dream and made it happen. If I was so devoted to my love from the movies, I must have a heart of gold, right? I must be the kind of man everyone woman needs and wants!

People would admire me for what I'd done. I would be a role model, a hero. By taking out the president, I would step into his place. I would be our new exalted leader.

President Hinckley. I liked the sound of that, even if I was just talking to myself.

And then the only thing better? First Lady Foster. Jodie Foster. Forget being a world-famous movie star. How might she like becoming the most important woman in America?

Dreams. So many hopes and dreams. But fate and reality kept teaming up to keep them from me. A month later, they would work even harder.

I'd failed in my attempt to take out Jimmy Carter, and then he'd been voted out. What was I to do now? If I killed him, it wouldn't make much of a difference. It wouldn't make me stand out.

But now I had to wait. I'd come so close to accomplishing my goal a few weeks before, and now I had to start all over. I had nothing to do. Our new president wouldn't take office for months, and I was apparently supposed to stay in a holding pattern until then?

What was I supposed to do? Just sit there and wait and wait until someone else got into the White House and then kill him? Now I had to start all over, and I was bitter as all hell. It seemed so unfair.

Honestly, I almost said screw it right then and there. It was too much trouble overhauling my plan to take out one guy. It wasn't worth it to have to go back to the beginning and plot out the patterns of someone who might have totally different interests than Carter and might hardly be out in public at all. That, along with the months of waiting for him to hurry the hell up and vow his way into office, made me just want to give up.

Well, at least to broaden my hopes. Not to end my quest, just to expand its goal a little bit.

After Thanksgiving, I was back in DC, not far from the White House. I was thinking about stalking out Reagan, but still not sure. He wouldn't take office for another month, and I couldn't imagine how I would occupy that much of my own time.

Well, maybe one. Let's make this quick and easy, if not neat.

In the span of a few minutes, one can get from the White House to the Hay-Adams Hotel, even if you don't walk very fast. Looming like an old Italian Renaissance castle, it's one of the most popular spots to stay in the nation's capital. By the time I walked through the lobby in December 1980, the place had been there for over half a century.

And now I would make it infamous. I would paint the whole goddamned building black. Every time Carter or Reagan or whoever else was living at the House across the street, they would feel a chill. They would remember what I was about to do.

I walked through the building and made my way to an elevator. Some people got on with me. No one smiled or said hello. No one really noticed. I was sort of hoping that someone would see the large guitar case in my hand and think I was a famous rock star, maybe there to warm up for a spot at the Reagan inauguration, but they didn't.

I guess I'm glad that no one took too much interest in me. If they'd started asking questions, they might have noticed that the object in my case was actually a huge rifle.

Yes. I was going to start blasting. I would aim for the White House. Maybe, just maybe, I would hit some big names. Maybe Carter or Walter Mondale or someone from the cabinet. Or maybe some other political bigwig. Someone important enough that I would be remembered for taking them out.

A decade and a half before, Charles Whitman had done this very thing, venturing out on the University of Texas's observation deck, armed to the nines with enough weapons to take out half the city. I always wondered why he'd bothered to bring a machete with him that day. Maybe he was going to try to throw it at someone.

With the same weaponry he'd almost perfected as a Marine, just as Lee Harvey Oswald had when he'd taken out Kennedy, Whitman had murdered 15 people and injured twice as many others before the police could take him out.

I didn't want to do exactly that. I wasn't going to go up there and just start randomly firing. First off, I didn't have Whitman's background, so I would probably have missed anyway. Secondly, I only had one weapon, not a damned arsenal like him, so I had to be conservative with my bullets.

Finally, I saw no reason to kill or even harm people I'd never seen before and would never know. I was going to aim at the White House, and people would already know the names of my victims. I was there for recognition. You get that by taking out the well known.

Unlike with my attempt at Carter, I knew I wouldn't survive this day. I had no illusions that someone would climb up and arrest me. I would feel the sniper's bullets, just like Whitman had. I still wanted to impress Jodie Foster, and maybe this would, but at least for the time being, I'd given up being around for her to fall for me. I couldn't wait so long. Maybe she would just admire me in my death.

As I stepped out onto the roof that day, I wondered what nickname they would give me. How would I be remembered? I thought Whitman's moniker of the Texas Tower Sniper was a little redundant. Maybe I would get something more interesting.

"Angel of Death?" No, too many people had taken that one. That was a cop-out nickname.

"DC Sniper?" Maybe, but that would sadly be snatched up by John Muhammad and Lee Malvo two decades later.

"John the Shooter?" God, I hoped people could do better than that.

In any case, I was ready to go out in a hail of glorified bullets.

I took my gun out. I drew it into my hands. I was ready to cock it.

Another few seconds, and the White House would be getting riddled with holes. Panic would ensue. I would see terrified throngs run out onto the White House lawn. Secret Service would be rushing in to protect them. The entire DC police department would arrive.

And, I was certain, very quickly, someone would see me, take their own shot, and send me down for good. I'd seen my last morning. I could literally count down the final seconds of my life.

And then I realized I couldn't. Decades later, I'm honestly not sure why I stopped then and there. Maybe I was afraid that I would kill a nobody. Really, I was probably concerned that such a random act wouldn't be enough to grab Jodie's attention.

But I think I just got a little scared. I'd been planning out the presidential assassination for some time, and I'd gotten close enough to Carter that I could have acted on it, but this was the first time there was nothing in my way.

No crowds. No shields. No protection for my targets. I had as good a chance as I ever would, as clear a shot as anyone ever had, and now all that was left was for me to pull the trigger.

I couldn't. Maybe I'd been lying to myself. Maybe I wasn't a killer after all. Maybe the reality I'd forced myself into was all a dream, one that I needed to hurry the hell up and wake up from. Get back to the real world. As sad and depressing, even frightening, as it was, millions of others were there and doing as well as they could. Maybe I was nothing special, no more so than them.

I headed back to my hotel.

The next night, I clicked on *Monday Night Football*.

And from within and without, the world almost exploded.

14. LENNON DEATH

I wasn't a big fan of either team that night, but as I'd been doing since football came to Monday nights in 1970, I was in front of that TV.

And I'd gotten pretty lucky. Miami and New England had battled it out, and now the contest was coming down to a last-second field goal. Can't ask for a more exciting outing.

I was already in a pretty good mood, sports-wise.

When I was a kid living in Dallas, my dad had scored Cowboys season tickets, and I'd sat next to him and my brother for years of Cotton Bowl contests in the 1960s. Sadly, my Boys had decided to wait until we'd moved away to *finally* win their first Super Bowl in early 1972.

But that night, December 8, 1980, I had something to celebrate. My squad had won its fourth straight contest the day before, and they looked well on their way to making the playoffs. I just knew they would.

On this game, things were coming down to the wire. One good kick would hand New England the win.

"It's suddenly been placed in total perspective for us," Howard Cosell's legendary, charismatic voice told the audience. "I'll finish this, [New England] is in the hurry-up offense."

Perspective? What did that mean? Finish what? What sort of perspective does one need in an NFL game, beyond which play to run next?

Probably no big thing. New England was about to try for the win.

"Remember," Cosell continued before the field goal could be tried, "this is just a football game, no matter who wins or loses."

Okay, that sounded strange. We were quite aware of that. Strange that he felt the need to preface his next statement like that.

"An unspeakable tragedy, confirmed to us by ABC News in New York City," he continued.

Oh no! What had happened? Had someone bombed Times Square or the Empire State Building? Had the president snuck north, and someone else taken him out? What was going on?

"John Lennon, outside of his apartment building on the West Side of New York City," Cosell said, his voice hardly different than 10 minutes before, when he'd been describing first downs and rushing yardage, "the most famous, perhaps, of all of the Beatles...."

Oh, shit. This was going to be bad. This was going to be horrible. It was obvious that he was putting off the message he had to convey, and that was always a sign of horrible news. I only hoped it wouldn't be what I pretty much knew it would be.

"Shot twice in the back, rushed to Roosevelt Hospital, dead on arrival," Cosell rushed. "Hard to go back to the game after that news flash." But he and the rest of the announcing team did, and moments later, they were all about the blocked kick and the game heading to overtime.

I didn't feel a thing. I hardly reacted. Didn't blink, didn't pass out, didn't feel much at all. Maybe because of how poised Cosell was. From his voice and from those of the other announcers, you could hardly tell they'd just learned some of the worst news a person could receive, and had it happen on national television.

I just sat there staring. It was strange, seeing so many people cheering, or even booing, in the stands that night. It was like I felt that they should have known that Lennon had been murdered, should have reacted the same way I did, or even as Cosell had. Of course they didn't know, couldn't know yet, but it was weird being in on something ahead of thousands of people who were in the same stadium as the guy who'd made the announcement. It was like knowing the punchline of a joke so dirty it made you want to puke.

I was in shock. It was like Cosell's other longtime friend, Muhammed Ali, was blasting me across the face with one blow after another. John Lennon was dead. Not just dead, but stolen. Robbed from us. Would it have been easier if he'd dropped from a sudden heart attack or even a car accident? Tragic, yes, unexpected, sure, but not like this. Who would want to do this? Who could hurt him enough to blast him to eternity like that? What would cause a person to do something so violent, so needlessly? It elevated the unthinkable to near impossible.

I sat there, watching the rest of the game. I wasn't stupid enough to think that it was a joke or misunderstanding. No way would Howard Cosell, or anyone else worth a damn, do something like that. I think I was just trying not to think. I felt that if I sat there and focused on what was happening on the field, rather than what I was thinking or hearing, I wouldn't have to handle it.

But I couldn't. As the extra period rolled, I heard Cosell's sad voice again.

"In case the folks missed the earlier news flash, ABC News has confirmed, that John Lennon, a member of the famed Beatles, maybe the best-known member..." Even after going through it once, he was still stalling for time.

"Was shot twice in the back outside of his apartment building, in the west side of New York tonight, rushed to the Roosevelt Hospital, dead on arrival. An unspeakable tragedy. Details on *Nightline*, thirty minutes after the end of this contest." Then, again, he went right back into sports announcing mode.

That's when I did lose it. Started crying and couldn't stop. I was heartbroken that one of my heroes had died. I'd built John Lennon up as something above human, so much better than us mere mortals. Now he was dead. Someone had the power to take him away, to end his life and rob the music world of his presence, his talent.

And I hated it. I was furious. How could anyone do this? How big a piece of shit would one have to be to take out John Lennon? What had he done to deserve this? If I'd been standing in front of the guy who'd committed the crime, I wouldn't have hesitated at all. I would have reached into my guitar case, taken out the rifle I still had, and given this SOB his just desserts. No self-doubt or nervousness on this one.

And I would be a hero. That certainly would have made me beloved. Hell, I wish I had. I wasn't sure if Jodie Foster was a Beatles fan, but I don't think she would have had a problem with what I'd done. The millions in mourning right next to me sure as hell wouldn't.

Mark David Chapman's name would live in pitch-black infamy as much as mine. A few months later, I would sort of follow in his footsteps. I think that's why, while I still pretty much hate his guts even today, I could understand what he'd done. I saw some commonalities in us, mainly caused by my worsening psychosis.

I don't think anyone knew how personal that moment was for Cosell himself. He and Lennon had been friends under the radar for years, and six years before (with one day's difference), the two had chatted on *Monday Night Football* during a game in Los Angeles, only to be joined by California's then-governor, none other than Ronald Reagan. Having to sit there and tell the nation that someone whom millions idolized and you knew personally had just died, and not just died, but been violently stolen, must have been unthinkable. It's interesting that the other announcers didn't say it themselves, instead basically telling Cosell he had to. When I found out how close he and Lennon were, that kind of pissed me off. Even when I went back and watched clips of the announcement, I admired how gutsy he was in doing that. I guess when you spend as much time in media, in front of cameras as he did, you get into a mindset that allows you to keep your cool in situations like that. I'm sure it hit him as hard and probably harder than it did so many others, particularly those like me who were "just" fans.

Of course, the world went crazy, not only the music world. Especially there in the nation's capital, everyone was running around crying, praying, staring off into space. Posters, shirts, all sorts of memorials to Lennon started popping up. Every TV station, every newspaper, so many people could talk of nothing else.

I felt like a passenger in my own body. It was impossible to ignore this. It was also impossible to comprehend, to deal with the matter. I could hardly talk or think at all. Who could? Three people even committed suicide over Lennon's death. I felt that way myself—and, as you'll read shortly, came within a small decision of acting on it, more than once.

I was so thankful when Central Park held a memorial a week later. As sad as it would be, at least it gave me, and thousands of other fans, something to look forward to. We would have a place to go where, while we would all be uncomfortable and heartbroken, we would at least be around people who were feeling the same thing, who were there to mourn, just as we were.

The night before I went, I was feeling lonely. That was hardly new for me, but with the wave of hopelessness flowing across the entire nation, it was worse. So much worse.

I decided to go to my regular standby in the matter. Like I've said and always will, I was never much of a drinker. I didn't do drugs, although I might have at that moment if I'd stumbled across any. I didn't run to the gym and bodybuild, or go for a 10-mile run in the frosty pre-Christmas weather, which wasn't a safe thing to do in Manhattan then.

No, I went outside my hotel. It didn't take long for me to locate just what I wanted.

Or, in this case, who I wanted.

There were always lovely ladies milling around the area, and none made the slightest secret of who they were and why they were there. I'd drowned my sorrows in ladies of the night before, so I figured I would try it again. I would have an easier time snaring a paid woman than Travis Bickle had, although I sure as hell wasn't prowling for anyone Iris's age, as *Taxi Driver* makes sadly clear that many had before Travis appeared on the scene.

The first lady I met was *very* easy on the eyes. She told me her name was Kelly. I didn't care if that was true. If she'd called herself Iris, I think I would have keeled over from shock. I would have seen some divine intervention in that.

She was there to make some quick money. I was there to grab some quick relief, some escape from the sadness. Like I said, she wasn't the first woman I'd taken off the streets, if only for a few minutes. I had one hell of a reason for needing her that night.

The next morning, I headed straight to the train station.

DC to New York City isn't a long ride, but it certainly felt like forever. It didn't matter. My parents had moved to Evergreen, Colorado, just west of Denver, right after I'd finished high school, but I could have been with them, or in California, or, hell, in another country. You couldn't have kept me away from that event if you'd locked me in solitary confinement, a situation that, sadly, would become very plausible a few months later.

We cried. We hugged people we'd never seen before and comforted people we would never see again. Many of us sang Beatles songs, especially "Imagine" and other tunes Lennon himself had done. "We All Shine On" proved sadly uplifting for such a moment. We all hoped that the instant karma John sang of in that song would come and visit Mark David Chapman very, very soon.

15. "I READ THE NEWS TODAY, OH NO!"

John Lennon is dead and people continue
to laugh and dream and live…
Oh, listen to the comedian tell his jokes…
The audience is laughing, so he must be amusing,
But I'm not close to a smile. John Lennon is dead!

Seventy-five thousand people with brains are
Watching the all-important football game…
Isn't it fun and exciting! No, no, no, a thousand
Times. A man died on December 8, 1980, and nothing
Will ever be the same…

For an entire week after the assassination
Of John Lennon I cried like a sick baby…
What I cannot comprehend is the fact that
People are trying to carry on with life now.
What's the use?

In America, heroes are meant to be killed. Idols
Are meant to be shot in the back. Guns are neat
Little things, aren't they? They can kill
Extraordinary people with every little effort.

But don't say a word about it to the NRA.

John Lennon died a couple of weeks ago, and I
Did too. Bang, bang, we're all dead. The stupid
Earth keeps revolving and the stupid people keep
The faith, but they are actually walking corpses.
Everyone is dead.

Ronald Reagan never missed a beat. Of course he's
Not in favor of gun control. How can you make a
World move without guns, guns, guns?

I think the Charter Arms people are so clever
To produce guns that are so small, and yet have
The capacity to kill famous people.
Every red-blooded American
Should send a Valentine card to the good folks at
Charter Arms, and the good folks at the NRA.

Speaking of red blood, I heard from an eyewitness
That the stuff was coming out of Lennon's mouth
And body at an alarming rate after he was shot.
And all it took to produce such a spectacle was
A little toy gun and an American pulling the trigger.

I am an American and boy am I proud! Let's see
How many more idols we can wipe off the face of
The earth....
The dream is over.

I died. You died. Everyone died.
America died. The world died. The universe.

John Hinckley Jr.

16. SLIPPING FURTHER AWAY AFTER LENNON

My mind was gone. My rationale was destroyed beyond repair. I knew it. There was nothing left for me. I was spiraling downward, and even I knew I was too far gone to ever get back to the surface.

And yet, I still managed to hide it. I don't know how. I think that's actually a common trademark of the psychotics of the world. We seem normal, or just slightly off, to those on the outside. People have this stereotypical view of us psychopaths. They envision someone laying in a corner, clumps of their hair in their hands, their body coated with a layer of dirt and grease, wiping the drool off their face long enough to blare out the next verse about the dangers of the Whore of Babylon, pointing out the 20-legged tarantulas crawling up and down the wall.

That's not how we are. We go psycho, yes, but we don't turn into monsters. We don't live in your reality. We don't live in the regular world. We see things, feel things, know things that others don't, but they make sense to us.

People have always scoffed at me and many people similar to me. They wonder how in the hell a guy could ever think that killing the president could impress anyone, let alone a famous actress. They write me off as another nutjob, and that's it.

That's sad. That's lazy. And we're not crazy. We're insane. That is the difference. That is why I didn't go to jail, even for committing one of the most horrific acts in world history. We'll come back to this later.

My parents are two of the smartest people I know, smarter than me in most ways, but when I went back to see them after

John Lennon died, they couldn't tell how far my mind was gone, and how fast it was still dropping.

That's not their fault. They're not psychiatrists, and even those in the mental health field fight enough among themselves that there's rarely one solid, unshakable conclusion to a mental illness.

I was still living in my Jodie Foster-obsessed world then. I was still out to kill someone—and no, I never felt the urge to harm my parents or anyone else I knew on a personal level, aside from myself. I just did what I'd always done around them: not speak very much about anything. They would ask me what I'd been up to, why I hadn't gone back to school, what job I had, and so on, and I would either lie or be so evasive that they would give up. They were used to that, so they didn't pursue it. I just wasn't one to brag about or even discuss myself much at all. They occasionally queried me as to whether Lynn and I were even talking anymore, and I would tap dance around that one as well.

That's something else psychotics can do pretty well—hide our symptoms strongly enough that people don't pick up on them. Psychosis can be tough to catch if you don't know what to look for, and most people aren't prepared to go searching. That's part of why some very ignorant people still crow about mental illness being able to be "switched on and off" by the sufferers. They honestly think we would act that out if we had a choice, which is ridiculous.

Then, a few weeks after I was home, their hand was forced—by none other than yours truly.

I hadn't been feeling right for some time, and taking that one-two punch so recently just added to it. I'd failed at killing Carter. One of my idols had been murdered. What would happen next?

Nothing I wanted to be around for. For all I knew, someone could have tapped into my own mind. They were reading my thoughts. They could look at me and tell what I was planning, dreaming of.

And what would they do? Kill me? Take me out before I could act? Maybe they were worshippers of the president, and they wanted to protect him.

Or, even worse, what if they jumped all the guns and got there before I did? What if one of them was planning to hole up on a roof nearby the Capitol, or maybe at a building down the street, like Oswald did for Kennedy? Maybe someone was planning to take Reagan out as soon as he finished the oath.

Taxi Driver had been a very popular movie. I'm sure I wasn't the only one to take more of an interest in Jodie Foster's work after it. Maybe someone out there felt stronger than I did.

And maybe his plan would work as well as my own kept *not* working. He would take out the president, and she would find out about it. Hell, maybe Reagan himself had been into her, had invited her to sit in the audience as he vowed? Perhaps she would see him fall. I was sure she would be shocked and upset, at first. But then the proud partaker of the act would come out and pronounce his love for her, and she would be so touched she would become his forever!

Some asshole, doing my deed to steal my true love? I couldn't believe someone would stoop so low. But there I was, heartbroken on the other side of the country, and I couldn't just hop on a plane and head over to do my work, especially with some time to pass before the inauguration.

Maybe I should give up. I'd had too much blow up in my face lately. I didn't want more of that.

These thoughts weren't constant. They came and went. Sometimes I felt like I had just one way out, and other times, I would kick myself for feeling that way.

But one day, they got a little strong. Too strong. I figured this was it. I'd been on antidepressants for a while, but I hadn't actually been taking them. I stored them up, only taking them when I really, really felt down. Still, I'd never fallen this far.

Home alone, I spread my pills out, looking over them thoughtfully. I wasn't a hundred percent sure that I wanted to die, but I wouldn't have minded it. Like many of those on their first attempt at suicide, I decided I would leave it up to chance. Maybe fate would send me a message of whether I should stay or go.

Rather than grabbing them all up in my hands and wolfing them down too quickly for my system to process, I took them slowly. I shot well past my recommended dosage, but I kept going.

By the time I'd passed the halfway point, I already felt dizzy. I noticed that my skin was getting clammy. Then my stomach heaved, and it was time to go.

Seconds later, I was hunched over the side of a toilet, returning the meds I'd taken and everything I'd eaten from that day and even the one before. Stuff was coming out of me that I had no damn clue what it was. I must have lost 12 pounds in those few moments.

I stood up and almost fell backward from what I saw in the mirror. My face was paler than all the ghosts in the world put together. I was shocked. What had I done to myself?

And then my mother was there. I didn't know what she'd seen, but she certainly knew what I'd been doing. When she saw the meds on the table, she put it together very quickly.

Like most parents then and now, my folks had lived in denial about my mental issues for a long time. They just kept trying to chalk it up to immaturity that would fade. But now they couldn't turn their backs anymore. I think my father would have rather thrown me to the wolves and told me to come back when I grew a backbone and a sense of tenacity, but my mother had had enough. Whether I'd wanted to die or not, she wasn't taking another chance.

She told me about a psychiatrist they'd found nearby who'd been working out some biofeedback treatments that had worked on some co-workers and friends of my dad. Not him personally. Like most men of his age and time, he didn't have much use for the shrinks of the world, or doctors in general.

It's a form of alternative medicine (a phrase that, in and of itself, still scares people today) that combines mental and physical health. Rather than laying on a couch and describing your deepest secrets, or not just that, you get up and exercise. The doctor monitors your heart rate, muscle tension, breathing, and other factors to help your anxiety.

Fine, why not? If they thought it would work, I would give it a shot for them. I didn't think it would work, but I didn't really care if it did. I figured the best that could happen would be that I would learn to control (i.e., hide) my symptoms so that my parents and everyone else would quit bothering me long enough to complete my murderous mission.

That's when I met Dr. John Hopper. I'm only mentioning his name because you'll see him again later in the story.

He would have me taking long walks all over the neighborhood, with a monitor on my hand managing my heart rate. I would sit in his office, listening to beeps on my headphones, hearing them move up and down with my heart.

I told him about feeling isolated and depressed and anxious, stuff I was sure he already knew. I mentioned Jodie, but certainly not what I had planned to win her heart. What was I, crazy?

Well, yes. But I don't think he ever thought so. He could tell I had some serious anxiety and depression issues, but he didn't believe I was mentally ill.

He assigned me a short autobiography of myself. There wasn't much to tell.

"Because I have remained so inactive and reclusive over the past few five years, I have managed to remove myself from the real world," I wrote, coming *this close* to opening up the doors to my new mind-altered existence and leading him in. "I have two obsessions in life now: writing and [Jodie]. I care about nothing else! My mind was on the breaking point at all times. A relationship I'd dreamed about went absolutely nowhere. A disillusionment was complete." Like anyone else who heard me spew out these rants up to the point of the shooting, he probably just saw me as a fan who had gotten too into his affection object but would move on to someone else as soon as the next beauty showed up in the movies.

As the last days of 1980 ticked away, I could tell that this was going nowhere fast. On the last night of the year, I holed up in a little motel.

Why alcohol, for a guy who hardly ever took a sip? And why peach brandy? It tastes fine, but it's kind of specific, especially for a non-drinker like me, right?

Well, because I could feel John Hinckley Jr., the person, slipping away. Actually, I didn't really want him around right then. I was becoming something else. Someone else. Someone who'd done what I wanted to do, who'd been where I wanted to go.

Travis Bickle. Yes, I was becoming him.

Not Robert De Niro, the man. Great actor, yes, but I didn't want to be rich and famous like him. I wanted to be the guy he'd played. I started listening to the *Taxi Driver* soundtrack on an almost hourly basis. I read and re-read the 1967 same-titled Richard Elman book the film was based on to where I could almost recite it.

Man, can an actor really be *too* good at his work? It seemed like De Niro actually had been, in this case. If he'd given a crappy performance as Travis, would I have been so inspired to become the vigilante with a heart? That's a real dark side effect of immense talent, isn't it?

But this particular booze type had been Travis's lifeline during his quest to save Iris. Now it would become my own. I hoped it would make me as courageous and brave as Mr. Bickle.

Between sips, I sat at a table. In my hand was a microphone, snaked down to a huge tape recorder. I'd been keeping a diary for a long time, and this was an audio entry.

"John Lennon is dead. The world is over. Forget it. It's just gonna be insanity, if I even make it through the first few days…. I still regret having to go on with 1981. My life is screwed up. The world is even more screwed up. I don't know why people want to live.

John Lennon is dead. I still think, I still think about Jodie all the time. That's all I think about really. That, and John Lennon's death. They were sort of binded together before December 8, they been binded together since last summer, really. John and Jodie and now one of 'em's dead."

I took out my guitar and did some strumming. It was my own personal version of John Lennon's "Oh, Yoko," his tribute to his wife named Ono.

"In the middle of a dream," I sang, "in the middle of a dream, I call your name. Ohhhh, *Jodie*! Ohhh, *Jodie*! My love will turn you on!" Like I guarantee *many* men had to their true loves since the song's 1971 release, I adapted it to fit my own desires.

"You've been through the storm," I sang to Jodie in an original creation of mine. "You have seen it all. I've been nowhere at all. Jodie, Jodie, could it be that I'm the one? Jodie, Jodie, don't you know it's done?"

"I hate New Haven with a mortal passion. I've been up there many times, not stalking her really, but just looking

after her.... I was going to take her away for a while there, but I don't know. I am so sick I can't even do that.... It'll be total suicide city. I mean, I couldn't care less. Jodie is the only thing that matters now. Anything I might do in 1981 would be solely for Jodie Foster's sake.

My obsession is Jodie Foster. I've gotta, I've gotta find her and talk to her some way in person or something.... That's all I want her to know, is that I love her. I don't want to hurt her.... I think I'd rather just see her not, not on earth, than being with other guys. I wouldn't want to stay here on earth without her.

I can't go the whole year 1981. I don't care anything about the decade, the '80s or the future or anything because the dream is over now just as Lennon said ten years ago, but it's really over now. Jodie Foster is the only dream now.

I read about Jodie and, and look at her pictures and just, my heart screams with love. I hate to think of her being with other guys. It just kills me, just devastates me to think about that. Sometimes I think I'd rather see her not, not on earth than being with other guys... but I have to go with her. I wouldn't want to stay on earth without her on earth. It would have to be some kind of final pact between me and Jodie. I think about that a lot. That's all I really think about.

Jodie is the only thing that matters now. Anything that I might do in 1981 would be solely for Jodie Foster's sake. And I mean that sincerely. I want to make some kind of statement or something on her behalf. Just tell the world in some way I worship and idolize her ten million times.

I just want to say goodbye to the old year, which was nothing; total misery, total death, John Lennon is dead, the world is over, forget it.

It'd have to be some kind of final pact between Jodie and me. I think about that a lot. It's time for me to go to bed. It's after midnight. It's the New Year, 1981, bye.

Hallelujah!"

17. LENNON SUICIDE

Did God Die?

The God I was told to believe in would never have

Permitted the murder of John Lennon. God didn't

Die. He never was alive in the first place.

John Hinckley Jr.

I still remembered John Lennon. Of course I did. I always would.

But for the first time, I hated what I was thinking. All the music, all the good he'd done for so many for so long, just seemed like a waste. He'd always worked so hard at that, always trying to get people to live in peace, in harmony, in and beyond his music, and he was just violently snatched away. Been forced to suffer in shock, in terror, in his last moments.

If he'd dropped dead of a heart attack, or even a drug overdose like so many of his colleagues from the music world had and have since, yes, that would have broken my heart, but it would have been easier to accept. It would have been a sad acceptance that death comes for us all, one way or another, and life ends for us all.

But like this? What a selfish piece of shit this Chapman guy was! What right did this scumbag have, making himself the judge, jury, and executioner of a guy he'd never met (well, he'd met him, as we've all seen that sad photo of Lennon signing an autograph for his assassin), and who had done nothing to him or to anyone else? What a needless act, which served zero purpose at all. Not just to kill an innocent man, but to fill him with lead from behind!

Didn't even have the guts to look the man in the eye before killing him.

But then there came a bigger question. If my mind had been hanging by a thread before, the shock and panic over John Lennon's murder, emotions that by then were almost foreign to me, severed them quickly.

My new mystery, one that could never be answered, became the matter of how anyone would want to live in a world?

Who the hell was this God guy? What gave him the right? Why would anyone want to worship, to be under the control of someone who would do this? If God was running things, he was just standing there while one of his greatest creations was destroyed. He could have stopped it at any time. He didn't have to let it happen. But he did, and that made me feel like this guy wasn't worth giving a damn about, let alone praying to, coming to in times of need. We didn't want or need help or guidance from someone who would do this sort of thing.

The world had become a sad, dark place. Not because John Lennon himself had been killed, or not only that. Just knowing that we lived in a place where the best get rewarded by violent, sudden death. Just knowing that no one's really appreciated. People don't give a shit about each other, to the point that they harm themselves to take down those who do right simply because it's right. This guy had painted his own name pitch black, and now he would spend the rest of his life in jail, probably surrounded by people who'd liked John Lennon themselves. I'm sure I was one of many who wished that the death penalty could have been reinstated for just one day.

I hated living then. I hated the world. I wanted to escape. For a brief period, I forgot about killing the president. I didn't care about impressing Jodie. I wanted a way out of this hellhole known as Planet Earth.

I wanted Mark David Chapman to die. No one else in America, probably the rest of the world, deserved it more.

But as much as I hated what he'd done and why, I actually considered things from the "how" perspective. He'd maneuvered his way close enough to his target, pulled out a specific type of firearm, then sat there and waited for his reward to come around. The clown knew exactly what he was doing, but he didn't see it as malicious. He believed—or *said* he believed, which his jury ended up not buying—that by killing Lennon, he would receive all of John's fanfare, stardom, everything else. Forget working so hard and obtaining it himself; he wanted everything handed to him, and he was willing to kill, needed to, to obtain it. Ironically, a guy who had never considered a music career was murdering for stardom, while myself, who had been banging on the door to music success, a knocking that continues today, wanted to be an assassin for other reasons.

My family, along with many others, celebrated as President Reagan took his oath of office on January 20, 1981. I pretended to share in the enthusiasm.

Right around that time, I contacted a local gun seller about him buying a few of my weapons. Smack in the middle of the parking lot of his center, no papers, no ID, no signatures, nothing legal at all, I handed over the rifle I'd carried in December, my trusty .38, and a few other firearms.

I kept the .22 pistol. I hoped it would be all I needed.

But this time, for the first time in months, I wasn't thinking about using it on the president. I seriously considering putting it to my own head, getting the hell out while the getting was great. I didn't know how anyone could stand living anymore, but that was their concern, and I didn't have to share in it. Lennon's violent, pointless death had been a sign that I needed to head out myself.

One of my most infamous portraits, much more so than the White House shot in 1980, had actually been taken just as my mental slide began. I'd taken it myself.

In the midst of my college career, which was never stable and ended far too early, I'd suffered a severe depressive attack. I can't even remember the exact year, only that it was in the late 1970s— as in, after my obsession with Jodie Foster had begun, but not to the level that I'd fully decided to murder for her.

It was my birthday, no less. Talk about adding insult to injury for those who loved you, even if I wasn't sure anyone did at that time. My life had just been going poorly, if it had been going anywhere at all, for years, and I didn't want it anymore.

For whatever reason, I decided that life wasn't worth moving on for. I took out a gun. I stood in front of my mirror in the Lubbock apartment I was about to get kicked out of.

Then I realized that I wasn't sure. I really thought I wanted to die, but not 100%.

I decided to make it a matter of chance. This way, if I did die, if my brains ended up all over the wall, it would be *mostly* my fault. Not quite all.

I flipped out the bullet casing and removed all but one shell. Then I spun it and pushed it back in, all with my eyes closed.

Yes, this was a not-so-friendly game of Russian Roulette. But if I was going down, I wanted people to know how, if not so much why. A photo can't convey that much. But they knew that *I knew* that I was finished, and that I was okay with it. I'd planned it out, and now I was showing them the last seconds of my life. I wanted them to see it.

With the gun squarely planted at my temple, I set up a camera for a snapshot. If you look at my expression in the photo—and it's easy to find all over the internet, even today—I didn't look upset or even angry, but more resigned. Like I wasn't necessarily happy or eager to put a bullet through my skull, but that I'd accepted that it was the tough, right choice.

I don't remember if I closed my eyes for the finale. I just know that, obviously, I heard a click, not a shot. Looks like I'd hit on one of the lucky five empty spots.

I took that as a sign, or maybe I didn't. Maybe I just realized that I needed to quit screwing around and buckle down.

When my possessions were raided after I shot the president, that photo was found. It's still one of my more infamous images, partly because it makes me look like the head case everyone wanted to portray me as. I'm sure there were quite a few people, probably still are, who wished my attempt had succeeded.

But a few months after Lennon was killed, I was determined to go a little further.

I kept going through the motions with my psychiatrist and my parents, but enough was enough. I wasn't playing any more games. I was tired of putting on an act for this guy. On Valentine's Day 1981, I was back in New York.

And it was going to be my last trip.

A Reluctant Swan Song

Criticize you may, this act of mine;

I trust you'll appreciate the romantic reasons.

One final stand, and the poet shall die.

A moment to pour out my feeling.

We all abhor the end result.

We all wonder about such outcasts.

But explanations do nothing more than raise questions.

Study not the reasons for the outburst.

Simply look into my eyes and say a prayer.

Bury me deep with your proper rage.

Remember my expression of love till the end of time.

Pick up the pieces and pack up the pain.

Leave the greater battleground a million miles behind.

But never forget that I didn't die in vain.

Writing from the day I went to commit
suicide at Lennon's apartment

My gun in my pocket, I stepped up West 72nd Street in the Big Apple. Then I saw it.

The Dakota. It was a lovely building with a dark past. It would forever be known as the place where a hero had fallen.

Not surprisingly, many people were milling around it. Many were taking pictures. I even saw a few laying down in the very spot where Lennon had laid, like it was some sort of pitch-black dramatization. Did these people think that was cool or funny?

At the time, I didn't really ask. I didn't think much at all. All I knew was that I had a few minutes left to live.

At the same place, with the same weapon that had been used to take out my main music man, I was going to follow in his footsteps. No more roulette—this gun was loaded, and all I would need was one good shot. I wasn't sure why Lennon's other fans had committed suicide after his death, but I sure as hell knew why I wanted to.

I had it all planned out. Back in my hotel, I'd written a long letter to Jodie, trying to justify what I was about to do. I think I tried to assure her that my reasons were strong enough, that it was for the best, right then. I probably apologized that she and I wouldn't get a chance to live out our love.

I had the note in my pocket. Soon, it would be found, and everyone would know how much she'd meant to me.

For I don't know how long, I just stood there and stared. I looked at the archway where Lennon had been shot, and the sidewalk where Chapman had stood to fire the shots that killed him. I looked up and down the streets, where so many fans had gathered that very December night to say a sad and shocked goodbye. What I wouldn't have given to be a part of that crowd.

Now all that was left was for me to do it. Just go right over there, sit down, or even stand, like it made a difference, and pull the trigger. The gun was loaded this time. No chance for chance. I was going down myself.

So many "if"s that day. If it had been a dark, rainy day, I might have taken it as a sign that I should go. The rain might have added to my blues enough to push me over the edge. If someone had been a jerk to me, that might have been another sign. There I was on the spot where my hero had been snatched away, and people were still going out of their way to be assholes.

Except they weren't, and they didn't. Not too many people noticed me. I think the doorman might have given me a few looks, mainly because I was just standing there staring, but he didn't say anything. No one said hello, asked how I was doing, nothing. But no one was a jerk, either. They must have figured I was just another heartbroken fan who'd come by to see his hero's last stand.

I was. And then I decided that that was all I would be. Standing there on a nice day, everyone apparently in a good mood, took me right out of the mindset myself.

I'm not sure what I was thinking. Only that this wasn't right. Not then. I don't know if I decided that I would never commit suicide from then on, and I don't think I felt that way, as I would try to take my life after that. I'm not sure if I decided that that wasn't the right time or place to do so.

Or it might have been that my mind switched back to the quest I'd been following for months. I was still going to save Jodie. I was still going to win her heart. And I was still going to do so by taking out the president.

Or get as close as I could. About an hour later, I was back at my hotel. The next day, I was down in DC.

It was time to kill. If it wasn't going to be Reagan, I had someone else in mind.

18. ALMOST KILLING KENNEDY

With that mess out of the way, my horrific goal of murder just kept getting clearer.

Honestly, I thought back to being on the roof of the hotel, and all I could feel was regret. Anger at myself. I was disappointed that I hadn't had the guts to carry it out. If I'd known one of my heroes was going to get murdered so soon after, I would have. I was ashamed that I didn't do what I'd climbed up on the roof to do, only to chicken out.

That wouldn't happen again. The next time I got a chance, I knew nothing would stop me, from within or without. I only knew that I would kill. After failing to take President Carter to his eternal rest, my mind started to spin even further. I was going to take a life. I just wasn't sure whose.

I didn't even care, and that lack of direction almost got me into even more trouble. It almost destroyed everything I'd been working toward. But murder was all I had left and, I kept realizing, all I'd had for a very long time.

After what had happened at the hotel in New York, I vowed it wouldn't be my own. Not yet. I wasn't important enough. No one would care if I committed suicide. Even if I were to kill myself at the spot where Lennon had died, people would just write me off as some obsessed Beatles fan. Someone so weak that he couldn't live in a world that his hero had been so violently stolen from. Beatles fans around the globe would see me as a disgrace. Many would probably have a lower opinion of me than they did of Chapman, who at least had the guts to face his consequences for the crime.

Back home, I would be hardly a blip on the local obituary page, and then people would forget about me, intentionally. My family would probably be so ashamed of what I'd done that they would try to push me out of their minds, and their friends and family sure as hell wouldn't be bringing it up.

A death by natural causes is hard enough to bring up with people, but you can't really talk at all about a person's son and brother's suicide. There's too much of a stigma. It's the most awkward of conversations. They're already feeling guilt and pain about it, and to bring it up is to just make it worse. So, people avoid each other for a time. When suicide is involved, people walk away until they feel safe, and then they often act like nothing happened. There's really nothing that can be said to make someone feel the slightest bit better when a loved one takes their own way out.

Besides, that wouldn't get Jodie's attention, would it? Even if I left a tome-length suicide note full of my love for her, she probably wouldn't even know about it, and if she did, she would brush me off as some unhinged nutjob who believed too much in the wrong things. Much less than she would eventually think about me after what I did.

I was going to take someone out, some way, even if I ended up taking myself out in the bargain. I didn't much care if I died, as long as I got to take someone important down with me. Someone's life would be mine, and people would remember both of us. Mark David Chapman would forever be known for a heartless, senseless crime, and I was going to outdo him.

But at that point, who knew? Who even cared? I'd lost all touch with reality at that point, and I wasn't interested in finding it again.

All I wanted to do was kill. That was the only goal I had left. I wanted to take someone out. As long as it was someone famous, I needed to be the one to end a life. I knew I would probably get taken out too if I did. I didn't care. I didn't necessarily want that, but I didn't give a damn anymore. I would wake up in the morning planning my murderous rampage, one person or many. It was all I could think about.

As before, I wasn't going out alone.

The very next day after my failed suicide attempt at Lennon's apartment, I flew right back down to DC. I wasn't sure if Reagan was in town, but if he was away, I could certainly find some consolation. I stood in front of the Capitol building, remember how I'd failed there a few months before. I wasn't going to have that happen again.

Because there would be no random shooting, no sniper-type working this time. I was going to walk right up to someone, or get as close as I could, and take them out. I wanted them to see me. I wanted the last thing they ever saw to be my face. I wanted them to know it was me. That, as much authority as they might have had in the political world, at that moment, they had no power. It was up to me, a nobody whose existence never meant a damn to them—if only because they didn't know me—whether they would ever see another day.

My mind zeroed in on one family. One family that, despite the political power they'd wielded in America for decades, was used to tragedy. It had happened to them enough that they wouldn't be surprised or upset about this, just sadly accepting that it had happened again.

Like everyone else old enough to remember the sad November 1963 day, I could recount just about every minute after I learned that John F. Kennedy had been shot so close to my home. Five years later, my best friend and I were celebrating the end of school by jetting off to Los Angeles to visit his sister for a few weeks.

As we made our way through the airport lobby, I could see a ton of people crowded around a newsstand. Many already had their own editions wide open. Most of them were just staring. Some looked like they were crying, or about to start. But no one, no one at all, was saying much. Everyone looked like they were in a trance.

I stepped close to the stand. Then I saw the huge black headlines.

Robert R. Kennedy was dead. Not just dead, killed. Violently murdered, just like his brother had been. The day before, he'd been killed right in the midst of a crowded hotel ballroom.

This was on my mind as I rode through DC on that day. These tragedies, along with all the others that had hit the Kennedy family, made me feel like I was following some sort of sick tradition. I truly believed that I was just taking one more step in a trend, as horrible as it was.

Pulling into Senator Ted Kennedy's office, I felt that this was appropriate. Two of his brothers had been murdered. It was fitting that he be next. It was no big deal, nothing new for them. First it had been Oswald. Then Sirhan. Now Hinckley would be the next name to darken the Kennedy legacy. Maybe Ted would be remembered as favorably as his brothers.

I went to his office. I stood outside the door, gun in hand.

And then I didn't go in. I suddenly felt nothing. It was like I was killing just to kill. I wasn't going to do that. I wasn't going to tee off and kill someone just because they were known. Yeah, committing the third Kennedy assassination might make a splash, but I really didn't want to. I felt like I was just going to blast the first well-known person whose office I drove by, and I liked to think that, in all my jumbled mind, I could be a little more rational than that.

This wasn't a grand enough gesture. If I'd set out to kill the president, that's what I was going to do.

Instead, I went out and bought a postcard with the White House's newest residents beaming out from the front.

"Dear Jodie, don't they make a darling couple?" I wrote to my lady. "Nancy is downright sexy. One day, you and I will occupy the White House and the peasants will drool with envy. Until then, please do your best to remain a virgin. You are a virgin, aren't you? Love, John."

Even with a mailbox nearby, I didn't drop it in. Never sent it at all. I went back to my hotel room and tucked it away. I don't know if I forgot to send it or never meant to at all. The point is, it was never mailed. I wouldn't see it again until my trial.

And then, right out of nowhere, my rationale exploded. I had a break from reality I'd never felt before. I don't know how it happened, but just after that, my entire mind went completely to shit. Psychosis reached in and shoved my desperation over the edge.

Another Beatles song kept rushing through my head. Like many songs that would follow, this one used a light tone to cover up some very dark lyrics.

"Well, you know that I'm a wicked guy," Lennon had written for his band, "and I was born with a jealous mind, and I can't spend my whole life trying just to make you toe the line."

Any Beatles fan worth their salt can read those lyrics and probably figure: a) where I'm going with this; and b) why "Run For Your Life" wasn't as big a hit as most of band's other tunes, with even Lennon downgrading it later on.

"I'd rather see you dead, little girl," the song promises, "than to be with another man."

With everything crashing down around me, that was how I suddenly felt about Jodie. The sadness that I still felt over John Lennon dying. My desperation to make a difference for Jodie that kept falling short. The betrayal that I felt over her not responding to my notes or calls, and taking time off from acting to deprive me of seeing my true love on the screen.

For a brief—fortunately, very brief period—my anger was now narrowed on her. My obsession had changed.

There was nothing that I wanted more than to win her heart. But if mine was going to keep getting broken, hers was as well. If I had no reason to go on, she shouldn't either.

For a short while, the longtime object of my psychotic attention became my target.

19. LEADING UP TO THE ACT

"There is a plot underway to abduct actress Jodie Foster from Yale University dorm in December or January. No ransom. She's being taken for romantic reasons. This is no joke! I don't wish to get further involved. Act as you wish."
Letter I wrote to the FBI, 1980

I was just doing Lennon's work. Following his words. Wasn't that what I was supposed to do? Wouldn't he be proud of me?

A psychotic mind doesn't stay focused. It bounces from one topic, one justification to another. Things that don't make sense today are in perfect clarity tonight. Something that appeared too ridiculous, or too sad, to even consider a short while ago now seems like the only thing to do.

As the month that would change my life, President Reagan's life, and American history forever began, I was back in Colorado at my parents' house. On March 1, they arrived home to find me gone, with just a note left behind. I informed them that I'd gone out to exorcise some demons.

I'm not sure what they made of that. I don't know what I would have figured if my kid had written something like that to me, then disappeared forever. I'm sure they never in a million years thought I would be out killing someone, let alone a famous actress or the damned president of the United States (like anyone ever could), but I don't think they would have been surprised if I'd turned up dead by my own hand. Not much had gone right for me in the past few years. My college career never got going. My music career had never found a spark. I'd tried and failed again and again and hadn't really established much for years. As heartbreaking as it must have been for them, as I'm sure it would for any parent, I bet they were as ready as any parent could be for some cop to show up on their doorstep to inform them that I was gone, and that I was both the victim and the culprit.

But that wasn't on my mind. I will forever be ashamed of what was.

In the first weeks of March, not for very long, I was back in New Haven on the Yale campus. I wanted to get lucky again.

"Jodie Foster.

Love, just wait. I'll rescue you very soon. Please cooperate."

Letter I sent to Jodie, March 6, 1981

I'd run into Jodie once, and I knew I could find her. It was, after all, my life's goal in the works for years. Even if my final result had changed.

In my warped mind, we would be recreating the love story for the ages. Our own Romeo and Juliet! Two tragic, violent deaths leading to an eternal life together in Utopia.

My gun hidden in a holster on my waist, I perused the campus. I ventured by the dorm in which I'd left notes. I searched all over near the spot where I'd seen her. As soon as I did, it would be all over.

I wasn't sure what I would do just yet. I didn't want to walk right up and shoot her, especially over and over like Chapman had to Lennon. That would be barbaric. I figured I might meet her. Maybe act like I was shaking her hand. Then kneel down and blare out some heartfelt declaration of love that convinced her that what was happening was simply the right thing to do. Not just for me. For her as well. That there was no greater act of devotion than to go to a better place and take her with me.

Then I would take her away. One quick shot to the head, or maybe the chest. No suffering for her. Hopefully, I would do it fast enough that she would never know what was happening. Just here one minute, and painlessly gone the next.

And I would follow suit on myself. Probably sit right down next to her as she slipped away. And the moment she was gone, I would put the gun in my own mouth and blast.

And then we would be together forever in eternity. It would be worth it for both of us. She would be okay with it. Her acting career, her college education, all of it would become miles in the secondary past for our love.

I can't believe I even considered that. As warped as my mind was, and it would get worse, you would think that even through the ruined caverns of my mind some sort of rationale might emerge.

It didn't. In a few days, in one of luckiest break of my life, and certainly Jodie's, I ran out of money again and had to hop a bus down to New York. My father had a business associate there, and he put me up in an apartment long enough for me to get back home.

Ironically, Jodie's life might have been saved by her commitments to being in the play *Getting Out*—where she played *a prostitute who kills a taxi driver*. Becoming the exact polar opposite of Iris might have saved her life.

This was March 7. Just weeks away.

"Jodie,

After tonight, John Lennon and I will have a
lot in common. It's all for you, Foster."

Lonely, Hinckley

That Hopper doctor I was talking about not long ago? Here's his first re-entry into this piece, although not his last.

He'd pronounced me all but cured, certainly not dangerous. I'd hidden my symptoms from him well enough that I could have gotten an Academy Award. He was convinced that I was just a dreaming drifter, that I needed to find some stability, some direction in my life.

And, said he, my parents could help me put boots on the ground by yanking my world out from under me. He recommended to them (I'm sure they didn't need much convincing) to show a little tough love. To kick me out and tell me not to come back until I knew what I wanted and how to get it.

Well, I certainly had the answers to those questions, and had for a while. But damned if he or they would know it until they saw it firsthand.

Right around the middle of March, I flew back to Denver. My father met me at the airport.

Like I said, he'd probably been eager to show me the tough love card for a while. Right then and there, he handed me a little bit of money and not-so-diplomatically informed me that I was on my own, and would stay that way until I changed my circumstances.

I wasn't surprised or upset. He'd always been of the opinion that men shouldn't whine or ask for help. That was weak, and men couldn't be weak. Part of being a man was to take care of your own issues by yourself. He claimed he'd never needed any assistance, and he saw no reason I should get any.

At that point, I felt like I'd landed right back at rock bottom. 1980 had ended horribly and 1981 had started just as badly. I felt as hopeless as ever.

But I didn't consider taking the same way out that I'd almost completed in front of John Lennon's apartment a few weeks before. I found a cheap flophouse hotel in West Denver.

Then I saw another sign of fate. Within walking distance of the hotel was a movie theater—and guess what *happened* to be playing at that time?

Yes. The story of Travis and Iris. The cinematic life that I was going to reach out and pull across the line to reality, to the extent that I signed in as "J. Travis" at the hotel where I was staying.

I screened in several times during that period. I hunted down some magazine articles focused on it. It was like I was being reminded what needed to be.

***

"[The FBI] wanted to know if Hinckley had ever been in touch with me, and I think he had, because once when I was out of town, my office received a letter from someone in Colorado who went on at length about how he'd like to be introduced to Jodie Foster. My secretary read it and threw it out, but I suspect it was him... the connection here between Hinckley and *Taxi Driver* is one at the psychological level, not a violent level."

Taxi Driver screenwriter Paul Schrader

One night, I was heading back to my impromptu home after a late showing. Out of nowhere, I saw flashing red and blue lights. A cop car pulled right up to me.

Oh, no. This was it. Someone had tipped them off. I'd been dead silent about my plans, but maybe law enforcement had made some kind of mind-reading tool. They knew what I was thinking, what I'd been planning for so long. Maybe they'd seen me at the Carter event and had been chasing me ever since. Maybe they'd seen me see *Taxi Driver* so much and figured out my Iris obsession. Just one more obstacle in my plan.

An officer stepped out and asked the basics: who I was, what I was doing, where I was going. I guess my jaywalking had made him suspicious.

He was about to ask for ID, which could have tipped him off to my previous record, if nothing else. But a call came over his radio, notifying him of a happening more important than some late-night loner who couldn't be bothered to find a crosswalk, and he hopped back in the car and sped off.

It took me a few steps back up the sidewalk to remember to breathe again.

My mother was more sympathetic than my father had been. When he was at work, she let me come back to the house and grab some of my possessions. I would go out and sell them to raise a little bit of money for my future. All the while, I'd been filling her head about looking for work in Denver. She didn't come right out and say I would be welcome back when I got a job, but she implied it. I know she didn't want to make this issue with my dad any worse than it was.

Goodbye to my guitar. Farewell to my Beatles albums. Just about everything that I could get someone to hand me a quick buck for was gone.

I had nothing left. Nothing but one last goal. By this time, it seemed like the only thing left to do.

I'd all but given up on my music career, but my mother didn't know that. I told her a load of garbage about establishing connections in the Los Angeles area. That the job market was better there than in Denver. That it was the place to go for those looking to make it in music. That all I needed was to meet one right person, and that I was lined up to run into several.

My father didn't come with us to the airport. I'm not sure if that was by choice.

It didn't matter. By that point, I had it all planned out.

Just before I boarded the plane—I'm not sure why, but my gun didn't get caught this time around!—I turned to her. I wasn't sure if it would be the last time. This needed to be more than just, "Bye, Mom, see you later." Because I wasn't sure if I would see her later... or ever again.

"I—I want to thank you, Mom," I stammered, "for all the things you've done for me all these years."

That was true. I did appreciate what she'd done. I knew that I hadn't been an easy kid to raise, even there in my mid-20s. She'd worked harder than a mother should have to, and that was mostly because of the person I was. But people don't say things like that unless there's something larger behind it. It's not just a goodbye. It's a farewell. It's something you say, the kind of lasting impression you leave, when you know, or at least have reason to believe, that you won't get to see or speak with this person for longer than a few days or weeks.

Once that tidbit got out, many people called it the end of any sort of rationale in my mind. No one believes that a person goes insane in a few hours, but if my mind had been heading out before that point, that was the end. Here is the moment when I actually stepped all the way out of reality, society's reality, and into the one I'd created. I'm not a hundred percent in agreement, but I can see that logic.

I'd reached the level of all or nothing at all. I had nothing left. I wasn't going to kill myself. I wasn't going to kill Jodie. I wasn't going to hurt innocent people. I was going to take out the president because I felt like I didn't have any other options. When I'd come close in the past, I'd had a choice. When I'd changed my mind in Nashville, I could try again. When I'd chickened out in

DC, I could try again. Now I couldn't try again, because there was nowhere else to go, nothing else to do.

That's why, all through the plane ride, first to a connection in Salt Lake City and then on to Los Angeles, I never wavered. As soon as I got off the plane, I didn't even think about leaving the airport, grabbing a cab, and hitting the city.

I went straight to the Greyhound bus station and spent what little money I had on a cross-country ticket all the way to DC.

I was on that bus for at least three or four nights. I was so broke, and so intense, that I slept on the bus. Other people would get out for an inn, but I just stayed right there and closed my eyes until the sun came up and the trip continued. It was inconvenient but not too bothersome.

Strangely, I found some pitch-black guidance in David Bowie's tune "Heroes," the tale of two forbidden lovers who risk death to see each other. Bowie got the idea from watching a couple kiss next to the Berlin Wall. It wasn't quite Jodie's and my story, but we could sure find that kind of love if we tried.

I knew I stopped once in Cleveland and again in Pittsburgh, but I hardly noticed. I could hardly say anything or do anything. Just stared straight ahead, my mind focused. On Jodie. On what I had to do for her.

Okay, maybe not all the way. I'd been practicing a tale of owning Denver's Independent Record Shop on other people for a while, and I let it slip to a fellow bus passenger. From the witness stand later on, the prosecution would use him to show the jury how little time I spent in reality.

And here is where things almost ended. Or, at least, came that close to changing altogether.

20. ALMOST TURNING AROUND

When the trip hit Wyoming, I actually almost had a vision. A realization. It was like life wasn't just tapping me on the shoulder. It was more like it was death-dripping my arm and screaming in my face, "Get rid of this! You have one chance left to not screw everything up! Take it! End this before you hurt anyone! It's not worth it!"

I almost listened. I wanted to listen. One choice here almost turned everything around. My one last shot was right in front of me. I could have taken it.

Standing at a bus station between jaunts, I saw that there was a new bus heading back to Denver. I had every chance, as well as the means, to get on it right there. I even had a plan.

Back in or around my residential area, I could have landed somewhere. Without bothering my family anymore, at least for a while, I could have gone right back to Denver and opened a new business. Maybe not even opened one. Just gotten a job in a bookstore or a record store. I could do that. People with much less work experience and formal education than myself had done that. It could have been the start of something great. Maybe if I got in on a record store, the manager or the visitors or someone else local could put me in a small venue to perform. Most record stores had connections like that.

I might have even found love. Not with a famous person who had more important things to worry about, like Jodie. Not with a wannabe performer who only made time when it suited her, like

Lynn. Just someone who wanted to settle down, just like I should have long ago.

I could have done all of that. If I'd switched buses right then and there, this book wouldn't be written. There would be no assassination attempt. No innocent people hurt or dead. No stigma in American history. No trial. No verdict. No incarceration or institutionalization.

Maybe none of that would have occurred. I might have been Normal Norman from Nowhere. After I got into the public eye, every guy who fits that description was rejoicing.

"Maybe nobody knows who I am," they said. "I may not be known outside the neighborhood. But I wouldn't trade places with that guy for anything!"

One choice. A ten-second journey. A few steps over to the bus, up the stairs, into the seat, and back to Colorado. Right there in Wyoming, I could have changed history forever for the better. But of course, I didn't. Got right back on my regular bus and sent my life, and several others, straight to hell.

Finally, on the afternoon of March 29, 1981, I hopped off the bus on New York Avenue and roared straight to 18th and G Streets to the Park Central Hotel. I was thrilled. I'd made it so far, put in so much time and effort. After my failings in college, my musical career, and most of the jobs I'd had, many people were all too anxious to slap certain labels on me, monikers like "directionless" and "lazy."

But I'd been proving them wrong all along, even if I didn't realize it at the time. I'd had one direction home, and I'd been on my way there for years. I'd worked as hard at getting this done as any college student working on a major project would. For almost five years, so much had been dropped in my way. So many reasons to quit, issues that would have turned away so many lesser men or women.

But not me. I'd never given up on this dream. I was going to make it happen, and now I vowed that nothing would stand in my way.

If I'd been lucky enough to run across President Reagan right then and there, I would have had my trusty .22 out and firing as soon as I got off the bus.

That wasn't the case. I guess I could give him a break. It was, after all, a Sunday, and even those running the country deserved a day off. He had some big plans coming up; I'd snatched up a newspaper and read that he was going to spend the next week or so flying all over the country to talk about cutting taxes and the federal budget.

But first, he was visiting the Washington Hilton Hotel to talk to the AFL-CIO's National Conference of the Building and Construction Trades Department about fighting inflation and helping the working man.

That would be the last act of his administration. It would be the finale to his life. Aside from William Henry Harrison's death after a month in office way back in 1841, Reagan was going to be our shortest-reigning president. Time for me to revel in the benefits of hard work.

He would never have to worry about energy crises or unemployment or foreign policy again. Less than 24 hours from then, he wouldn't be the president anymore. But I was the only one in the world who knew that.

Ironically enough, I later learned that, less than two weeks before, Reagan had visited Ford's Theater for a fundraiser. The same Ford's Theater that had been thrust into infamy over a century before when John Wilkes Booth put a bullet through the head of President Abraham Lincoln as Lincoln laughed along to the play *Our American Cousin.*

Like I'm sure everyone who has visited that theater since that dark moment has, Reagan checked out the box where the man who'd ended the Civil War had been stolen from his country.

"As you look up there," he remarked, "you can't help but run those events of 1865 through your mind. You imagine the figure of John Wilkes Booth bursting through the door at the rear of the box, shooting the president, then leaping onto the stage and running away before a stunned audience.

"It occurred to me that, until that night, probably no one had ever given much thought to the possibility someone might want to kill the president.... I thought about all the security provided Nancy and me and the children and how different things were now. Looking up at the flag-draped box, I thought that, even with all the Secret Service protection we now had, it was probably still possible for someone who had enough determination to get close enough to a president to shoot him."

Probably? That was an understatement. Had he not been around when two crazed women had nearly gunned down President Ford in September 1975 alone, only weeks before Reagan made his first run at the White House? Hell, I'd personally been close enough to take out Carter twice. I knew I had more than enough of the determination he'd mentioned. Now it was a question of putting actions to words and thoughts when the toughest moments arrived.

I killed the evening wandering up and down the nearby streets, stealthily creeping in and out of one porno shop after another. I checked out a peep show in one. I almost knocked the hell out of a bookstore clerk who wanted to put on his own show with me.

Eventually, I made my way to the Park Central Hotel, less than a half mile from the White House. Like I had so many times before, I rehearsed Travis Bickle's legendary "You talking to me?" monologue in front of a mirror, knowing I would be acting it out very, very soon.

"In most cases, [the film] has helped purge people of antisocial behavior. I just regret it didn't work that way for Hinckley."

Taxi Driver **screenwriter Paul Schrader**

Rifling through my suitcase, I grabbed my copy of *The Catcher in the Rye*. As much of a piece of shit as I thought Mark David Chapman was, the book had kept him focused enough to not run after he'd blasted John Lennon to eternity. I wasn't going to try to escape either. Whatever consequences I would face— arrest, getting shot myself, even praised—I wouldn't run away. That was the one aspect of my cinematic hero Travis Bickle, who'd lost his nerve and skittered off before his own assassination attempt, that I wouldn't emulate. That's what a coward does, and cowardice wouldn't impress anyone, least of all my beloved Jodie. I intended to take the book with me, and knowing I had it would calm me, or so I hoped.

Ironically, I also happened to be carrying a biography of Lennon himself, one of many that had been hastily tossed together after his shocking passing. I even had a piece on Ted Bundy, who'd taken more innocent lives that I ever intended to do. *Romeo and Juliet* was there, appropriate for a guy who still saw his next action as that of love.

I needed a good night's sleep; I had a big day ahead of me tomorrow.

But I needed to let someone know. Just in case things didn't work out too well, there was one person who deserved an explanation and declaration.

Looking over a magazine story about Jodie leaving Hollywood for school, I knew I would never be able to do what I must without one last message to her. I had a little time. I could put more depth and detail into this piece than the small notes I'd slipped up Jodie's dorm door.

Time for endgame.

21. REGARDLESS

Regardless of your lovely life
I am still here writhing in pain
I am still reeling from the truth
Regardless of the outside sun
I remain the far side of crazy
I remain the mortal enemy of Man
Regardless of a million smiles
I can't escape this torture chamber
I can't begin to be happy
Regardless of your dream come true
I continue to grovel for normalcy
I continue to scream inside
Regardless of everyone's friends
I plot revenge in the dark
I plot escape from this asylum
Regardless of Disneyland
I follow the example of perverts
I follow the long-lost swine
Regardless of Miss America's attitude
I stagger from day to day
I stagger toward the future
Regardless of the laughter of children
I cannot continue to pretend
I cannot continue to live.

John Hinckley Jr.

March 30, 1981

22. MORNING

President Reagan eats breakfast with some of his appointees. He chats with his Chief of Staff members. He has a phone call with Helmut Schmidt, Germany's chancellor. He meets with Vice President Bush. Then comes another meeting with the Chiefs of Staff. James Brady, who became his press secretary at the same time Reagan took office two months before, is at the meeting.

***

I rolled over in bed at the Park Central. The clock pleasantly informed me that it was still early, so there was no need to rush. I lay back, closed my eyes again, and tried to relax. I had a busy day, but I knew it wouldn't be a nice one, so I wasn't quite anxious to get going.

I didn't feel sad or nervous. I didn't feel much of anything at all. The issues I'd had when I'd gotten close to killing Carter, when I'd nearly blasted the hell out of the Capitol building, even when I almost took my own life, didn't really bother me that much. I was surprised about that. I knew, as I'd been planning for a long time, that I would change American history, and probably the entire world, forever on that very day, but by that point, I just wanted to get it done. I only hoped I wouldn't lose my nerve or my way at the last second like I had before.

Like I always did, I hopped in the shower and shaved my face. I had a feeling that many people would be seeing it soon, and I didn't want to look unprepared.

Strolling over to a local McDonald's for my breakfast, I grabbed up a newspaper. The president's schedule was right there in living black ink for me to check around, and I was pleased. He would be out of town very soon, like maybe even later that day, but for the time being, he was almost within sight.

I don't remember if *The Washington Post* put his day out in print, but *The Washington Star*, which went out of business later in 1981, certainly did; that's where I found out where he would be. There was also a toll-free number people could call to get a recording of his daily doings. That sounds a little weird, or at least irresponsible as all hell, considering the attempts on President Ford, but I guess the press had more trust in the American public than they do today. I know that these practices came to a sudden halt after I used them to hunt down Reagan.

"Pretend you are

Satan's long-lost illegitimate son,

A solitary weed among carnations,

A child without a home, the loser of a one-man race

Are we supposed to be happy or what?

We're on the verge of nuclear holocaust
and millions are starving,

And the American dream is a joke,

And America is fast becoming a joke.

Are we supposed to be happy or what?

Welcome to the truth.

Welcome to reality.

Welcome to my world."

Writing found in my DC hotel room

Afternoon

Regan takes care of some business in the Oval Office. He works on one of his legendary speeches with writer Kenneth Khachigian, probably over some seriously pending issues between Russia and Poland that are going on. He has some lunch and walks around the White House grounds with David Fischer, his assistant.

He has just had his final meal. But it's time to go. He hops in the presidential limo and heads off to the Washington Hilton Hotel.

***

Back at the hotel, I sat down and transcribed one of the most infamous letters in American history. It would be seen soon afterward in the media, at my trial, and is still easy to locate today with a simple Google search.

It was my final letter to Jodie. If it was the last communication I would ever have with her—and I truly believed it would be—at least she would know why I did what I did. How much of a mark, a difference she'd made in my life. How much she would always mean.

Dear Jodie,

There is a definite possibility that I will be killed in my attempt to get Reagan. It is for this very reason that I am writing you this letter now.

As you well know by now, I love you very much. Over the past seven months, I've left you dozens of poems, letters and love messages in the faint hope that you could develop an interest in me. Although we talked on the phone a couple of times, I never had the nerve to simply approach you and introduce myself. Besides my shyness, I honestly did not wish to bother you with my constant presence. I know the many messages left at your door and in your mailbox were a nuisance, but I felt that it was the most painless way for me to express my love for you.

I feel very good about the fact that you at least know my name and know how I feel about you. And by hanging around your dormitory, I've come to realize that I'm the topic of more than a little conversation, however full of ridicule it may be. At least you know that I'll always love you.

Jodie, I would abandon this idea of getting Reagan in a second if I could only win your heart and live out the rest of my life with you, whether it be in total obscurity or whatever.

I will admit to you that the reason I'm going ahead with this attempt now is because I just cannot wait any longer to impress you. I've got to do something now to make you understand, in no uncertain terms, that I am doing all of this for your sake! By sacrificing my freedom and possibly my life, I hope to change your mind about me. This letter is being written only an hour before I leave for the Hilton Hotel. Jodie, I'm asking you to please look into your heart and at least give me the chance, with this historical deed, to gain your respect and love.

I love you forever,

John Hinckley

I worked as hard on that writing as any essay or other writing project I'd ever done for school, on my novel that sputtered out so quickly, on anything at all.

I'm not sure why I didn't mail it. During my walks around the local area, I certainly saw quite a few mailboxes. Maybe I didn't have an envelope and stamps handy. Maybe I was just in a hurry.

Maybe I thought that they would find it on me, on the corpse I left behind as I moved on, and pass it to her. Of course she would be moved enough to make me her personal martyr, her hero who gave his life for her. She would tell the press, my family, even the president's family, what a heartfelt man I truly was, herself so moved by it that they would be as well. She would make me her main man for the rest of her acting career. Maybe her life.

I took one last look around the hotel room. It might be the last thing I would ever do on my own. It might have been the place I'd spent my last night. Picking up my belongings, I flipped through a copy of a novel I'd picked up. Called *The Fan*, it tells the story of an obsessed, deranged man who stalks his favorite actress. Mostly told through letters between the two, the 1977 work ends with the two having a violent confrontation that only she walks away from. Reading that book, I was amazed at how people like this guy existed. What was *wrong* with such nuts?

I put some pictures of Jodie into my wallet. There was also a pin with John Lennon on it there.

Ironically, the story would make its way to theaters less than two months after my infamous act. It's a good bet that my actions probably caused its poor showing there.

Without a limo myself, or even a car, I hopped a cab over to the Hilton. It was less than 10 minutes away.

***

The moment I step out, there's already a small group of people milling on the sidewalk. Some are clearly with the press. Others are tourists, or maybe locals, just trying to get a close look at the man who will lead their land to a golden age. I see enough cameras to open a shop.

There's a light rain moving in and out, so I slip on my jacket. But no one asks for my ID, my press pass, anything like that. Apparently, this guy was elected by so many millions of people around the nation that the concept of someone disliking him, even wanting to harm him, is unfathomable to so many. We wait and wait.

Now, just before 2:00 p.m., it's time.

The limo pulls up, and the cheers go up. Many applaud or call out their personal hellos. Those cameras I witnessed start flashing like crazy, both from the press and the visitors.

I'm ready to finish my work. I reach into my pocket, where my trusty .22 is waiting. Time for all the years of waiting to become reality.

And then he looks at me. His ever-present smile flashes right into my eyes. He waves, and I think he's singling me out while doing it.

Suddenly, I can't move. My hand, centimeters from the gun, stops right where it is. By the time I get my bearings, he has passed into the building and the crowd is already thinning out.

What happened? Did I fail again? Did I choke? Was fate trying to tell me that I should end my quest then and there? He was obviously a nice fellow, everyone said that, and now he, the leader of the greatest country around, had personally acknowledged me.

Had I been wrong all along? How could I hurt, let alone kill, someone who'd not only never done anything to me or anyone I knew, but who had gone out of his way to show friendliness he didn't have to? What the hell was I thinking, going to just kill someone like that?

As I he stepped through the hotel entrance, I followed him in. I didn't go to the ballroom where he would be speaking; the Service people had that spot under everything but lock and key. I hung out in the lobby, pretending to flip through magazines and other reading materials, pondering my next move.

I felt something coming back, the obsession I'd felt for years that had gone into this. How horrible I'd felt when I'd fallen short. How desperate I was to prove myself to Jodie. What an accomplishment it would be to do this. What a weight would be off my chest and shoulders.

Hearing some applause from the ballroom, I figured it was about done. Time to go back into character.

Back outside, I stepped into the midst of the same size crowd, the same people I'd been next to about a half hour before. Members of the press told me to back away or leave, that this was the media spot. I said no. I'd been here first (even if I hadn't), and damned if I was going to let this chance slip away again.

As the cameras started flashing again, I figured he was coming back out. It was now. Right now.

***

My day to address the Bldg. & Const. Trades Nat. Conf. A.F.L.-C.I.O. at the Hilton Ballroom—2 P.M. Was all dressed to go & for some reason at the last min. took off my really good wristwatch & wore an older one.

Speech not riotously received—still it was successful.

From President Reagan's diaries of the speech.

***

2:24 p.m.

Only seconds away from my name going into history books for generations. Mostly for the wrong reasons, yes, but it'll be there.

Unless someone stops me. I don't necessarily hope so, but there is a small piece of me that hopes this won't happen. Maybe someone will brush against me, feel the gun, and snatch it away. Maybe some huge cop or bodyguard will run around the corner and accidentally knock me down. Maybe whatever. If something or someone from the outside stops me, I might abort this.

I stand. I wait. I'm standing right around the corner from the door to the hotel. His limo's right in front of me, so I know he can't get away without me seeing him. He'll have to pass me to get out, and he won't be making it.

The president steps around the corner. Just like before, he's smiling and waving. If he's in a hurry, I'll fail again.

He takes a few steps forward. Then he hesitates, still waving and calling to his voter friends.

And then he does it. Turns his head. Smiles at me. Waves again.

I don't know what he's trying to do. Mock me? Let me know that I can't get him, even this close? Or maybe he's daring me to try. He's looking at me. He knows I'm there. Probably even knows why I'm there. It's him and me, and this wave is his way of spewing, "You're here, but you can't get me. Because you just don't have the guts."

For a moment, he's a slight distance away from his glorified bodyguards. It's the chance I need.

Now's the time. I have to do it right now and very fast. If anyone sees me, they might step in front of me. They might grab my gun. They might blow my head off. Anything can happen.

I've had my hand on my gun since the crowd started cheering. Now it's out and up. Pointed right at him.

> "Their eyes were on me. They saw the gun. Now I
> have no choice. I have to go forward and shoot."

My later description of the moment to a psychiatrist

Blast! Blast! Blast! Blast! Blast! Blast!

People will say later that it sounded like firecrackers, but there's no mistaking this sound. In less than two seconds, my gun is empty.

Reagan turns his head to look at me. That smile that he always wears has suddenly become a frown. I can't tell if he's shocked that something so out of nowhere is happening, or terrified that someone is taking his life, or whatever else. That image will appear on the cover of the next editions of both *Newsweek* and *Time*, the latter of which will also carry a shot of me being driven away from the scene.

People are already freaking out. A few Service members shove him into the limo. A mass of people are all over me.

Fists smash me in the face, the back, everywhere. Some people slam me with kicks and knees. Others pin me down. I'm getting hit by cops, reporters, passersby, everyone. An agent jumps on top of me. I can't tell if he's trying to protect me from the crowd or holding me down so they can get in some more shots.

I'm still pulling the trigger. My bullets are long gone, but I keep going *click, click, click*, until my gun is knocked from my hand. I don't know who has it. The next time I see it will be at my trial.

As I fall backward against the wall, I can see a man slump over the pavement. It's James Brady, though I don't know that yet. Reagan's limo is already speeding around the corner and up the street. I can't tell if I hit him or not.

As I drew my gun and used it, I hadn't felt much at all. Just the completion of a task. Now I'm getting hurt. All I can think of is protection. My hands and arms are across my face, trying to ward off the next blow, which is coming from somewhere I can't try to guess.

I still might get killed. Maybe someone, in all the mess, will press his own gun right up against me and pull the trigger. Maybe my head will get bashed in. Maybe I'll get choked to death right here and now.

"I'll kill you!" a guy screams as he pounds me with one hand and chokes me with the other, actions for which Reagan would later thank him face to face. "You shot at my president! I'll kill you!" Another guy punches the hell out of my head, and blood's coming out of both my skull and his hand.

It maybe goes on for a minute. It seems like forever to me. In my fleeting moments of clarity, I keep wondering if my mission was accomplished, and who it will affect. How they'll respond.

Finally, a few Service people reach into the crowd and yank me out. Cuffing my hands, they shove me into a car, a hell of a lot harder than Reagan's people launched him. They don't even search me to see if I happen to have another gun in my pocket.

Cameras caught me getting manhandled by the crowd and being whisked away in the car. I looked dazed, like I was as confused and shocked as anyone by what the hell I'd done. I think my mind and body were trying to transport me away from the trauma long enough to regain some sort of composure.

Sanity? Not a chance. I was as far from that point as anyone had ever been. If I realized and understood what had happened, it sure as hell wasn't going to occur for a long while. I just knew my life would never be the same. Neither would much else. Still, it's not like it had been going so wonderfully for a very long time before that.

"I'm relieved," I would later describe the moment to a psychiatrist. "It's over."

I don't think it took us a minute to get to the police station. The Service agents were shouting at me the whole time, but I didn't respond. I don't even recall what they said, my mind was so far gone. I think I asked them to loosen the cuffs because my wrists were hurting. They told me how lucky I was that that was my only problem.

In another span I can hardly recall, they yanked me out of the car, strip-searched me, and all but javelined me into a cell, though they were nice enough to let me redress first. I stood and sat and stared. I might have been in shock. My psyche might have been so broken that I couldn't know what the hell was happening.

Pretty soon, the FBI showed up. By then, I'd regained enough sense to sort of know what had happened.

"If you want to understand what I did," I taunted them, "go to my room. It was a matter of love."

Over at the FBI headquarters, I was sat down for some interrogating. I didn't mind, and I didn't clam right up. The agents were assertive, but not rough. They didn't try to steamroll me into submission. I had no issue spending hours discussing the bus trip I'd taken, my college failings, just about everything. But when they asked me about earlier that day, I finally lawyered up. I might have already been in too much trouble to get out of, and I didn't want to make it worse, if such a thing was possible.

I asked them if the president had been hit. They said he had, but they didn't know how bad it was. They also told me that I'd shot three other people.

I guess I shouldn't have been surprised. I'd wildly fired in a jammed area. But I still felt bad. I'd never set out to hurt anyone innocent, anyone I didn't know.

"I accomplished everything I was going for," I exclaimed. "I should feel good now that I accomplished everything on a grand scale... the circumstances were just unbelievably perfect. I just didn't have time to get nervous or anything."

Honestly, I was kind of surprised at how professional everyone was. I'm sure many of them would have loved to place their badges in the other room and give me a beating that would send me to the hospital or worse. Why give any sort of due process to a guy who'd just tried to take out the president?

But they were fair. Maybe they didn't want to jeopardize anything later on. They didn't want anything I said or anything they found thrown out because of any unprofessionalism on their part. They wanted me to have fair treatment and probably hoped the justice system would do its worst. Ironically, I even helped a detective spell "assassinate" when he was writing up my police report.

However, early on, I did ask for a lawyer. They didn't say I couldn't have one, not even that I couldn't have one yet, but chose to deflect the conversation away from the day and delve back into my past. That statement would make a huge difference as my trial drew near.

Two public defenders showed up quickly and talked to me for a little while. They told me what would happen next. We would go to court, I would be charged, and I would spend the night behind bars. Probably not there in DC, as it wasn't safe—see what I mean about being professional?—but not far away. They also told me something interesting: they were hoping to haul the case to court as soon as possible. Not just because I had a right to a speedy trial. I was 25 years old and wouldn't have my next birthday until the end of May. In Washington, DC, someone my age could still be tried as a youthful offender. If they could get things going by the end of the next month, whatever sentencing guidelines I would face, if any, would be strongly reduced.

My parents managed to call. I can hardly remember what I said, only that my wrists were sore from the cuffs. They would tell me later how amazed they were at how normal I sounded, especially at such a time.

Then, out of nowhere, my thoughts returned to my original reason for doing all this. The Oscars were scheduled for that night. I knew Jodie wouldn't be winning, as she wasn't nominated, but I hoped she might show up to present. I know I wasn't the only one who wanted to see her one last time before school started.

They were held the next day, but no one really cared. Like the rest of the world, Hollywood was too focused on my act to get too concerned about some awards. Ironically, Reagan himself, who had done some acting before his political career, had already taped a speech welcoming everyone to the show. If he'd died, the show almost certainly would have been canceled, or at least his message removed.

Show host Johnny Carson decided to forgo his legendary comedy gifts, explaining why the Oscars had been put on hold. His announcement that the president would be okay got one of the loudest ovations of the night.

Ironically, my hero Travis Bickle himself, none other than Robert De Niro, took home his second Oscar for *Raging Bull*. That film losing Best Picture to *Ordinary People* was absurd. Ironically enough, when my trial came around in 1982, many people tried to draw some commonalties between the Hinckleys and the Jarrett family of *Ordinary People*, the sad story of a family who can't recover after the sudden loss of their beloved son, a tragedy that ends up separating the parents and cutting the cord between the mother and a son who survived. My parents' marriage would barely survive my actions, and I'd been estranged from them for years, though more from my actions than the horrible events in that film.

Jodie wasn't there for the ceremony. My interest in her had already become common knowledge, so there might have been reasons for that far beyond personal.

Strangely enough, two years later, De Niro played an unknown wannabe standup comic who ends up stalking and taking hostage a Carson-level TV talk show host in *King of Comedy*. (Reagan's own daughter, Patti Davis, nearly got a role in the film.) Many people labeled that film as one of De Niro's rare misfires and badmouthed Scorsese for making a stalker the main character in an attempted dramedy. You have to think that some people saw some remnants of me in his work.

"I think a lot of stuff is gratuitous, and I don't like it personally. If there's a reason for it, and it is what it is, then that's what it is. It's a complicated one.... Seeing things that are done in movies are like dreams. You see things you couldn't do in normal life. It's a collective dream for an audience. It's not like it's real—they know it's not real. Unfortunately, there are some people who take it as real. They're unbalanced, unhinged, or whatever."

Robert De Niro on movie violence, 2012

Right before midnight that night, I walked into a crowded courtroom to face a magistrate, who formally charged me with the act and ruled I would be sent south to Virginia's Quantico, where some U.S. marshals would watch over me 24-7 in the brig. Even FBI director William Webster was there to witness the happenings.

That's when I found out what I'd done. To that point, I thought—hoped—I'd just hit Reagan. But they informed me that I was being charged with the attempted murder of not only him, but Brady (whom many news outlets had falsely reported dead), police officer Thomas Delahanty, and Secret Service agent Tim McCarthy, who'd leaped in front of the president and taken a bullet in the chest. Had he not thought so fast, or been a half second slower, that shot might have taken Reagan out then and there.

Also, my Devastator shells that were supposed to explode on impact hadn't worked—not in the way they should have. They'd simply blasted into their targets, not causing nearly as much damage as I'd intended. I doubted such bad luck would garner me much sympathy.

I didn't react to anything. I was so removed from reality that I couldn't comprehend much. I was so overwhelmed, not just with that day, but everything else leading up to it, that I barely knew what the hell was happening.

For all the time it took me to get driven down to the Marine base, I didn't say a word. The ones driving me didn't either. I think they were pissed about what I'd done—just like millions were—and to even speak to the guy who'd nearly murdered their president would have been a sign of disrespect to Reagan.

They carted me in there and loaded me into a brig, just like I'd been shoved into the cell earlier in the day.

I wouldn't sleep a wink that night. What the hell had I done? In public, in front of hundreds of people, I'd almost killed the president of the United States and three other people.

I'm sure millions of people already hated me. I'm sure millions more thought I was out of my fucking mind. They were more right than they would ever know.

But just before I lay down, a marshal handed me a note.

"We love you," it said. "From Diane and Steve." In the midst of everything, my sister and her husband had somehow managed to get me a message. How nice of them.

It was one of the few feel-good moments I would have for a very, very long time.

"They need to get the electric chair lined up for that boy."

Brad Feller, Louisiana

"When they caught Hinckley, I was overjoyed.
At once, I wished I could shoot Hinckley."

Paula Buckwell, North Carolina

"I would have him shot just within a week's time."

Jim Magner, Louisiana

"I think John Hinckley Jr. should be put in a pit
of poison scorpions, take him and put him in a
guillotine, cut his head off, then put Hinckley in a pit
of quicksand and let him disappear forever."

Roger Feverson (fifth-grader), Missouri

"Americans, kill John Hinckley and what he stands for. If
the attempted assassin is to remain alive, the fact that he is
alive keeps alive the presence of the assassination attempt."

Mark Renier, Florida

"Whoever shot him is a nut and a half."

David Ogle, Texas

"These dastardly crimes must be stopped. That can only
be done by the swift execution of Mr. Hinckley and
others like him, not by gun control. If a murderer knows
he will lose his life when he takes another, he will think
twice before using a gun on another human being."

Larry Harris, Alabama

"They should take the man that did it, sit him down
every day, and torture him for twenty years."

Jim O'Brock, Louisiana

"Punish him promptly, preferably by public execution
by hanging, firing squad, or even beheading. Perhaps
it might serve as a deterrent for some other person,
sane or deranged, from attempting it again."

W.C. Betz, Florida

Word spread like a wildfire on fast forward. On the other side of the country, my mother was already heartbroken. She'd just learned that a president she and my dad had supported and stood behind might soon be gone forever.

Then, moments later, another call had come. The press had some new questions.

Their own son had been arrested for the crime. For all they knew, I was still in California. I hadn't told them about my bus trip back east, let alone my purpose for it.

Ironically enough, many national outlets first claimed that it had been my dad who had shot Reagan. They didn't know I had a "Jr." attached to my moniker. How horrible would it have been if some personal avenger had hunted my father down to take revenge? Like my actions hadn't caused enough pain and suffering already.

What in the *hell* does one think or say to that? They had no idea, as if anyone ever could. It's not even remotely possible to handle such news. The FBI arrived at their home. So did their friends and other family members. As I was on my way to imprisonment thousands of miles away, my family was being grilled about my friends, job, career, schooling, whatever. They needed to know if I was a lone gunman or the end of a chain reaction. They had to check to see if I was a serial killer with a list of bodies that had ended in Washington.

In the nation's capital alone, about 150 FBI agents were dumped onto my case. Across the country, hundreds more joined in, along with the local cops, the Secret Service, anyone with a badge. They investigated every single thing they could, every person they could interview, anything anywhere that might help them in any way. By the end of the month, they'd put together over a thousand pages of information about John Hinckley Jr.

Not surprisingly, the world "conspiracy" kept jumping up all over the place. Like John Wilkes Booth, who'd been assisted in his murder of Lincoln, or Lee Harvey Oswald, whom many today believe was a patsy for many, much more powerful men, there was no way I could have pulled this off alone, right? A guy who often looked, in media photographs, like he couldn't remember what day it was or how to spell his name, could never have planned all this out, gotten the weaponry, and snuck close enough undetected to take out the president and several others by himself, right?

That went on and on. Jim Garrison, whose crazy ideas about the JFK assassination had pushed him to the American forefront, enough to bring about the only trial in the Dallas tragedy that had happened so close to my home, was busy as a judge in Louisiana, so he didn't get involved. Over and over, the FBI and others were so desperate to find that there was more to my act than had been caught on camera.

Okay, so maybe some of that was my fault. I figured that my life was over, nothing left to lose or do. Why not screw with people and waste their time? The crimes I was charged with carried enough fines that even the wealthiest of men couldn't pay them. Why not add to it?

I was playing games with the guards. While they stood and watched me in my cell like they were transfixed, like I would disappear if they blinked, I was scribbling down some information.

I drew ridiculous-looking maps. I wrote notes to people with fake names and initials. I scribbled out plan after plan to bump off Reagan, and maybe even some others. I talked about deals I was willing to make as the law closed in, hinting that I might turn in some co-conspirators if the prosecution dropped or lowered my charges.

One day, when I was strolling off to the shower, I *happened* to leave all these notes out in the open. The guards, as they did every time I was out of the cell, searched through it and found them. Now they were sure that my minions were going to continue my work, our work, and make it so much worse. The FBI went right back to work, as hard as ever, determined to find out who I was writing to, what I was planning, who else was involved.

But, per usual, there was nothing. There never had been. My motive, my actions… people just kept finding shock and awe about the repeated lack of climax in my story. It had given me one hell of a sense of power, to go from being a lifelong nobody to being able to dictate the actions of so many powerful people. I'm surprised the guards didn't arrange for me to get jumped in my cell and beaten severely one night after lights out.

My parents told the FBI about Lynn. She was about my only friend of whom they were aware. They gave out all the information they had on her and recommended she be called. Problem was, they didn't have a phone number or an address for her. Not even a physical description. Remember, they'd never met or spoken directly to her.

My hotel room already having been torn apart and a certain letter found, agents asked my folks about Jodie Foster and any connections I had with her. From the letter, the FBI thought she and I had already had a Hollywood-level affair.

Mom and Dad were dumbfounded. Who the hell was Jodie Foster? A girl I'd met at Texas Tech that they didn't know about? A neighbor I'd hung out with in the area? Not big movie fans, they'd never heard the name before.

Almost instantly, the death threats began. The city switchboard collapsed under the pressure of so many calls at once. Pathetically, a bunch of morons from here and there were promising to do all kinds of obscene things to my parents, other family members, everyone. These people were pissed and terrified enough that they felt they had to do *something*, and harassing an elderly couple was best they could act upon. But the local cops and FBI came through, showing up to establish a human blockade around the home. The Rev. Billy Graham, a personal friend of Reagan's who'd prayed at his bedside, called, as did Senate Chaplain Richard Halverson. Friends and neighbors poured in to assist.

Right after two in the morning, an agent showed up to ask if he could search the home. They figured to just get it done.

Looking around, he dug up a couple of books. One on John Lennon. A few on Hitler. Some on the Kennedy assassination. A diary by Democratic presidential candidate George Wallace's attempted assassin Arthur Bremer, and an article on the "Texas Tower Sniper," Charles Whitman. Pretty appropriate for guy who had just tried to pull off his own presidential murder.

He found the photo of me standing in front of the White House. Two days later, newspaper readers around the world would see it.

Reaching into the closet, he pulled out a green suitcase. Laying it on the bed, he unzipped the top. Right there lay a pistol box. An empty pistol box. Several full cartridges. There was a black ski mask. And a few papers.

I'd sharpened my skills at a Denver firing range. I'd shot at silhouettes, and I could tell I was getting better at it. When I first started, my bullet holes were all over the place. Eventually, they'd grown closer and closer to the target.

The one that he pulled was in the shape of a man and absolutely riddled with holes showing seriously rehearsed marksmanship.

Not surprisingly, the media descended on everyone who had ever known me or my family. Our friends' friends. My elementary school classmates and teachers. My dad's co-workers. My former professors. Basically, anyone who had been in the presence of a Hinckley in the past two decades was up for grabs with interviews. Why had I gone bad? When did it start? Whose fault was it?

And I'm sure the media was shocked at what it couldn't find. Didn't find, because there was nothing to find. I'd come from a well-off family full of morale, all do-gooders. My father was a hard-working businessman who'd earned his millions without cutting a single corner. My mother was a friendly community face. They lived in a six-figure house with a swimming pool in the back yard. My siblings were both accomplished.

Me? I hadn't done much, but what little I'd done hadn't been much wrong. I had no criminal history. I'd been an okay student. I had at least gone to college a few times, even if I hadn't finished. I was into music, like most people were, but not to any huge degree. Sure, I'd dreamed of being a famous musician someday, but, hell, so had millions of others.

Like I said, there was nothing to find, not right away. Yes, I was a hardcore introvert. Sure, I was aimless, irresponsible. Lazy as all hell. Probably a chronic pain to my family, the dark horse that so many families are ashamed to discuss.

But a murderer? A presidential assassin? Hell no. The media and general public probably expected to find some guy who'd grown up on the streets between stays at the local psychiatric hospital and/or prison. They hoped I was living in some abandoned shack wallpapered with posters of Reagan, his face probably X-ed out or graffitied over. They wanted to hear stories about me wandering up and down the streets all night long, babbling about the end of the world. Maybe I was just a nut hooked on the thrill of the gun, looking for the adrenalin rush of using it on the world's most well-known target. A drunk or drug addict so hammered as to not know what was going on.

Hardly. I was on a drug when I shot the president, although not anything illegal or street-related, like the marijuana that America was still stigmatizing at that time, especially a few years later when Nancy Reagan launched the "Just Say No" program to get and keep kids off drugs. Just a little Valium, which was normal for me. I needed something to stay calm in the midst of the most chaotic of situations.

I'd touched marijuana once in a while, but it wasn't a regular thing and hadn't been for a long time. Several people from my past got their names in a paper by spreading rumors about me being a pothead or even a dealer back in grade school, but none of that was true.

They found people who'd known me in school. They talked to librarians and bookstore owners who had seen me read. People who had waited on me in restaurants. People who had sat near me on the cross-country bus ride I'd taken.

All of them said the same thing: that there was nothing there. Literally, nothing. Good or bad, there was nothing to find. Nothing memorable for any reason. I was a person they'd encountered, and as soon as I'd left, they hadn't spoken to me or even thought of me ever again. Had they lived another century, they probably never would have, except when millions of people were forced to.

"By 1975, virtually all of us had lost contact with John… John had drifted into sequestration so smoothly that nobody noticed he was missing.

"What if we hadn't lost touch back in college? What if one of us had thought, 'What's John Hinckley up to today?' and picked up the phone to find out? Would we have shaken John loose from his self-imposed isolation? We all shake our heads and wonder."

Kirk Dooley, former classmate, April 5, 1981

The media took a few aspects of my past and blew them up like bombs. The psychiatric treatment that I'd undergone voluntarily for a few months turned into a huge issue. My Nazi interests that had come and gone and led to nothing suddenly became huge. They made up stories about me following Reagan to California (one paper swore up and down it had a photo of us shaking hands) and even to Canada. People were desperate to find something, anything at all that might offer some logic as to how my name had suddenly splashed across America and why. I'm sure they were frustrated about not being able to lay the groundwork for why a man commits such a psychotic act.

Photos were the same way. They were desperate to portray me as someone that people could literally see was off his head. If I was seen in a newspaper, I was always unfocused. Never looking at the camera. No expression on my face. Certainly not smiling, but not really frowning or looking sad or anything else. It was important to show that I was off on some other world. In hindsight, that may have helped my eventual legal defense. It's easier to plead that someone's mentally ill if they keep being made to look like they don't have the first clue what's going on.

That's what the media does. When it can't find a real story, it invents one. The truth didn't matter. I could have been a straight-A Ivy League valedictorian who'd earned a military Purple Heart and then become a doctor who'd saved thousands of sufferers, and the media wouldn't have touched it. I was a wannabe presidential assassin, and they were going to make sure they showed me as someone just screwed up enough to commit such an act. If that meant misrepresenting so much about me, my past, everything else, that was the price I would pay for being one of the most evil, hated humans in world history.

Then, somehow or other, my letter to Jodie jumped straight into the public eye. Someone just *happened* to leak it to the press. It was all they needed. Now everything would turn around.

23. SAVING JODIE

"A girl beyond words

To know her is to love her

To love her is easy.

I can't escape this torture chamber.

I continue to grovel for normalcy.

I continue to scream inside.

I stagger from day to day.

I stagger toward the future.

Regardless of the laughter of children,

I cannot continue to pretend.

I cannot continue to live.

A kind of heaven waiting for us.

I'm not going to stay around here much
longer and continue taking this abuse.

Only fools believe is gladness;

My sadness is a fate that will not end.

Don't send me a sympathy note.

I wrote my way into this mess.

Oh, yes, I'll accept all the blame.

The shame I create is unique.

I know myself to be damned.

On my knees, please, oh, please,

Consider this disease I've contracted from
a wretched fool I call myself."

Writing found in my DC hotel room

On the very morning I shot Reagan, Jodie Foster had signed off to return to the screen for the first time since *Carny*. Working back into the movie game with a small role, she would be Edward Asner's daughter Barbara in *O'Hara's Wife*, in which Mariette Hartley's title character, actually named Harry, comes back in ghost form to help Barbara and Ed's Bob through her loss.

As news of the shooting spurted across America, Jodie drowned her attention and time in an extended study period. Like everyone else, she hoped that the president would be fine, and that the person who did it, certainly evil, crazy, or a bit of both, would pay dearly. Exams were coming out, and Yale gives out some of the toughest in the nation.

Then, that evening, Jodie's roommate grabbed her. My name was screamed in her face. It sounded vaguely familiar.

"John Hinckley," her roommate gasped.

"What about him?" Foster asked. "Did he write me again?"

"He's the one, I think. It was on the radio."

"Bullshit. You're imagining things."

I was hardly the first to send her some fan mail, even if my methods had been extreme. But they'd probably blended in with the rest. I'd just talked about how much I admired her, what a great actress she was. Same as probably a mountain of other messages. Even before the shooting, she was getting a few thousand every single week. The Yale post office must have loved her.

No threats. Nothing obscene. Certainly nothing about what I had planned for her, and for us.

However, she'd gotten more communication from me than from most. When more and more notes started showing up with my name on them, she'd handed them to the dean. Now they were in the hands of the FBI—as were her photos of address that they'd yanked off me after I'd shot Reagan.

The very FBI that had interviewed her the day of the shooting, and the day after that, along with some higher-ups from Yale had found my letter to her, and they wanted to know everything.

Like, the phone conversations we'd had. Were they legit? Had she responded to my communication? Had she and I been meeting in secret? Was she actually offering that place in her heart that I'd all but begged for?

She said no. To everything.

"I'm very scared," she said the day after the shooting, between productions of *Getting Out*, a play being put on by students from Yale. "It's quite a traumatic thing." She held a news conference and denied that we'd spoken on the phone, a mistruth that she corrected when the transcripts came out in September 1981.

But hey, that just meant she was putting on an act, right? Secretly, she admired what I'd done and was planning to respond favorably. Maybe secretly, but in the most positive way. Even when she claimed that we'd never spoken or met, I knew it was a show. That's what actors do, right?

Or maybe she was responding from emotion. Maybe she was shocked and frightened. But that was just the impact talking. We can't know how we'll respond right away in a situation like that. She wasn't being rational. Once she calmed down enough to appreciate the steps I'd taken, the devotion I'd shown, she would realize that it was all for her, all for the greater good for us. The entire story landed her back on the cover of *People* magazine on April 20, and I was sure she would be grateful for my effort to help her get there.

But then came my turn to be terrified.

The staff tried to hide this from me, but it came through. One week after I'd shot Reagan, some piece of shit called the Yale police and promised to blow up Welch Hall if I wasn't released by that afternoon. The very Hall where Jodie lived, the exact one whose halls I'd perused to look for her, would become a pile of rubble full of innocent bodies because someone attached my name to it.

Across America, death threats against both Reagan and Vice President Bush were popping up like land mines. Both men's daily schedules were torn away from the public. Hundreds of people were calling in and shouting out threats to take them out, and several people were arrested. The FBI and other such associations were on the highest alert. I was getting blamed or credited, depending on who was asked. Ironically, as I got ready for trial, a teenage girl was arrested for calling in a threat to Reagan—from a nightclub less than a mile from Yale! Many people probably double-checked her age (she was too young to go to the school) to make sure it hadn't been Jodie!

"John Hinckley wielded a tremendous amount of power," explained UCLA psychiatry professor Dr. Irwin Ruben, "and that's very seductive, especially to those who have violent tendencies, but feel weak and small." Well, I knew as well as anyone that Jodie was neither violent, small, or weak, but I sure as hell hoped she would find me seductive. On April 9, a guy named Leonard Anthony Bariana robbed a San Diego bank, armed with a note that said he needed a paltry $80,000 to compensate my acts.

For every one that was openly expressed, there were almost certainly many more than were silently considered. People who intend to act on their threats tend not to call or write ahead of time.

And then another came about; one that, to this day, stands out too far to me.

On April 3, a letter arrived on the Yale campus. It carried Jodie's name.

"I will finish what Hinckley started," it vowed. [Reagan] must die. [Hinckley] has told me so in a prophetic dream. Sadly, though, your death is also required. You too will suffer the same fate as Reagan and others in his fascist regime. You cannot escape. We are a wave of assassins throughout the world." Unlike me, the dirtbag hadn't even had the guts to put his name on it.

As Jodie acted her way through *Getting Out* that night and the next, the author was in the audience both times. Perhaps noticing the heavy police guard she was under at the time, even he wasn't stupid enough to make a move, only labeling himself, "Int. People's Court." Her dorm and the school dining hall were also under heavy surveillance, and she would eventually be given a bodyguard. In the darkest form of irony, some idiot left a note on the lobby bulletin board during her performance, proclaiming that, "By the time the show is over, Jodie Foster will be dead." The guy was quickly exposed as a harmless, worthless troublemaker, pissed at the overabundance of security at the event.

"I was too pretty to kill, he had said as he was arrested," Jodie claimed. "He saw me in my play and simply couldn't. The bearded man in center left? Ten feet from death? Ten feet from a loaded pistol held by a sick and perhaps 'insane' man? Ten feet? I don't care to know for sure."

Two days later, a maid at the Sheraton Park Plaza found some bullets and pictures of the president with "X"s on his face, marked "Targeted for Death." It wasn't the same room I'd spent time at, but it was the same building.

There was also another note.

"I depart now for Washington, DC, to bring to completion Hinckley's reality," it read. "Ultimately, Ronald Reagan will be shot to death and this country turned to the 'left.' If I cannot get at the president, I am prepared to slay some other prominent 'right-wing' political figure."

But now there was a name. It was from Edward Richardson, of the "Inter. Peoples Court." The same cretin who'd threatened to kill Jodie, both with a fake bomb and a theater visit that put him right next to her, was now promising to take out the president.

Fortunately, they got him before he could hurt anybody. Carrying a pistol and a photo of Lynette Fromme, the Charles Manson follower who'd tried to kill President Ford, Richardson was nabbed at a New York City bus station. A landscaper and wannabe street preacher from Drexel Hill, just west of Philadelphia, he may very well have intended to keep going south… all the way to DC.

But I was just worried for my beloved Jodie. What had I done to her? What was this SOB, and maybe others, trying to do to her? It looked like she did need rescuing after all.

I was furious. She wasn't safe, and it was my fault. All I'd wanted to do was love and protect her, and now some nutcase was trying to destroy the finest lady alive and making it sound like I'd set him on the path.

And here I was, locked away. All I could do was steam. They needed to get her out of there, take her away from the public eye, give her a new name, new identity, whatever. Just save her. Get her out of harm's way. Millions of people had already known her, and now they were associating her with me.

I'd always dreamed of that in some capacity, but now people were trying to harm her? Was that what they thought I wanted? Did they think she'd done something wrong? After my letter from the hotel room had run in news around the world, they should have known how much I cared for her. Why everyone should like her. And now some sicko was trying to hurt her?

That wasn't going to happen. Damned if I would allow it. The FBI or the local police should have come to get me and, if not apologize for getting between her and me, set me free with my new mission. If they weren't going to protect her, I would do it myself. I would never let this Richardson asshole, the bomb callers, or anyone else lay a dirty hand on her.

"Her voice and smile put stars in my eyes and send shivers everywhere," I'd remarked in my Casanova-esque letter to *Time*. "I only hope Yale doesn't destroy Jodie. Four years at that place is enough to ravage anyone. I tried to rescue her once, and it looks like I may have to do it again…. It's now six months later, and she's playing it cool again. I can't take much more of this silent treatment."

Yes, I'd thought about harming her myself, but that hadn't lasted, and it was my life's biggest regret by far. I wasn't feeling remorseful about shooting the president just yet, but I would always wish to high heaven I hadn't done that. Getting the hell out of there, getting to Jodie, and taking her off to safety would be my ultimate redemption.

Of course, the press tried to jump all over this one. Richardson and I were relatives. Best friends. Former roommates. Conspirators. I'd been behind his actions all along, cheering him on, letting him know how proud I would be if he could finish *our* work.

Bullshit. All a bunch of crap. I'd never met or heard of this guy, and if he'd said those things about Jodie directly to me, I would have practiced my killing ways much earlier!

Perhaps realizing the shitstorm he'd thrown himself into, Richardson tried to shift the blame. He talked about visiting Colorado and getting very close to my family, making it look like we'd known each other. Hooked to a lie detector, he swore up and down that we'd met and had the deepest of discussions.

Wrong. Way wrong. He couldn't be bothered to research his lies. Yes, he'd been near my family home, but the cops quickly learned that I hadn't even been in the state at the time. Had we met? Sure—in his *freakin' dreams*! Literally, that's what he said—that he'd dreamed of meeting me, and that was good enough for his warped mind to go to work.

That July, back up near Yale, Richardson got a year in jail for threatening Reagan. I wish to God and every saint that they'd put him in the cell next to me.

Sadly, all of that only became clear in hindsight. Many things seem valid to the psychotic mind. It took me far too long to realize that. Everything I'd just written, I myself didn't understand until much later. I feel that way today, but I didn't for a very, very long time. I was never off enough to think that I was Jodie's only fan, but I certainly believed I was her biggest, definitely her all-time favorite.

I never considered that I myself might inspire a copycat, someone who would follow in my footsteps and take the next one too far. I should have picked that up pretty quickly, as Fred Robert Wise Jr., who'd been arrested for calling the FBI, had then admitted in an interview that he planned to kill President Reagan. The April after my shooting, Harold Thomas Smith strolled into a Raleigh bus station and asserted to a cop, "President Reagan won't live long. If I get my hands on him, I'll blow his brains out." Both Wise and Smith were housed right there with me at Butner Federal Correctional Institution.

And that wasn't even the end. In the summer of 1982, I got the exact same type of letter that I'd sent to Jodie, even more so.

"You are not alone in your quest to find that one special person," I was informed by Chicago college student Penny Lynn Bailey, "that you are willing to die for or be killed for." She and I started corresponding. I asked her to mail me a gun. She told me she planned to kill Jodie. Instead, I recommended we (simply!) hijack an airplane and all three of us—she, I, and Jodie, fly off to Utopia.

I didn't even learn about Richardson until after I'd been found not guilty. Right out of nowhere, his sister contacted me and told me his story. Just a month after I'd been transferred to Washington, DC's St. Elizabeth Hospital for my long trip to (I can't even say *back to*, I was so screwed up) sanity, I started communicating with this piece of shit.

> "Because of the many revelations that came out at my trial, Jodie is now scared to death of me. My feelings about her are quite mixed; one day I love her and the next day I want to kill her. It was revealed at the trial that I was stalking Jodie the first week of March 1981 and I was actually on my way to New Haven at the end of March, when I detoured to Wash. D.C. and shot Reagan. I had planned to shoot her and then myself. One week later you were stalking her. Jodie is pretty damn lucky to be alive, isn't she? Oh, how I wish you could have gotten her when you had the chance. Now she walks around with bodyguards and gets as many threatening letters as me."

John Hinckley letter to Edward Richardson, July 22, 1982

Like so many other things I did during that period, I can't explain any of it. There's nothing to justify that, nor could there ever have been. When that came out, I'm sure many people wished they could go back and try me again. I'm sure some of Jodie's fans wished they could get her own revenge. I'm sure it reassured people that I'd never see the light of free day.

I'll go more into this later, but being the most notorious man in America, maybe the world, for what I'd done and what had happened to me (and what hadn't, conviction-wise), I was getting letters from all over the place; mostly hate mail, but some in praise, probably from people as insane as I was. I believed then, as I do today, that there are plenty of people in society more unstable than I ever was, and many of them have never been near a courtroom or hospital. I was just trying to make connections. I liked the letters, and I wanted them to continue. I may have figured that, since this guy was locked up too, he couldn't get her, so I knew my ridiculously obscene "encouragement" couldn't be acted upon.

I never figured that he might keep it in mind and do it when he got out; a year in jail isn't that long, especially when one behaves. I didn't understand then that my stupidity was adding to Jodie's danger. Fortunately, he didn't. I don't know what happened to him after he was released, but he apparently stayed away from the law.

Sadly, he wasn't even the worst guy I would be writing to. Again, keep reading.

But even with one guy who'd tried to kill for her and another making the most obscene of threats, Jodie didn't let it disrupt her. She kept studying at Yale. She kept working in plays. She was given a special single dorm room to stay under surveillance, although she wouldn't hire a bodyguard. She showed a hell of a lot more balance than a lot of people who'd been far less affected by the past weeks' actions.

"Who'd want to hurt me?" she rhetorically queried, hanging out at a pizza parlor not far from the bar I'd drank at, bragging to her classmates about our supposed relationship. "[I'm] not particularly upset. I'm such a nice guy. You just have to go on. I just don't think about it."

God, what a strong woman. What a beautiful powerhouse, inside and out. I admired her so much for that. No matter what happened to me over the next months, no matter how battered my mind had already become, she would never leave it all the way.

24. INSANITY

"A lady wrote me a letter right after it happened. In the last paragraph, she wrote something like, 'Please don't stop making the films, because, remember, that for the one crazy or stupid person who acted that way after seeing *Taxi Driver*, think of all those who saw it and were enriched my it.'

And that's why I'm glad I read my mail. Because I had thought of not continuing. I wasn't going to do anything for a while. It was very strange.

As for the bigger issue, I don't know what people want to do. Are they saying, 'Don't show these films'? Then you might as well start pulling books off shelves and telling people not to say anything. And, you know, there are some plays that can give people ideas too. Let's get rid of those, and the plays by the ancient Greeks. What about the play about the guy who [marries] his mother. Get rid of him. Bay, can he give people ideas.

I mean, how can anyone really believe that that's the one reason this guy really did that? Are people looking for answers that simple? They've got to be crazy if they are."

***Taxi Driver* director Martin Scorsese, November 1981**

Two days after the shooting, I met Vince Fuller. He'd been a friend of the attorney of my father's company, and now he was working out of the firm of Edward Bennett Williams, the same firm that had represented Jack Ruby after he'd killed Lee Harvey Oswald two decades before. Ironically, Williams, who'd been president of the Washington Redskins since 1966 and the Democratic Party treasurer during the 1970s, was quite the heavy hitter in the nation's capital. If he and Reagan weren't close friends, they were at least personally acquainted. I was lucky that my father had some legal pull in the area. My parents had yanked some strings and footed the bills, and I was reaping benefits I'd hardly earned.

I could tell that Fuller was a no-nonsense guy, and that he wasn't going to be friends with me. He was there to do a job the best he could. He knew he wouldn't be popular for doing it, and again, he never had to like me as a person. I'm sure every defense attorney who sticks around will eventually defend a person, maybe several people, that they can't stand, that they would never want to see or even speak of again after the trial. I don't know if he felt that strongly about me, but it was obvious that I was his client, and he was going to try to get me acquitted. This was business. If it was personal, it was only so to him. He knew he was going to get paid, and he intended to earn it. If there was an ethical issue, it was that he gave his clients and their families what they were paying for. He was never going to be accused of giving less than his best.

His co-counsel, Gregory Craig, was like the connector between Vince and me. He was friendly. He and I could talk, about the trial and whatever else. He would go to Vince and talk to him, removing any reference to anything but the courtroom.

My parents had already come to town, and Fuller had taken them through a deposition that would be as tough as any court. They'd talked about my childhood, my college life, everything. They'd told him, basically, that I'd never really done anything.

Not good. Not bad. Anything whatsoever. They did, however, point him toward Lynn. Surely, she would be a new wealth of information.

Then they got some more horrible news, enough to convince them yet again how far over the edge I'd gone, and how long I'd been falling.

As my folks got ready to testify before a grand jury, they glanced around, looking at the other people nearby. Perhaps that pretty lady down the hall was Lynn. Maybe that one was. Was this the woman who could show the jury that I still had a few grasps on sanity? It would be nice to finally meet the person who'd kept their son grounded for so long. Maybe they could take her out for a bite afterward to grab some information about my life that I'd hidden from them.

Just before they and my lawyers went in to speak their minds, Vince pulled them aside to reveal a sad truth that he'd known for a while.

Lynn Collins didn't exist. She never had.

She wasn't someone I knew in passing that I'd created a relationship with in my head, not far from my Jodie fantasies. She wasn't a person I'd dated once or twice and then broken up with.

She was a figment of my psychosis. Never real.

There was no actress looking to take or surpass Jodie's place in Hollywood. No trips to New York or California. No family in Chicago. No meeting in a laundromat. No visits to Texas.

Nothing. No one. No one whatsoever. I'd also never taken a writing course at Yale. Not at Yale, not near it, not sponsored by it, nothing.

Oh, and that LISTALOT shit? It didn't really exist either. I'd had some ideas for it, maybe talked about it with a few people, but it had never come close to getting off the ground, certainly never to the levels I'd lied about. Just one more falsehood that I'd managed to pull, to convince them and everybody else, least of all me, that I had at least some stability.

In Vince's presence, I'm sure my parents broke down. Maybe they didn't; they were probably so worn out by my garbage that they might not have even had the strength. But they didn't really bring it up to me. I'm sure they were really angry, very disappointed in their liar of a son. But they knew that I'd gotten myself into enough trouble and had the common decency not to add to it. Not yet.

Vince and I started talking defense possibilities. It was a pretty short conversation.

I actually wanted to plead guilty. I just wanted the whole thing over with. I was too sad, too tired, too far from reality to even imagine going through a trial. Sitting there for hours a day and days at a time, watching lawyers babble and argue, seeing one witness after another (maybe even Reagan himself) describe what I'd done, even getting on the stand myself and trying to convince a jury that, even after almost killing the president, I really wasn't that bad a guy; none of that sounded too appealing for me. Like President Ford's attempted assassin Sara Jane Moore already had and John Lennon's killer Mark David Chapman eventually would, I wanted to plead out and hope I wouldn't be locked away forever. Of course, I was still sure that Jodie would show up and help me get out earlier.

That's another reason I wanted to plead guilty. I wanted her to know how proud I was of the deed, the strength, inside and out, that I'd shown while planning it out and pulling it off.

Not because I was remorseful. Not really because I had some desperate need to stay in jail for the rest of my life. Mainly because I felt that, by pleading not guilty, I would be admitting to doing something wrong. I would be saying that my actions weren't justified. To me, they were. There was a great reason behind them, and I still couldn't fathom why more people couldn't see that. Doing something to win the heart and love of another was a great reason to do what I'd done, and if I'd pled not guilty, I would be disgracing my actions. I would let myself down. More importantly, I would be letting Jodie down. I couldn't have that.

I didn't see a real difference between facing consequences and taking responsibility. I was still proud of what I'd done, and I was more than happy to tell everyone who wanted to listen, regardless of why.

The insanity defense would be a tough sell to any jury, or anyone else. It sure hadn't worked for Sirhan Sirhan after he'd killed Robert F. Kennedy, or for Arthur Bremer, who'd almost murdered presidential candidate George Wallace, or for Jack Ruby, who killed alleged JFK assassin Lee Harvey Oswald on national TV. Serial killers David Berkowitz and John Wayne Gacy had also tried to hide behind it and failed. Eventually, though, my lawyers, my family, and I realized that it was our only option.

"If you demonstrate that a defendant is a mad dog," explained Los Angeles attorney Paul Fitzgerald, "the jurors want to put the mad dog to sleep."

They didn't want to offer a guilty plea. They knew I needed psychiatric help, not confinement. They also realized that such a plea would almost certainly put me in jail for the rest of my life anyway. Even if I wasn't officially sentenced to life in prison, I would never see the light of freedom again. Even if I bargained to a lesser sentence, no parole board in the history of the universe would release a guy who had almost killed the president and several others. Something like, "Twenty years to life," would have meant, "Life, even if he lives to be 150!"

But not guilty? Only slightly easier.

I was on tape doing it, with hundreds of witnesses, so we couldn't say that someone else had done it. Reagan had been unarmed, and even his bodyguards hadn't been threatening me, so self-defense wasn't going to work. I'd bought the gun, brought it there, and pointed it straight at him to fire, so anything about it being an accident was out of the question fast.

Insanity would be our only defense. They hoped I could pass the M'Naghten rule, a standard legal test defining the defense of insanity.

There are two factors to M'Naghten that apply. We had to either prove that I didn't know what I was doing, or that I didn't understand that it was wrong.

The first one was out fairly quickly. My pursuing of Carter quickly became common knowledge, as had my cross-country bus trip to Washington, DC to stalk Reagan. Those and other factors, including all the preparation I'd taken for the assassination date alone, showed that I was conscious of my actions.

But their legitimacy? Maybe we could try that. I'd felt that my actions were justified, if not legal. Perhaps my mind was so scarred that my personal reasoning could override the law, at least in the eyes of the 12 people who would be making up their own minds about me.

They told me that the authorities would want to examine me right away. Not to determine my sanity as a whole, but to see if I even had the competence to go to trial. Fuller told me that an insanity defense was likely, but not his final verdict. Lawyers, it appears, need to wait until the last minute to make any decisions. They never know when something might pop up out of nowhere.

The shrinks were about to take me through the mental wringer, and I would spend the next few months getting grilled by people who would argue whether my mind was stable. During that process, a person is kept in everything but solitary confinement and, of course, with a guy in the world's public eye, everything would get kicked up a few notches.

Therefore, I wouldn't get to see my folks for months. After flying all the way across the country and undergoing Fuller's impromptu interrogation, my parents were finally allowed to see me—for all of one hour.

They brought me a Bible (my father had just undergone a serious religious experience, which he would carry the rest of his life) and some letters from friends and family. I told them about my cell, like how the guards kept the lights on all night. We could have been having a picnic from the way we were chatting.

Except, of course, for the shooting. We managed to go the entire hour without hardly bringing it up. I think they could see that, despite everything that had happened, very little had sunk in with me. I still came across like I'd just gotten into a little issue, and everything would be okay soon. The possibility that I would never leave the place was nowhere near my mind.

That must have been tough for them. Up until the very moment of the shooting, they'd still believed that I would find a silver lining in my directionlessness. That I was one realization, one good choice away from getting my feet on the ground and running to success. They'd never considered, as no parent ever would by choice, the possibility that there was something seriously wrong with me, to the point that I would try to take human lives.

But if they were in denial about it, they never showed it. They told me that they would always love me, always be there for me, as would the rest of the Hinckley family.

"We simply ask that you realize that John is a sick boy," they told the press, "and that you give him the benefit of the doubt until all the true facts concerning his mental health are known."

In court the next day, Fuller argued to put my examination back a bit to give us more time to prepare. He was probably afraid that I would be a little too honest with the doctor and endanger my case, but the judge said no.

Later that day, I sat down with Dr. James Evans, a local forensic psychiatrist. I don't remember much about that particular conversation, but I'm sure we went over as much as we could with a magnifying glass from hell.

For the most part, I guess it was kind of fun. If people hadn't necessarily avoided me for most of my life, they certainly hadn't gravitated toward me. I wasn't someone that people wanted to come up and chat with, or invite me most places. I'd had a small set of friends who had a small list of interests, and I was fine with that.

But this was different. Now people actually cared enough to chat with me. They were interested, even for the worst reasons, in my past. They were asking my opinions, my thoughts. They wanted to hear from me, to recognize me. I was significant. I was important to many people who themselves carried a great deal of authority.

There was still one wild card to all of this: the accused himself. Me. Even when we'd talked about the insanity plea, it being my only chance to remain out of prison for the rest of my life (not that a mental institution would be a five-star resort), I wasn't sold on the idea.

But that was one of the few pontifications I would keep inside. If the prosecuting detectives got any hint that I thought I was guilty, that even I believed myself to be sane, they would have run with that like lightning, and my upcoming jury, were there one at all, would hear it over and over.

Of course, Evans declared that my mind wasn't decimated enough to avoid trial. Now Fuller went to battle with the government to decide who would examine me first, between our psychiatrists and theirs.

And we also got a bit of good news. DC courts had a less stringent view of M'Naghten than most in the nation. Assuming we would plead insanity, in typical legal jargon, we only had to prove that I lacked "substantial capacity" to tell right from wrong. Basically, we wouldn't have to convince a jury that insanity had taken me so far over the edge that I was totally delusional, all the way away from reality, only far enough to *not* realize that this particular act was wrong.

The prosecution would be sure to argue that all my premeditation showed that I was at least moderately stable, but the revelation that I'd already been under psychiatric care, as little as I felt it had done, could help me. The obsession with Jodie might also be enough to show that I was at least partially off the mental radar.

Might. That was always a word that everyone used in my case. No lawyer would ever guarantee a single decision, let alone a full verdict, but Fuller and his colleagues stayed optimistic while reminding me that we were fighting one of the most uphill battles in legal history. The 12 people who would decide my fate had almost certainly seen on TV and in newspapers, probably over and over again, me nearly killing the president. Him rushing away in fear. James Brady and my other innocent victims lying on the ground in pain. My detached, remorseless face as I was driven from one location to the next. They'd undoubtedly seen on TV and read in the newspapers one columnist, one common man and woman, calling for my head.

Many of these writers had already jumped to the conclusion that I would be using an insanity defense, and they went out of their way to destroy it themselves. Psychiatrists, sociologists, psychologists, even other lawyers and politicians were in newspapers, magazines, on news stations on the radio and television, destroying an argument I hadn't even had the chance to make. They were ridiculing things we hadn't even said yet. Clearly, they were demonstrating, quite enthusiastically, that the whole "innocent until proven guilty" proverb only exists in the walls of a courtroom, and trying to persuade others before they even reached that point.

"The so-called 'temporary insanity' defense should not be allowed in federal criminal trials," proclaimed State Senator Walter Mengden. Ironically, as a Texas Republican, he was exactly the kind of fellow my parents would have supported, politics-wise.

The jurors would only be human. They were very likely to decide that, if people with such a background, professional and educated, were willing to put their name and degree behind an opinion and express it to millions, it must be worth listening to. Who would they be to question the word of people with doctorate degrees, who'd personally seen patients who demonstrated insanity, and others who didn't, who taught college classes on the subject? It would be simpler to just listen and agree.

On a personal level, many of these people would love to be the president's self-appointed avengers. What a cap feather it would be to be able to say or brag, "This evil cretin tried to take out the man we elected to run the country—and I made him pay!" How could they maintain any semblance of impartiality in a case like this?

My lawyers did express the opinion, though, that this case was going to drag out far beyond the end of May, so any youthful offender status I might have enjoyed would probably be gone. But we would give it a shot anyway.

Right after I was deemed competent to assist, I was tossed into a limousine and surrounded by a motorcade of officers. As I was driven to an airfield, I couldn't help but feel that I was receiving my own form of presidential treatment.

A helicopter flew me to North Carolina's Butner Federal Correctional Institution, a place for the mentally ill. Butner would be my home until just before the trial.

Down there, I felt a sense of manic. On one side, it was exciting. Everyone in America and most of the world knew my name. I'd gone from defining obscurity to notoriety. And I would be there for a while. Right now, I was only charged with attempting to kill the president. Reagan was improving, but he wasn't out of the woods yet. If he died, I would be even more known. As I went toward trial, as I was tried, and whatever happened afterward, the name of John Hinckley Jr. would be part of Americana. Days before, no one had known me. Now no one would ever forget.

And then I would flip over to the worst side. My life as I knew it was ruined. Over. Barring a miracle, which I, in all my psychosis, still hoped for, I would never be free again, at least not for a while. Most people didn't or wouldn't understand what I'd done. I wondered if being known was worth being hated.

The FBI was trying to question me, but my lawyers made it clear to me and them that we weren't going to be communicating. The only people I would be talking to for much of the next year would be my family and the people in my case, as in, the doctors and lawyers.

After Charles Whitman's killing spree in Texas, an autopsy dug up a tumor in his brain, and some people had blamed that for his psychotic acts. I guess they were thinking I might have the same affliction. People with mental illnesses like schizophrenia commonly have strange wrinkles in their brain, and they wanted to see if there was something there. One night, I was taken to Duke University for a brain scan.

Interestingly, the guards attempted to get the staff to leave my bulletproof vest on even when I was getting scanned. I knew I would probably never be able to step outside without it, maybe for the rest of my life, but I had at least hoped that a medical procedure would give me a break.

Not at first. The staff tried to scan me with this heavy vest on. It took a hyperventilation attack by my body to show them that even this precaution wasn't necessary.

Soon after that, I was choppered off to Johns Hopkins Hospital in Baltimore, this time for a spinal tap. I wasn't sure what information my backbone could give about my mind, but apparently the procedure can check to see if one's brain has been infected, if not outright ruined, by diseases like meningitis or encephalitis. Maybe there was a medical cause for my insanity. With all my past prostitute dalliances, I wonder if they checked for syphilis, just as deadly as the diseases I just named.

And here came that interrogative onslaught. On a daily basis, I chatted with one doctor, then another, then some more. Sometimes I talked to those working for our team. Others, I would be with the prosecution's assistors. I spent my off time strumming a guitar that Greg Craig had managed to convince someone I deserved.

We talked about my childhood. The schooling I'd done well in, and that which I hadn't. Jobs I'd held. Relationships I hadn't had. My music. My jobs, real and imagined. My actions, physical and mental, in the days, even in the moments, leading up to the shooting.

I never knew in advance which doctor from which team I would be talking to. They didn't want me to be too prepared. Spontaneity can help a person's impartiality.

"It was almost a blessing in disguise. The roller-coaster ride ended March 30. Now, I'm only depressed because I'm cooped up here."

Writing from my Butner sessions

As the sessions went on, I could see some strong distinctions between my doctors and the prosecution's. Those trying to help me get convicted showed their objective almost at once. They were more pointed, more confrontational with me. Clearly, they'd already put a tremendous amount of time and preparation into ensuring that their exam would end with the decree that this guy was as normal as John Smith and apple pie. One of them was Dr. Jonas Rappeport, who'd examined Arthur Bremer and testified that Bremer was clear as the gunshots he'd fired into George Wallace. He'd also sat down with Sara Jane Moore, who'd shot President Ford.

One of his colleagues was fellow examiner Dr. Park Dietz, who taught at Harvard. Credibility was clearly a hardcore objective in the prosecution's eyes and mind.

Strangely, of everyone I talked to, I spent the most time with Butner psychiatrist Sally Johnson, herself just two years older than me, along with being heavily pregnant. I guess being a local made her more accessible. With a Harvard professor on the team, I guess the prosecutors felt they could trade closeness for experience on this one.

My doctors, who'd actually been selected by Vince and my parents, were more open. They were more impartial. They were much more honest. They appeared to have walked in with a wide-open mind. They were on my side, but I could tell that they didn't automatically assume that I was insane, or that I wasn't, like the prosecution had. They came across more that they legitimately wanted to know. I could very easily have imagined one of them resigning from my team if they decided that I wasn't insane after all.

Hell, I didn't mind anything. I never refused to answer any of the questions. Like I said, I didn't feel I'd done much wrong, so I didn't have an issue holding forth the details. I may have even stretched out some of the conversations. Remember, these doctors were about the only human contact I was enjoying those days.

In the midst of it all, with only a few days left before I was out of the age range, Vince Fuller decided to take a shot in the dark, offering for me to plead guilty to a few of the charges if I could get sentenced under the juvenile laws discussed earlier. Not shockingly, the prosecutors told us there wasn't a chance in hell.

I shouldn't have been surprised. In reality, I don't think I was. I'd been feeling down in the days leading up to that, in part because I would be imprisoned on my birthday, and I guess I'd been naive enough to get my hopes up a bit. When the prosecution, without a nanosecond of consideration, gave the most emphatic "NO!" they sent a major depressive wave blasting through my cell.

And it happened again. I went back to my medication in the hopes that it would take me too far. I spent some time stockpiling a load of Valium and Tylenol, whining about taking them for headaches. Right around my 26th birthday, I decided to take everything away. I gulped down a couple of handfuls.

I was sitting there, waiting for things to end. I think I remember falling backward. A psychiatrist said I confessed what I'd done, but I don't remember that. Anyway, the guards found me laying on my back, shaking, vomit and other bodily fluids everywhere.

They took me to the hospital and pumped everything they could out of my digestive system. They were getting shit out of there I couldn't even recognize. They were worried my liver might be damaged, so they medicated the hell out of me for that.

Then they put me in a suicide cell. No reading materials, no phone calls, nothing whatsoever. Just a toilet, mattress, and bed. Butner's the most minimum of security institutions, as my fellow inmates were hanging out, watching TV in rooms with no bars, playing tennis. Not me. I was back under heavy watch and would stay that way for a very long time.

Well, not quite. When my parents found out about my attempt, they complained to the staff, and I at least got a TV to watch. But the guards even controlled that; a long extension cord ran from my set into a guard's office nearby. Every time the news came on, he would yank out the cord to keep me from catching up on the world's events.

With so many doctors fighting over an opinion, along with the time crunch I'd caused by self-imposing capital punishment, everything got pushed back. The testing had been scheduled for 90 days or less, ending in July. When it became clear that that wouldn't be near enough time, the courts pushed the deadline back to the beginning of August.

In the interim, Vince came up with another plea deal. He and I would be willing to plead guilty to enough of the major charges that I would get an automatic four life sentences.

But remember, in legal talk, life rarely means life. It typically means the legal system takes enough of your years to ensure that, even when you get out, you'll never do anything that matters. A life sentence is the epitome of legal ambiguity.

Under the deal, my sentences would run concurrently, not consecutive. Rather than completing one and starting another the next day, I would basically do them all at once. Like I said, even with my arrangement edging closer, I wasn't certain I would plead insanity.

So I liked the idea. My parents seemed okay with it too. Hell, I was only 26. If I could behave myself behind bars and get a sort-of-friendly parole board, I could be back out sometime in my early forties.

As he always did for me, Vince put together one hell of a zealous, well-researched argument to end the nightmare I'd caused and let everyone get back to healing while I rotted out of the public eye. But a certain someone on the other side said no.

Just after Reagan had taken over, his administration appointed an up-and-comer from New York as its associate attorney general—basically, the third most powerful American in the legal world. Now the guy was going to make his boss and his country proud. He wasn't handing out any kid glove treatment to the guy who'd almost taken out a man who'd done him such a big favor.

He turned us down flat and told us to prepare for World War Three when it came time for trial.

The guy's name? Rudy Guiliani. Yes, the same one whose name would become synonymous with New York City and ultimately the mayoral title itself across America, especially after he was named "America's Mayor" for his leadership right after the 9/11 attacks.

I was always thinking about Jodie. I was sure that she would be there soon. But I figured I would give her just a little more incentive to hurry up and show. To display my devotion enough that she would make me a main priority, I'd given some written interviews to *Time*, *Newsweek*, and other publications, vowing to be the man she'd always wanted, but she still couldn't find her way to me.

"The most important thing in my life is Jodie Foster's love and admiration. From head to toe, every square inch of Jodie attracts me. She reached her peak when she was 12, and then she reached a second peak following March 30, '81.

On March 30, I made my love known to [Jodie] in my own unique way. She did not respond at all prior to March 30. I blame her and I don't blame her. After March 30, I finally got a response out of her. It's now six months later, and she's playing it cool again. I can't take much more of this silent treatment.

The ultimate expression of my love would be to take her away from Yale and the world permanently."

My letter to *Time Magazine*, October 1981

I decided to try a new tactic. It had worked at a few times in the political world, so I figured I might have some success. Besides, I'm sure Jodie wouldn't mind me losing a few pounds.

The next time the staff brought me a meal, I refused. I don't know if I said why. I might have said I was sick or just not hungry or whatever. I said no to my next meal as well. And the one after that, and the one after that as well.

Yes, I was off on my own hunger strike. I could stand to drop a few, and I was a strong guy, or so I believed, mentally if not physically. I could focus enough on my goal to withstand the difficulty of a few days, even weeks, without a solid meal.

The next time I ate, I vowed it would be looking across the table, straight into the eyes of the lovely lady who'd finally shown up. Heck, Jodie didn't even have to go that far to placate me. I would have been happy with a few phone conversations, hopefully with more time, depth, and detail that those we'd had back on the Yale campus. My lawyers refused to help me, blowing me off when I demanded they call Jodie or send her some letters I'd written, asking why she was playing "Little Miss Innocent."

But I'd forgotten where I was. I was certainly not the only Butner resident to try this sort of thing. The medical higher-ups had seen prisoners forsake their food for a cause, and they had a quick remedy.

Hey, if I didn't want to feed myself, fine with them. But they would make for damn sure I ate somehow. Like, being force-fed with feeding tubes. In all kinds of brutal detail, they explained how slow and painful this process could be. They were trained to do it comfortably to someone who legitimately couldn't eat, but for an idiot starving (pardon the pun) for attention for no reasons outside of his gutted mind, they knew just how to go the other way. The suffering I would undergo to get my nutrients by force would be a million times worse than a couple hunger pangs.

Okay, this wasn't going to work out. Reluctantly, or so I made it seem to them, I went back to the normal manner of consumption.

It was fine. I was sure Jodie would show soon anyway. So sure that I hardly even thought about the court case that would finally be taking shape later that month.

The psychiatrists' reports were starting to roll in. Not surprisingly, the three who worked for me were sure that I was a textbook psychotic. That I'd had no clue what I was doing, far too far into my own reality to understand the gravity of the situation. Too convinced of my own delusions to be held responsible.

And, shockingly, those on the prosecution's side deemed me totally sane. Absolutely aware of what I was doing. Not for the first time, I'd gone to kill the president, and this time, I'd stalked him all the way across the country and spent a few days nearly within sight of him. The best these people would give me was that I had a personality disorder—you think?!—but nothing ever near the levels of being insane. Not even close enough that I couldn't comprehend killing the president.

Interestingly, even with all this, my next court appearance would be extremely anticlimactic. Not because of what happened, but because of what was going on elsewhere at the exact same time.

There was never any doubt that I would be indicted. Even in my ravaged mind, I knew that no jury, grand or otherwise, would let me get away without at least some time and suffering.

As the counts against me were read out on August 24, I only sat and watched. Nothing else to do yet. Defendants don't usually speak at indictments, unless there's a snowball's chance in hell that they can keep from being tried. That was never going to apply to me, so my lawyers and I just sat there and heard the charges, if not the evidence, against me. Thirteen separate counts rained down, including attempted murder against Tim McCarthy, Thomas Delahanty, James Brady, and, of course, the president. Even if by some miracle I was acquitted of everything else, just getting convicted on a single one of those could put me away forever.

"I'm glad he was a poor shot."
James Brady, Reagan press secretary, January 1982

"I hope he stays behind bars a long time. A long, long time."
Secret Service Agent Tim McCarthy

I wasn't concerned about it yet. I was still considering how I would respond a few days later when a judge asked how I was pleading. I knew what was going to happen, so I let my mind wander.

I let it scurry a few states north. That very same day in New York, the justice system was throwing the book at America's most other well-known gunman, and I only wished I could myself have hurled it, and a few other things, at the scumbag as well.

Mark David Chapman, whose murder of John Lennon had broken the world's heart, and mine as well, the previous December, got 20 years to life. Everyone knew, as I'm sure he did, that there was no way he would be out in 20 years, or maybe not even life at all. Here in the middle of 2025, he's still locked up, denied parole 13 times.

His jury hadn't bought the insanity defense, and no doubt that, if I pled that way, the jurors on my case would be thinking about it. They might feel that, if these 12 people didn't buy the argument that mental illness caused this cretin to kill a famous musician to feed his own ego, they probably shouldn't buy that another guy would nearly kill not one, but four people to feed his fantasy of an actress.

But at that point, they might not have a job to do at all. I would be arraigned later that week, and neither Fuller nor my parents nor even I was sure what would happen there. There might be a long trial encompassing the nation. Or there might be a guilty plea and a defendant off to jail, almost certainly forever, by the weekend.

No one knew. Not even me.

25. "BUT NOT REALLY"

I'm feeling better now but not really
An attack of something has crippled me.
Hey doctor, there is a small problem
That I seem to have with communicating.
Shut up, and listen to my life story
Although I don't want to tell it.
I was born, I grew up and now
I've come to you for some guidance.
I'll call you a counselor instead of a shrink
The word psychiatrist scares people
Especially my neighborly parents.
Can you counsel me and tell me
That everything will be fine and dandy
Because you will help me to help myself?
Oh Boy! Now I have confidence
In myself.
Here I come world.
Ready or not, I can do anything now
Because my attitude had been turned around.
Didn't you say my attitude was everything?
Hey doctor, how can I thank you?
I'm feeling better now but not really.

John Hinckley Jr.

26. RONALD REAGAN

"Please tell me you're all Republicans."

**Ronald Reagan to the George Washington
University Hospital staff, just before
undergoing surgery after my shooting.**

Before we go forward, I would like to reiterate something I
touched on back on the introduction. I'm sure that, even today,
it will come as a surprise to many, although I've tried to make
it very clear, literally almost since the moment I shot President
Reagan.

I actually liked him very much. I never had a problem with
him on a personal level. This wasn't like John Wilkes Booth,
who thought he was some kind of one-man avenger for the
Confederacy when he shot Lincoln, or Lee Harvey Oswald, a self-
created Russian double agent who struck a Cold War blow for his
new country by killing the president.

Not for me. I never felt as such. As I've stated, my entire
family loved Reagan to death. He was going to be the savior
of a wrecked country. My brother Scott was planning to have
dinner a few nights later with Neil Bush, the son of Reagan's vice
president.

"President Reagan is the best president we've had this
century," I proclaimed in a letter to *Newsweek* in early October
1981. "Let's give the man a chance."

A chance? It had been six months since I personally had
almost ended the man's life, and now here I was sounding like I
was on TV campaigning for him? What the hell was wrong with

me? Where did I get off talking like that? I'm sure many readers felt the same way.

"I helped his presidency," I once bragged. "After I shot him, his rating in the polls went up by twenty percent." I'm sure that quip helped my standing.

I wasn't as into Reagan as my family was. Partially because I'm not especially political, but mainly because, by the time of his election, my mind had been so altered into a reality that was so far from everyone else's. My psyche was a few degrees from full destruction.

I'd blurred and broken the line between John Hinckley and Travis Bickle past the point of salvaging. After my failed attempt to take out Carter, I'd set my sights on Reagan. Bickle considered, but never actually attempted, to take out Palantine, whose bodyguards see Bickle before he can complete the act. There's not a day goes by that I don't wish Reagan's own protectors had grabbed me before I could carry out my own.

Reagan was an innocent victim in my quest. Innocent in the sense that he hadn't done anything wrong. Not to me or anyone I knew, or to his country or anyone else. He was a good man in the wrong place at the wrong time. With the wrong job.

He was the president and, whoever the president was, I was going to take him out as my final act to win Jodie's affection. It didn't matter who he was. If Carter had been re-elected, or if George Bush or John Anderson had beaten Reagan for the Republican nomination and ultimately the White House, any of them would have gone down.

For her. For Jodie.

"Unfortunately, Jodie is now at Yale, where sweetness and innocence are not allowed," my *Newsweek* letter continued. "Jodie is a bright girl and this overflowing brilliance used to intimidate me. But now I think we are equal and compatible.... In closing, I would like to say hello to Ms. Foster and ask her one small question: Will you marry me, Jodie?"

Now, yes, here's where things get even stranger, as though they had any kind of rationale up to this point. You would be amazed at the number of people who have gone out of their way to make this point to me. I guess they're just looking for some semblance of logic in the totally illogical.

When Bickle goes to kill Palantine, he's not actually acting on Iris's behalf. He's there to rescue Betsy (well, "rescue," as she's no longer into him). Only after getting almost caught does he suddenly remember Iris, and then he takes out some horrible people to get his and her own happy ending.

So, I get asked and rooked to high heaven, who was I rescuing Jodie from here? Just as I'd burned the distinction between myself and Travis, so I had that between her and Iris. She hadn't been taken in by the dregs of society for me to swoop in and be her savior. Reagan hadn't done anything to her, to me, or to anyone I knew.

Basically, not only was my mind gone by this point, but I wasn't even lining my fantasy up with my own role model. How could I even justify this back then?

I can't. I never could. It's a question that can't be answered, a mystery that only becomes clear in the mind of a psychopath. Things make sense to the mentally ill that no sane person could ever comprehend. We believe in ourselves, our actions, because they seem right in our mind, one that's already destroyed.

The one thing that I vowed I would never do was hide. I wouldn't be like Oswald, shooting from a building window several stories in the air and then running off into a theater, or Booth, scurrying away from Ford's Theater and spending a few days on the run before the local law took him out.

I had a clear motive that I couldn't wait to share with everyone, that I knew would make sense to all, especially to Jodie, if I could just get the chance to explain. I wanted to be known as the guy who'd taken these steps for the woman he adored. No matter what I did or who saw me, I was going to stand there and take the credit, the blame, and maybe the beatings and bullets. I fully appreciated that I might get attacked by Reagan's Secret Service folk or some vigilante trying to defend his president or, hell, even Reagan himself. I might even get shot dead right then and there.

I was okay with it. Hell, as destroyed as my mind was at that point, I might have been secretly hoping for it. My own sort of soldier dying in battle. I could become a martyr, a guy who gave his life for his quest and his love for Jodie.

Travis Bickle hadn't been concerned about appearances; he'd been ready to take out his target in the midst of a crowd. I wanted to be so brave myself. I wanted people to know my name and motive. I was sure I would have the same happy ending, become the same hero he was, get the same thankful letter from Jodie that he'd gotten from Iris's family.

But in the epitome of sad irony, Reagan himself would begin my journey to mental health, would reach out and pull me back to reality.

"Left the hotel at the usual side entrance and headed for the car—suddenly there was a burst of gun fire from the left. S.S. Agent pushed me onto the floor of the car & jumped on top. I felt a blow in my upper back that was unbelievably painful. I was sure he'd broken my rib. The car took off. I sat up on the edge of the seat almost paralyzed by pain. Then I began coughing up blood which made both of us think—yes, I had a broken rib & it had punctured a lung. He switched orders from W.H. to Geo. Wash. U. Hosp.

By the time we arrived I was having great trouble getting enough air…. I walked into the emergency room and was hoisted onto a cart where I was stripped of my clothes. It was then we learned I'd been shot & had a bullet in my lung.

Getting shot hurts. Still my fear was growing because no matter how hard I tried to breathe it seemed I was getting less & less air. I focused on that tiled ceiling and prayed.

But I realized I couldn't ask for God's help while at the same time I felt hatred for the mixed-up young man who had shot me. Isn't that the meaning of the lost sheep? We are all God's children & therefore equally beloved by him. I began to pray for his soul and that he would find his way back to the fold."

Excerpt from Reagan's diary in days after shooting

Just two months after I shot him (he was back at full work within a few weeks), Reagan was in West Berlin, giving one of his many talks about knocking down the Berlin Wall. This one wouldn't become as famous as his "Tear down this wall!" plea six years later, but it stands out for a different reason.

"By its very existence and character, Berlin remains the most compelling argument for an open world," he told a jammed U.S. Air Force base. "We're reminded of the many traditions of openness and democracy that have marked the history of this city."

Suddenly, a pop sounded nearby. We might have expected a barrage of agents to barrel in and yank him off the stage. America was still on the edge from my actions, and as extroverted as he was, many didn't want him getting too public.

But it wasn't the Second Coming of Hinckley. A balloon had exploded.

He didn't flinch. Didn't even look up. Instead, Reagan pulled out the improvisational skills he'd learned from decades in the acting business.

"Missed me!" he quipped.

The audience roared with laughter.

What poise. How brave. This guy had almost been gunned down in public, and here he could joke about it on the spur of the moment. Many people wished they had his guts. I know I did.

I didn't learn about this for a while, but Reagan apparently wanted to come see me himself while I was locked up. It was things like that that started to bring my mind back together, to pull me out of this fantasy I'd created.

I wasn't too surprised that he would forgive me, although maybe for him to do so as quickly as he did. Reagan was a deep Christian, even if he wasn't always public about it. Religion is a touchy subject for those who need millions of people to vote for them, even if they may not agree with them in the spiritual sense.

But when I learned what a moral person he was in that sense, as not just a president, but a man, my own mind began to change, in a good way. I began to see what I'd truly done.

I'd never considered him an enemy, but maybe an object. But that was far too superficial, so cold on my part. He was a man with a past. He'd worked very hard throughout his life, well before entering politics. He'd tried very hard to make things better for California when he ran it.

He had a wife. He had children. He had so many people who loved him on a personal level. I'd hurt them all. I'd nearly ruined their lives. And worst of all, I'd *tried* to ruin their lives. It had been on purpose.

That's what a murder does. It doesn't just remove a life. It steals a huge part of those around the victim. It violently snatches away a part of their lives they held so close. I'd attempted to take away Neil's younger brother and Nancy's husband; Nancy would pray every time her husband went out for the rest of their lives together. I'd nearly stolen Michael, Maureen, Patti, and Ronald Jr.'s dad. (Reagan's other daughter Christine hadn't survived infancy.) So many other family members. So many other friends who, again, knew and loved him as so much more than just American's main public figure, the man running the nation.

And, of course, I'd done the same to my other victims. Thomas Delahanty, Tim McCarthy, and James Brady had also had family and friends who nearly lost them as well, all because of me.

It was sad. The remorse I felt started to trickle down and nearly grew into a tidal wave. It took me far too long to realize it, but it was a major step in my mental health healing. These people had always been innocent, but now I saw them as exactly that: full people. People who had accomplished more than me. People who had done nothing wrong. The last people in the country who deserved what I'd done. Nothing was worth that. Nothing would ever be. Nothing could ever justify that.

And now all I could do was sit there and realize all of this. I don't recall the exact time this fully hit me, but very quickly, I started to realize the obscene extent of what I'd done.

I also realized the wrongness. The terrible mistakes I'd made. The terrible *real* mistakes I'd made. I'd spent far too long not being able to tell the difference between the movies and reality, and I wouldn't finish that journey for a very long time, but here was its starting line.

"I hope he'll get well, too. He seems to be
a very disturbed young man."
Ronald Reagan, back at work on April 22, 1981

27. PLEADING

"With one little squeeze of this trigger, I can put that person at my feet, moaning and groaning and pleading with God. This gun gives me pornographic power. If I wish, the president will fall and the world will look at me in disbelief, all because I own an inexpensive gun."

My writing "Guns Are Fun"

If the past few months had been tough on me, my family, my lawyers, and everyone else, the next three days magnified the effects by about a thousand.

My family, my lawyers, so many others kept trying to convince me to plead insanity. They could see and feel and know things that I couldn't or wouldn't. Those of us in the grip of psychosis see a perfectly logical world, and mine still made sense to me. I could still walk into a courtroom, look a judge in the eye, and proudly proclaim that, as a moral man, I was ready to stand up and take responsibility, not hide behind some façade that had been created for me.

With so much against me, I didn't think any defense would work, let alone one as typically unsuccessful as the insanity plea. At that point, less than 3% of felony defendants had even tried insanity and, of those who had, three out of four ended up getting convicted and going to jail anyway.

Chatting with them, having another in what was becoming a seemingly endless round of conversations with one doctor after another, in my moments of solitude at Quantico, even on my way to Maryland's Fort Meade for my long-awaited plea date,

I changed my mind. Then I changed it back. Then it went here and there and everywhere. With so little on my plate in basically solitary confinement, my mind was desperate for activity, and I'm sure that having so little to pick from damaged my psyche even more. Not that I felt there was much wrong with it at that point.

As much as everyone worked to show me that not guilty was the way to go, they made it clear that I was the final decision selector. If I could assist in my own defense, I could certainly make this choice. I didn't tell them how much I'd gone back and forth, only that I was leaning toward guilty.

Even as I walked into the U.S. District Court on August 28, 1981, wearing an oversized blue suit to hide the bulletproof vest under it, I wasn't sure which way I would go. My lawyers sat with me at the table, some large federal marshals just a few feet away. My parents were in the midst of a jammed courtroom. Everyone on my side hoped I would push through to trial. Those against me, obviously the extreme majority, probably wanted me to take my lumps and go straight to jail, to be done with this and let them, my victims, and the rest of the nation get on with healing.

The same long list of counts against me was read aloud. Then, court clerk Betty Flynn became one of the first to actually bring me into the proceedings. She asked how I wished to plead.

I don't think anyone there, including her and Judge Barrington Parker, whom I would get to know very well very soon, so much as breathed for the next few seconds. My parents clasped each other's hands, hoping that I would show more guts than I had for a while. My lawyers couldn't say anything to me anymore. For the first time since I'd shoved myself into the darkest of national spotlights, everything was shining on me.

I looked at the judge. I looked at his clerk. I glanced around. Then, for the first and only time of the day in court, I spoke.

"Not guilty."

A wave of whispers spread over the room. Many were scoffing at me. Some were wiping tears. Others tried to burn holes through me with their eyes. I saw my parents, and it was clear they'd felt the relief.

And then it was back to business. Vince told Parker that he wanted more time to have me examined, and Parker said okay. Vince agreed with the prosecutors that I was competent to help with my defense. He didn't mention insanity, probably because at that point, everyone knew it was going to happen. The examinations would continue.

Then I was back to Fort Meade, a military base about a half hour from the nation's capital. Like at Quantico, I was kept very far from the rest of the inmate population. No one wanted these guys to exact their own justice. My self-overdose still in everyone's mind, guards were watching me day and night. As everyone would find out later, that wouldn't be sufficient.

I was scared myself; from then on, just about every time Vince went to court for me, I chose to stay in my cell, pretty sure that somebody would love to try out the strength of my bulletproof vest. A few days after my plea, he attempted to get bail on my behalf, and I'm not sure I would have accepted it if he'd been successful.

"You and the other journalists make it sound like I was some kind of a hobo or something. My recent cross-country ventures were necessary because New Haven was so far away. I would have travelled to Budapest to find Jodie Foster. Now that I'm in Maryland, she and I are much closer in more ways than one."

My letter to *The Washington Post*, Sept. 7, 1981

In late September, Vince Fuller made the announcement that everyone had seen coming for weeks, even months: I would plead insanity. The facts were clear. I'd written what looked like serious premeditation in my letter to Jodie, then gone out and tried to kill the president, and harmed some others in the bargain.

Now it was up to opinion. The jurors would be the ones trying to get inside my jumbled mind and make sense of it. Each one might find something different.

Under DC's laws at the time, my team would have to prove that I "lacked substantial capacity to appreciate the wrongfulness of his conduct, or to conform his conduct to the requirements of the law." After I was acquitted, those laws were strengthened, both in DC and around the nation.

Then Vince went back to work, ensuring that his client would get the fairest of trials. Any great defense attorney can delay a trial until his client's great-grandkids die of old age, and Vince could do that to the highest. Right after my plea, he'd advised me to waive my right to a speedy trial. He needed some time, and he was going to use it right. My trial was supposed to begin right around that Thanksgiving—nearly seven months after the shooting, already a long time by legal standards—and he was going to delay the hell out of it, if the system could be challenged enough.

Of course, I had my own reason for not wanting to go to trial just yet. I was still hoping I wouldn't have to. In my dark, dark, completely insane fantasies, someone else would arrive soon to help me out, to finish the plan I'd started. All this court stuff was simply a formality. It would be over soon. All I needed was a little help from my special friend.

28. SUICIDE IN STOCKADE

"I felt very shocked, very frightened, and very distressed."

**Jodie Foster to *PBS News Hour* on learning
of the Hinckley letters, April 1981**

There was just one last piece of the puzzle. All that was missing was my goal, the object of my affection and my action. Everything to finish my work.

Jodie.

Surely, she was already on her way. I'd traveled all the way across the country to impress her; she would feel obligated to return the favor. Having hoped to attend Yale myself, I knew that her Connecticut school spot wasn't *that* long of a commute to my new involuntary home at Fort Meade. Surely, she could take a brief break to come south to see me.

And what a moment that would be! How majestic!

I knew she would pull up in a limo, surrounded by bodyguards and a huge entourage! This would be a special moment for her, and nothing would ruin it! She would rush right up to the gates of the base, inform the guards that she was going in there to see me whether they liked it or not, and barge right through! Who would dare say no to one of America's most recognized and certainly lovely faces?

And when she got in? It would be greater than any romance that even Hollywood could conceive of! She would rush to me, declare herself in undying awe of a man who took such steps to impress a simple gal with big dreams, and hand me her heart on a platter, far fancier than I'd handed to ungrateful guests during my busboy days at that club in Denver.

Of course, everyone would fall right under her goddess-level spell, although not to the extent that I had. She would tell everyone who needed to know that I was her man, that someone who would go to these lengths for her had no business being cooped up in a place like this, and personally ride my arm right outside.

And, per Hollywood style, we would live happily ever after. Even those who were pissed at what I'd done would end up okay with it, and with me. So much better than Sport, or even Travis Bickle, was to her Iris, I would treat her right for the rest of our years and decades together.

Every day, I waited for her to arrive. I kept glancing out the windows, knowing that she was seconds away from pulling up. I knew that some drill sergeant, probably one who had been screaming in my face just minutes before, would meekly make his way up to my cell, informing me that this world-famous actress was on the phone, demanding to hear my voice again. A long love letter with her signature on it would be showing up in my box any time now.

Such bullshit. Such stupid bullshit.

That would become much clearer later on, but here was where it first started to sink in. Actually, I don't think I was so much upset because my plan to impress her hadn't worked, or at least it wasn't just that. I was also angry. I'd shoved myself into the darkest national spotlight, and people around the world were proclaiming me the most hated man in America. Maybe even on earth. I'd given up so much for her, thrown my own name 10 feet deep in the mud, and she couldn't be bothered to even respond, other than giving a PBS interview and distancing herself as far from me as possible, telling them that she'd never seen the letters I'd sent, or even heard of them until the FBI contacted her (which was only mostly true, as I would find out later). Depression and anger were teaming up to kick my psychosis into seriously high gear.

As the days ticked by that November, I sank further down. Every day, I could feel my dream not coming true, slipping more and more away from me. I was getting more and more quiet around others. Even when my parents came to visit, I hardly spoke. They thought I was upset because I was worried about going to jail for the rest of my life. I was hardly thinking about that.

I spent my days sitting in my room. I would stare at TV screens with no clue of what I was seeing, and look at books without giving a damn about the words. I would open a book, and then realize that two hours had zoomed by without me so much as turning a page.

Well, I was going to break Jodie's heart, just as she was shattering mine. I was going to end my legacy then and there. I would be forever remembered, and probably despised, for trying to murder the president. But it would be the last thing I would do. Maybe this would rub a little of the dirt off my name. Maybe I could go out with a little bit of sympathy.

And she would feel so awful. She would have to live with herself, knowing that her most devoted man had done so much, and she'd been too insensitive to care. She could have stopped it. She could have saved me. One phone call, one letter to me, even, yes, stopping by, and I would still be alive.

How could she hurt me so? It was a question I was sure she would be asking as she couldn't fall asleep every single night. The love I'd felt for her had switched into anger. Now for redemption.

I'd thought about harming her before, but I'd still managed to put a romantic spin on it. Romeo and Juliet took their own lives in what literature today considers the ultimate ending to the ultimate love story. That's what I'd felt when I searched Yale's campus for her for a brief period in the past. Now I was mad at her. Now I had moments where I wanted to harm her. Where I felt she'd betrayed me. I'd gone so far and done so much for her, for us, and now she was throwing me aside and going on about her life. Mine was, for all intents and purposes, finished, and she didn't care. My psychosis threw me back and forth between depression at having failed again, anger at her, and, still once in a while, naiveté that she would still come for me. But just as it had for me in the past, the depression won out.

Right around my first Thanksgiving locked away, I started planning my exit. Not my escape; even my fried mind knew that that would be a disaster. I was the closest-watched inmate in America, so there was hardly any chance I would sneak anywhere near the outside—and if I did, that would be even more dangerous.

There wasn't a more hated man in America than John Hinckley Jr. at that point, and people, even very well-known people, had been calling for my head since I'd shot the president. People would have lined up to get the honor of putting their own bullets through my head, and many would consider it the most justifiable of homicides.

I didn't want that. I didn't want to go back out in public. I was still thinking about what it would be like to kill a president, but I knew that neither I, nor anyone else in the general population, would get anywhere close to one for a long time. If the president had been highly guarded before, he had more security than anyone on the planet now.

And that wouldn't make the lasting mark that I so longed for. I wanted to go out in a blaze of my ego-created glory that would burn through Jodie's psyche and the American public forever. My departure would be the last one a person takes, and I was going to be the one to control mine.

I was under pretty heavy lock and key, but not *that* closely watched. The marshals were checking in on me every few minutes. Suicide watch wasn't as stringent as it is today. I had access to a couple of materials that didn't look dangerous, but a man who very much wants to go out can always find a way.

I'd worked it out pretty well. I'd heard one conversation after another about the guards battling it out over their favorite gridiron squads. Many of them spent as much of their Saturdays and Sundays in front of the TV cheering and booing football as watching us. As the second round of NFL games kicked off that day, I knew I'd seen my last afternoon.

A guard glanced in on me, and I did my best to ignore him. I didn't give him any grief, but I didn't make much eye contact or look sick either, which might have made him suspicious. I knew what I had planned, but I didn't want to give him any reason to double-take. The less attention I drew, the better.

As he walked away, I went into action. I'd torn apart a small box and jammed the cardboard into the lock. If someone tried to open it with a key, I knew it would stick or even break the key off. Just what I wanted.

Yanking off my T-shirt, I tied the top of it around my bunk and the other half around my neck. I didn't even hesitate. It was time. I stood next to the bed and then slumped over.

My timing was great. As I fell down, the knot held perfectly. I didn't even struggle. As my air and vision started to slip away, I hardly minded or even felt it much.

Hanging there, I was actually pretty calm. I was sad, but I was ready. This was tough, but it was the right thing. I knew I'd made the toughest decision a person can choose with his life, but I was okay with it. I wouldn't have to face all the hatred from the world. I wouldn't have to go through a trial. I wouldn't have to go to jail for the rest of my life, a new part of hell. I would get the last word in my quest for Jodie.

This was as courageous an escape as a man in my situation could make. A few more moments, and I would be on my way out, hoping that my next destination, my next life, would be a little happier.

I don't know why or how or what, but something must have occurred to that guard. He turned around and came right back.

Seeing me, he shoved his key into the lock. But my plan worked; it didn't turn. Others pulled on the key, then on the door, trying to get it open. But I'd outsmarted them.

Just as I was ready to start counting down my last breaths, just as I'd taken a mental picture of the last sight I would ever see, a loud noise startled me. Someone had smashed his way through the cell door window.

Now I was hoping that the process would hurry up. I was almost glancing around, looking for death to hurry up and take me away from this. Just as I lost consciousness, a guard reached in and opened the door from the outside. Another came in, then another. One hoisted me up, the other tore down the T-shirt.

They carried me to the dispensary. A few more seconds, and I would have been gone. If that glass had held for one more blow, it would have been too late for me. My neck and throat hurt, but not to the point that they were badly damaged. I could still breathe.

They strapped me down and shoved IVs into my arms and tubes into my mouth and nose. I couldn't see or feel, but everything from my neck up was purple and blotchy, and my eyes looked like red paint had been dumped straight into them.

As I lay there in intensive care, doctors were concerned about brain damage. I'd hung from that bunk for a few minutes, more than long enough to cause enough oxygen deprivation to scar my cerebellum permanently. The strain on my body could cause my kidneys to fail.

The next afternoon, I woke up with no clue where I was or why I was there. I guess I hoped it had all been a bad dream, a nightmare that had gone on too long. I could have been back in a DC hotel. I might have been back at my parents' house. Maybe I was in a regular hospital, and the doctors had given me the wrong medication, putting me in a coma for years. Perhaps my attempted murder had all been a pitch-black trick of the mind, and everything would be okay now.

The pain in my eyes and kidneys, both of which would stick around for some time, informed me otherwise. I'd also caught a horrible cold, which laid me up even further. My brain ended up being fine, although considering how warped my mind was, it seems weird to even say that.

When I finally left the hospital, I was taken to a different cell—and there was nothing in that room with me. My guitar was gone. The chair was gone. No paper, pens, or pencils to write with. No bed sheets, no shoelaces, sure as hell no T-shirts. Not even a bed or pillow. I was sleeping on a mattress with paper sheets on the floor in my underwear until the trial began.

I'm sure some of these guards had hated what I did, and me as a person for doing it, but their duties overrode their personal feelings. In hindsight, that took a ton of guts.

I would have to face justice and the law, but not for a while. My trial, which had been scheduled to start at the end of that month, was knocked somewhere into 1982. Ironically, Vince Fuller used the event to try to get me transferred to Washington's St. Elizabeth's Hospital. The prosecution, claiming to fear for my safety, said St. Elizabeth's wasn't secure enough, and they wanted me sent back down to Butner. Months before my acquittal would confine me to St. Elizabeth's, it almost became my home early. I thought my lawyers might use it to re-argue my mental state, which could have gotten me institutionalized before the trial even began and put it off indefinitely.

I'm sure, in a dark way they would never admit, my lawyers were glad I'd done this. No defense attorney is anxious to go to trial, and they'd already gotten one extension the previous summer. Now they had even more time to prep.

They didn't waste it, either. Maybe a week after I was back in the cells, I was already meeting with them and the psychiatrists again.

Not to mention that I'd just provided them with one hell of a new insanity aspect. How the hell could a man willing not only to kill others, but himself, for the love of a celebrity be thinking the slightest bit clearly? They would sure as hell be asking the jury that exact question, probably several times every day of the trial.

How many people who have attempted suicide have talked about how ashamed they were, how it was a permanent solution to a problem that wouldn't last? How it gave them a new outlook, a new lease, a new appreciation for life itself, the courage to move forward and face their problems head on?

I never felt that way. I wasn't necessarily upset that I'd been saved, but I wasn't thrilled about it, either. I certainly didn't find any new sense of inspiration. I'd already known that, if I had the chance, I would try to kill the president again. I'd also long since known that I could take my own life.

And I would try to do so again. But then I got the greatest news of my life, although I don't recall exactly when I heard it.

Jodie was coming. Not to Fort Meade, but to DC. She was actually going to testify. I knew she was there to help me out. My dreams and fantasies would all come true. Finally, I would get to look into her eyes, hopefully take her hand, know that it had all been worth it. After spending much of 1981 as the human persona of infamy, now I would be all about love and admiration. My savior, my heroine, would be arriving soon.

29. MORE DELAYS

"Hinckley didn't intend to fail. He intended to kill the president.
He failed narrowly—because of fast thinking on the part of
the Secret Service, because my father was strong, fit, a fighter,
and because God didn't intend for him to die that day."

Patti Davis Reagan, April 2000

Still, Vince Fuller and Greg Craig had some work to do. I figured
they were biding time until Jodie got there, tiding me over on the
way to that great moment. They'd informed me that she wouldn't
be there the next day, or even the next week or month, but she was
coming. I figured that all the preparation work he was doing was
just for appearance, that once she showed up, it would all be over.
That no trial would actually occur.

First, Vince filed suit to keep my private writings out of the
game. After my suicide attempt back at Butner, guards there had
done everything but tear my cell apart. Of course, they'd found
the writing I'd done. Along with my fiction piece about the
conspirators, they'd dug up my diary (I affectionately titled it *A
Diary of a Person We All Know*) and some other scribblings.

Guards admitted to looking at these particular works but
claimed they'd never gone into anything clearly marked as being
between my lawyers and me. They said, probably truthfully, that
they were worried not just about any assistance I'd had in the
murder attempt, but that I might try to take my own life again, and
they wanted to be ready to help me if I did. Now the prosecution
was trying to get these scribblings in front of the judge and jury.

Later that month, in the same court in which I'd pled, also in front of Judge Parker, I claimed that during my original interrogation, I'd repeatedly asked for a lawyer. A half-hour conversation full of info that could help bury me could disappear if Vince gave a strong enough argument.

Detectives testified that this was the case, but they'd only talked to me about my background, not about the shooting itself. My discussion of Jodie was a major subject here.

I hoped so. I certainly didn't mind word getting out about that. Maybe it would give her a bit of incentive to arrive early.

In any case, Judge Parker listened and agreed, ruling that these pieces couldn't come into court, and an appeals court upheld him. After my hanging attempt had knocked my trial into 1982, this debate delayed it even further.

Again, I'm pretty sure that these judges were just keeping themselves covered. Judges have to act impartial, but I'm certain than many of them, probably Parker included, both very much wanted me convicted and punished and were fairly convinced I would be. They were giving my team and me some serious breaks so my guilty verdict would be safe from appeals.

In the meantime, I would find myself a different sort of defendant. In February of 1982, Thomas Delahanty, who'd saved the president's life by taking one of my bullets, sued me for $12 million. Suffering from serious pain, as well as damage to his hearing, he'd been forced to retire later that year, and now he and his family were blaming me for both the damage done to his career and his marriage.

The very next month, James Brady, shot in the head and suffering injuries that he would never come close to recovering from, dropped a $46 million suit on me. Tim McCarthy, another of my victims, would sue me soon as well. Ironically, everyone but President Reagan himself tried to take me to court. Apparently, these men, as much of the country did, believed the hyperbole the media was spewing about my family being richer than the Rockefellers or the Gettys or whoever else.

Those cases dragged on for nearly two decades, until we finally settled out of court, well before I was free. I don't even remember the specifics of how, and I'm pretty sure I couldn't legally discuss them if I did.

By this point, everyone was getting irritated at how slowly my case was dragging. What many people thought would be an open-and-shut case, which I could have caused by pleading guilty, had gone on for literally a year. Even for the most visible crime in American history, one that had almost caused the violent loss of a president, that's a long time.

Put it like this: Charles Guiteau (killed President James Garfield in September 1881), Leon Czolgosz (killed President William McKinley in September 1901), Guiseppe Zangara (killed Chicago mayor Anton Cermak in February 1933, during his attempted assassination of President-elect Franklin D. Roosevelt), Arthur Bremer (tried to kill Governor George Wallace in May 1972), and Lynette Fromme (tried to kill President Gerald Ford in September 1975) *combined* didn't have to wait that long to stand trial—and those are just the ones who made it that far. We'll never know how long it would have taken to put John Wilkes Booth and Lee Harvey Oswald on trial, or if they would have pleaded out.

"John is truly ill," vented my father, John Sr., in March 1982, "and we're anxious to get that across in court." My brother said the same thing.

But then there came the perfect reason to delay the trial, one I would have waited another year for, at least. My dream would finally come true. For the first time in as long as I could remember, I would have something, someone, to look forward to and celebrate.

30. GETTING CLOSER TO JODIE

"This Thing Called Love"

Jodie squirms and pretends not to care.

I swear the end is very near.

Right here is a good place to start.

Your heart shall forget how to beat.

How sweet is this thing called love!

As I sat and waited for a moment I'd been dreaming of for so long, I knew it was almost over. This hearing, this conversation between a witness and a lawyer, would set everything right for everyone. Her words would set me free. A brief discussion, and I would be on my way home, with her on my arm very soon.

Jodie had been warming up for this. A few months before, in March, she'd appeared on the cover and pages of *High Society*, a *Playboy* wannabe magazine. Often wearing little more than a smile, her gorgeous eyes had teased away any memories of Iris's sad, unassertive youth. Now she was a sexy woman who wanted everyone to know that she'd grown all the way up. A marshal had bought the magazine and shown it to me. He wasn't allowed to hand it to me, instead giving it to one of my lawyers, who emphatically stated that I couldn't see it.

Yes, millions had seen the display. But I knew it was all for me. I knew I'd been the reason she'd done it. It was a secret message between us; this would be waiting for me when I got out, and she would help ensure that happened very soon.

It had been exactly a year since I'd shown my devotion to Jodie Foster by shooting the president and three others. I couldn't believe that was a coincidence. For me, it was the perfect irony; I hadn't enjoyed my time locked away, but it would be worth it soon. There was about to be a wonderful payoff for my difficulties, a thanks for my efforts.

Not long before, Vince had given me the greatest news of my life. Jodie would be showing up for questioning. Somehow or other, she'd been convinced to give her own deposition in the case. By now, my obsession with her had become public knowledge and media fodder, so of course she would have to show up. She'd spoken briefly to the press, but the tapes of our conversations had long since become public, and I'd certainly not been shy about my feelings for her and our communication, regardless if they'd been real or just a creation of my psychotic mind.

She'd claimed to be testifying, and allowing it to be videotaped, for her not being available for my trial. Along with *O'Hara's Wife*, she was working on the TV film *Svengali*, where she would portray aspiring singer Zoe, under the tutelage of Peter O'Toole's title character.

But that trial wouldn't happen. It was all a front to get near me. I could envision Vince or someone else asking her something, and then her raising her hand to silence him, roaming her stunning face all over the court, and proclaiming, "This man, John Hinckley, is of the soundest mind. What he did was an act of romance that even my next Hollywood adventure couldn't capture. He is love. He is sexy. He is everything that any woman could ever want and more, and even being a major movie star can't compare to the wonders of winning his heart. I am so lucky, and I want everyone to know it!"

Of course I'd been wrong up to and during my suicide attempt at Fort Meade. The waiting had just made my heart grow fonder. I was so ashamed that I'd believed for a second that she wouldn't be there for me.

"What Attracts Me"

Your face is what attracts me, sweet and
cute and capable of melting hearts.

Your [breasts] are what attracts me, ample
and pure and waiting to be caressed.

Your body is what attracts me, shapely
and firm and sexy as all get out.

I'd avoided court, and public life in general, since the shooting, but every Marine in the country couldn't have kept me out of the courtroom that day. I was hoping, though, that Jodie didn't have the strongest sense of smell—otherwise, she might detect that I'd vomited in the car on the way there that morning.

Few other people would be present, only those with a legal right and reason. As in me, the lawyers, the judge, security, and, of course, Jodie herself. No press. Not even my parents could get inside on this one.

Jodie walked in, and my eyes went to her like a magnet. This was the woman of my fantasies. I'd admired her from afar for years as Iris and in other films, and now she was there, in living, breathing, beautiful color.

She didn't look at me. That was fine. Maybe she didn't want to be distracted. Perhaps mere eye contact would have made her lose all composure and rush me.

She sat down, a hesitant smile on her lovely face. Her eyes slowly brushed the courtroom.

There! There it was! She gave me that same look so many had seen on the *High Society* cover! That alluring expression that screamed, "I would love for you to take my innocence!"

I knew it!

I still couldn't believe this. I almost jammed a nearby pen into my arm to ensure I wasn't dreaming. This was so far from our milliseconds-long encounter on the Yale campus, which seemed like years ago from another world. I was sure it was on her mind. I knew she regretted not making a stronger impression on me and was anxious to make up for it.

With a smile that made my mouth almost triple in size, I couldn't stop shaking. Shock that my fantasy had just become real. Nervousness. Anticipation and hope that she would return my love. As she was sworn in and started answering questions, I stayed just like that.

Any second now, she would drop the formal professionalism and become the lovestruck beauty who'd finally found the man of all her dreams.

Vince and the other lawyers talked to her about our phone calls that had been taped and the letters I'd left under her door. Honestly, I was hardly listening. I was waiting for the signal that she was there for me. I wanted to stand up and declare it myself. I almost nudged my lawyer to have him do so.

Finally, he seemed to be getting there.

"How would you describe your relationship with John Hinckley?" Vince asked.

There it was. Now she would look right at me and give me that amazing smile. It was time to leave this legal stuff behind and go off together.

"It's wonderful!" she proclaimed, her emotions suddenly rushing to the surface. "He's so amazing. From the moment I knew that he'd done what he'd done, all for me, I knew I would do anything to spend the rest of my life with him… and I hope it lasts another hundred years!"

That's what I heard her say. The problem was, she didn't. It took me a moment to realize that she didn't.

"I don't have a relationship with John Hinckley," she flatly stated.

What?! She couldn't have said that. I didn't want to believe it. I'd never believed I was insane, but for the first time, I hoped I was. I couldn't comprehend that what had just happened was real. After all I'd done for her. I couldn't fathom that this had just occurred.

I knew she was kidding. Putting on a persona. That's what actors do, right?

But she didn't speak again. Neither did Vince. Neither did anyone. At least, that's what my psychotic self remembers.

Everything I'd tried and failed, everything that hadn't worked for me, everything, everything, everything else, was nothing compared to this. It paled to the most colorless shade. I went dead cold. My smile vanished. I felt my heart shatter and then drop to the ground, like it wasn't even a part of me anymore.

She'd failed me. Stabbed me right in the back. Broken my heart and ripped it out. Destroyed a life that I'd been envisioning with her for years.

The lawyers said they were done. She got up to leave. Didn't say anything to me. Didn't even look at me.

How dare she.

The psychosis that had driven me to try to kill the president was gone. When I'd shot him and others, I hadn't felt much at all. Certainly not like this.

Now I was insane, for a different reason in a different way. Now I had absolutely no concept of reality at all. I hadn't been all that angry when I'd almost killed the president of the United States. This fury almost caused me to burst into flames.

Terrifyingly, I can say that, had a marshal been standing near me, I might have gone for his weapon. A taser, a club, even, God forbid, a gun, if any had been in arm's range, I would have grabbed something and used it on her. As she walked by, the only object I could see was a pen.

I fired it at her. I don't know if it hit her. I wasn't looking.

Because I was out of my seat. I was going to go at her and make her pay dearly. My hands were all I would need to get my revenge.

Fortunately, the marshals were ready. I'm sure they'd discussed what to do if something like this occurred. A few grabbed me. One stepped in front of her.

"I'll get you, Jodie!" I roared. "*I swear to God I'll kill you!*"

I was rushed from the courtroom and right back to Fort Meade. Apparently, a nurse had to come to help calm Jodie's nerves enough for her to be on her way.

What had I done? What effect would it have? Honestly, if I'd been Vince, I would have kicked my ass to the curb, walked out of the room, found another client, and forgotten me forever.

"John," Vince had sadly remarked to my parents, "is a lot sicker than any of us realized."

If I'd had a gun right there, I would have splattered my brains all over the wall.

The last words in my entire life that I'd ever thought I would use, and they'd come rushing from my mouth like some kind of vitriolic freight train. The last actions I believed I would ever take. The surrealism of it all.

I did the only thing I could when my mind was on overload. I called my lawyer and all but begged him to bring me those magazine photos. If Jodie the person would betray me like that, at least the image of her beauty would always be there. He hung up.

Of course, the TV networks jumped all over the tape, desperately wanting to spread it over the airwaves before the trial even began. Just about every major network filed suit to blast that footage all over the place.

But Parker had some extra reason for denying it. First off, Jodie was a witness, and that was it. If my actions hadn't put her in enough danger already, things were getting worse months later. Not long before, Jodie had gotten a note promising her, "Your death is also required. You too will suffer the same fate as Reagan." Like I've stated before, for every person willing to be so blunt about it, there were probably many more talking and thinking about such an act. Fortunately, he denied the request.

"Amen"

Jodie, please watch over me and protect me.

Have me do your will in this life of mine.

I repent for my sins and ask your forgiveness.

And I humbly ask all of this in your mother's name.

Amen.

**All poems in this chapter were found in my
DC hotel room after the shooting**

31. TRIAL BEGINS

"Legal observers agree that there is virtually
no chance for an acquittal."

TV commentator, first day of jury selection

Even after that, it appeared the trial would never begin. After being ruled against in the decision to exclude my anti-assassination statement and the writings from my cell, the prosecution considered taking the matter all the way to the Supreme Court. But, probably feeling that they had enough and wanting to get to the start of arguably the most important criminal trial in American history, they decided against it.

When my lawyers asked that the video of me shooting Reagan be removed from the trial, arguing that it wasn't necessary if I was admitting to committing the act, Judge Parker disagreed. By late April 1982, it was clear that things were going to get rolling soon. Nearly 13 months after I'd nearly killed four people, I was finally going to trial for it.

Floors beneath the courtroom, I waited in the U.S. District Court basement. This would be my home for months, throughout the trial. That was one reason I looked forward to the trial, getting out of this room. Here I was with no access to radio, TV, newspapers, anything at all for the non-trial parts of the day. At least being in court would give me somewhere to be, people to talk to, things to focus on.

As I looked out at the troop of officers guarding me, some of whom had police dogs with them, I couldn't help but wonder if

Reagan himself spent time under such heavy guard, at least until my actions.

And almost right away, we ran smack-dab into trouble.

With the trial taking place in Washington, DC (my lawyers didn't ask for a change of venue, which in hindsight, I think they should have), jurors would come from a mostly inner-city area, which clued us in that our selections might not be very well educated in the formal sense, if not the naturally intellectual one.

That, and they would almost certainly be mostly minority. Reagan wasn't especially popular with Black voters (less than 15% of them had chosen him over Carter in 1980), but he was still their president, and it might make them feel important to personally fight on his behalf. Here I was, a privileged White boy, who, as far as the press had portrayed, had had a rich life handed to him on a platter, been given chance after chance, and lazily flushed everything away to kill someone for the least personal of motives.

Our worst fears came true during jury selection. Judge Parker questioned the jury, doing what he could to alleviate any partiality, bias against (or for) me, anything that gave any impression that these people would begin with a wide open mind.

With all 90 of the potential panel before him, Parker asked a question that was probably intended to be a hell of a lot more routine than it came across.

"How many," he asked the potential jurors, "have not heard or read anything about this case?"

Not one hand went up. Not a single one. Not that I should have been surprised; these people hadn't been living on a deserted island or lying in a coma for the past year. But with all that time, and all the information (accurate or otherwise) that the American media had barraged the public with therein, these people had probably made up their mind, to a point, about my guilt.

As the numbers dropped, the news didn't get much better. Jurors were asked what they already knew, how they felt about mental illness, if they'd seen *Taxi Driver*, all sorts of questions. When the deciding group was finalized, it wasn't a welcome sight.

Of the 12 jurors, 11 were Black. One was a waiter, another a parking lot attendant, two were secretaries, yet another a janitor. These people were living paycheck to paycheck, and none had been to school for very long—except the sole White woman, who had a master's degree in college psychology. As these people heard about my lifestyle, my upbringing, and saw all the lawyers, doctors, and other experts my family could afford, it was doubtful they would be too sympathetic.

And then there was my admittedly short-lived support of and membership in a Neo-Nazi group. If a bunch of Black jurors heard about that, they were apt to destroy me then and there!

Looking at that jury, having them look back at me, I was pretty sure I would be found guilty from the moment they'd been selected. I'm sure my legal team and my family were feeling the same way.

Would the president testify? That had never happened before. Gerald Ford had given a videotaped deposition for Lynette Fromme's trial, just like Jodie had for mine, but no president had ever testified in an open criminal court event, though a few had testified before Congress. As opening statements began, no one was sure just yet.

Knowing he didn't have to prove that I'd actually committed the act, U.S. attorney Roger Adelman, known for his work on fighting the insanity defense, focused on my preparation methods. Calling me a "calculating assassin," he talked about the bullets I'd bought, some exploding ones designed not only to kill, but to maim in the bargain.

"He is waiting," Adelman said of me to the jury. "He is waiting to see the president. He is waiting with a gun in his pocket. The evidence will show you he is waiting to shoot the president, waiting to kill him."

He talked about all the shots I'd taken, even in so little time. He told the jury about how I'd kept pulling the trigger even after the ammunition was gone.

Now it was Vince's turn. Much of what Adelman had said was true.

"We all know what happened," he reminded the jury. "We concede."

However, it was the meaning behind it that he intended to use to fight on my behalf. He made it clear early on that Jodie Foster and *Taxi Driver* would be important aspects of my defense.

"There is no question the mentally insane can calculate and plan the bizarre," he warned the jury. "The more isolated Mr. Hinckley gets... the greater the fantasies become to fill the void. The fantasies... become the driving forces in Hinckley's life."

Then came the witnesses. Nine on the first day.

The prosecution had announced that President Reagan and James Brady wouldn't testify, and my team breathed a huge sigh of relief. Seeing the injured Brady up close, or hearing directly from the president, might fire up the jury against me so much that they would want to make me pay right then and there.

Tim McCarthy showed his emotion at being my victim. "All of a sudden, I heard a shot," he said in a wobbling voice. "I tried to place myself between the apparent danger and the president. A moment later, I was hit by a gunshot."

Fortunately, McCarthy hadn't been injured enough to even leave his bodyguard job, receiving a $10,000 award for his actions. Thomas Delahanty hadn't been so lucky, forced into retirement by my actions. After almost two decades on the job, he received the DC Police Department's highest honor of the Distinguished Secret Service award.

"I heard somebody say, 'He's coming. He's coming,'" Delahanty testified. "I heard a single shot, followed by four to five more in rapid succession."

The jury heard about my history of target practice back in Denver. They were passed photos of bullet holes and bloody clothes from the aftermath. They saw footage of me getting too close to President Carter in Ohio the October before the shooting, and they learned of my arrest after following him to Tennessee. Brady wasn't going to show up, but a surgeon slowly and painfully walked the jury through the path my bullet had torn through his skull and brain. (The prosecution attempted to show the jury some gory photos of him and the other victims, but Parker denied it.) A doctor who had operated on Reagan told the jury how much the president had suffered. They also saw the video of the shooting and heard my New Year's Eve tape about John Lennon and Jodie Foster.

As many times as I'd seen that, this felt new to me. I'd kept my head down and mouth shut while McCarthy and Delahanty had testified, but as that tape played, I couldn't help but look up a bit. For the first time, I was watching it around people who, while they knew what was happening, were the first who could actually do something about it. These jurors could be the ones who could punish me for it, and I didn't think this judge was going to show much mercy on a guilty verdict. People had analyzed it, talked about it, mainly grabbed every opportunity to use it to badmouth me, but that's all they could do—just spout off their opinions. Ironically, these 12 people, the few who were forbidden from expressing an opinion publicly, which could get them kicked off the jury, were the very ones who could actually do the disciplining.

The next day was more of the same, as seven witnesses gave fact after uncontested fact. The prosecution described the bullets I'd used, and other physical evidence that proved I'd done the act. An FBI agent described searching my DC hotel room and finding my postcard to Jodie, the one promising to make her my own First Lady someday, as well as my note about hijacking a plane.

"I dove for it," testified Secret Service agent Dennis McCarthy (not related to Tim), one of the first to take me down. "I heard at first what sounded like a pop. On first impression, I thought it was a firecracker. On the second shot, I realized it was a gun. At that point, I had a momentary feeling of panic… I remember the desperate feeling. I've got to get to it. I've got to stop him."

And just as we'd feared, but certainly anticipated, the prosecution shoved my racist rantings right in front of this nearly all minority jury.

"By the summer of 1978," an old writing of mine read, "I was an all-out anti-Semite and White racialist. I read a book from cover to cover called *Mein Kampf* by Adolph Hitler. This autobiography by the most misunderstood man in history is, after the Bible, the greatest book ever written…. The majority of my Nazi comrades are believers in God and Christ and have a high moral character." I caught the jurors glancing at me, and didn't like what their faces showed. When they saw my letter about John Lennon, which included me mocking him for not supporting gun control, along with that ridiculous line that "Heroes are meant to be killed [and] idols are meant to be shot in the back," those faces grew longer and darker by the second.

Vince didn't say much at the start, perhaps hoping the prosecution would use up enough of its emotional impact for him to battle back when the debates over insanity came around. But my trial was different than most, at least at the time. After the opening statements, the prosecution would go into all kinds of depth about the factual aspects of their case. Once that happened, things would switch over to the defense, who would present the same sort of aspects.

Then the prosecution would back over again, switching to the opinion-based elements; as in, the doctors and other professionals who would battle it out as to what was going on in my head during the shooting.

Vince, of course, tried to prevent this, as any lawyer would. Once the prosecution was finished, he immediately asked Judge Parker to acquit me then and there.

"Thoughts of such fantasy," he said after hearing and reading so many of my words, "could not be assumed as those of a normally adjusted person."

Called summary judgment, it's tried in virtually every major case by virtually every defense lawyer as soon as the prosecutors finish. And, as almost always in the legal field, the judge quickly disagreed, sending us straight into preparation mode.

By this point, it was clear that Reagan wasn't going to testify. The question that I'm sure the courthouse was wondering now was, would I?

Believe it or not, there was actually some precedence to this as well. Thirty years before Abraham Lincoln became the first president to be assassinated, a house painter named Richard Lawrence almost sent President Andrew Jackson to the punch instead. In the weeks of January 1835, Lawrence followed Jackson around. As Jackson left the funeral of Rep. Warren Davis in South Carolina, Lawrence jumped out and pointed a gun at him.

Fortunately for both of them, it misfired. So did the other one Lawrence used. Jackson didn't need any help from his bodyguards, beating the hell out of Lawrence with a cane before a crowd walloped him. That April, Lawrence got on the witness stand, showed the jury firsthand how crazy he was, and was acquitted for insanity. (The case prosecutor was Francis Scott Key, who'd written the national anthem a few decades before.) Lawrence would spend the last three decades of his life locked away.

In October 1912, tavern owner John Schrank followed President Theodore Roosevelt all over the country before getting close enough on October 14 in Milwaukee. Ironically, right outside a hotel, Schrank blasted Roosevelt in the chest. As his assassin was whisked away, Roosevelt chose to head straight to the Milwaukee Auditorium and speak for nearly an hour, where he gloated about surviving the shooting before finally getting checked for it. Doctors felt it would be more dangerous to try removing the bullet lodged in his chest muscle than to leave it in place; Roosevelt would carry it for the rest of his life. A judge deemed Schrank insane, and he lived out the rest of his days in mental hospitals.

We talked about it. My lawyers and I discussed me getting up there and taking the oath. But quickly, we all agreed that I wasn't getting on the stand. The prosecution would have a field day walking me through, probably over and over again, every single action I'd taken, every writing I'd done, everyone I'd ever met, up to that day and since.

Also, it would be a catch-22. What was I going to do, get up there and try to convince the jury that my obsession with Jodie was justification for what I'd done? If I tried to make such an irrational issue seem rational, I might look too lucid.

Dangerously, I might look *sane*. This was exactly the opposite of what my team wanted to convey. It was very important that I come across as out of my mind.

32. FAMILY TO THE RESCUE

"I seem to have a need to hurt those people that I love the most. This is true in relation to my family and to Jodie Foster. I love them so much, but I have this compulsion to destroy them. On March 30, 1981, I was asking to be loved. I was asking my family to take me back, and I was asking Jodie Foster to hold me in her heart. My assassination attempt was an act of love. I'm sorry love has to be so painful."

My letter to *The New York Times*, July 9, 1982, right in the midst of the trial

Like much of America, the jury probably saw me as a monster. All they knew about me was I was the guy who'd coldly snuck up and tried to violently kill people in public. I was John Hinckley Jr., the scumbag looking to take out the president. Nothing good. Nothing redeeming. Nothing whole. Certainly not deserving of any concern, let alone sympathy.

Vince hoped to neutralize that. He needed the court to see me as a complete person—someone with a past, with dreams, with emotions, with, well, as much reason behind the act as anyone could find.

So he started off with the one who knew me better than anyone else: Jo Ann Hinckley. My own mother.

My mother had been battling a persistent cough for days, which was probably caused more by the stress I was giving her than any bugs in the air. But almost as soon as she sat on the stand, that all went away. A mother's love can be pretty strong.

She talked about how I'd gotten off to a good start back in Texas, doing well in school and in sports. But she and Vince didn't spend much time there.

They wanted to give a full picture. Not to glorify me as a great guy who'd done everything right but this. She was there to preview the gist of my defense—the sad, lonely nature that had started to turn my mind the wrong way.

She talked about my girlfriend who had never existed, and Vince showed my Lynn-based lies to the jury. My circle of friends that had dropped nearly to zero by the time I'd entered college. My Yale education that had gone absolutely nowhere. The psychiatrist visits I hadn't stuck to.

Both she and my father had wanted to institutionalize me a few months before the shooting, she claimed, and I'd been okay with that. Then Hopper had stepped in and convinced them otherwise.

The doctor, Mom remembered, "kept saying, 'no, no, no.' That's really going to make a cripple out of him. He talked us out of it every time. Two or three times we tried to do it."

Hopper wasn't one of the doctors who had examined me after the shooting, so he wouldn't testify about my mental stability. But he did admit to trying to convince my family not to put me away.

Mom mentioned me dropping out of college for quests and destinations unknown. Me always coming to my family for money and help, far more than I should have needed. She talked about how she and my dad had decided not to help me anymore.

"John was becoming very, very depressed about school and things in general," she recalled of the spring of 1979, when my downfall was reaching full speed. "[He] looked so bad when he came home. He was very, very overweight. He was wiped out. He looked sick…. He was going downhill, downhill, downhill. [He] would sit for hours, staring out the window, doing nothing." She finished by sobbing her way through a detailed recollection of that infamous phone call from a reporter who informed her that the clown who had just shot the president was none other than her third spawn.

For two days of testimony, she sat up there and explained my life to the jury. When she burst into tears, it was all I could do not to follow her there.

Through it all, I felt very proud to be a Hinckley. I know all my family members must have been incredibly nervous. Having to talk in front of the entire world, especially about one's personal life, is excruciating for anyone. But they did. Not just my mother, but my siblings Scott and Diane, who followed her to the witness stand to state that everyone had wanted me in a facility for the time being.

They didn't have to do that. No one can be forced to testify against their will. They could have stayed home, remained silent, pled the fifth, or whatever else. But they got up there for me, a guy who'd been, although not necessarily intentionally, pushing them away for years. I felt a sense of family love I hadn't for a long time as I watched them testify. If I'd ever wanted to get on the stand myself, seeing what they went through convinced me otherwise.

My father was the last one up there. He talked about the arguments we'd had, of me leaving everything unfinished. He mentioned the issues I'd caused, not just between him and me, but between him and my mother, our siblings, everyone. My absenteeism had forced them to take my issues out on each other, and their relationships had suffered in the bargain.

He talked about our final meeting, the one just a few weeks before the shooting. How we'd met at a Denver airport, and how he'd explained to me, for what he vowed would be the last time, what a disappointment I was to my family, and to myself, and that I wouldn't be coming back around until I got my head out of the sand.

"He just left us no choice but not to take him home again," he recalled. "We had to force him to go on his own."

And then, for maybe the first time in my 26 years (at least, in my presence), he lost control, burying his teary face in a handkerchief.

"I'm sure that was the greatest mistake of my life," he admitted. "I am the cause of John's tragedy. We forced him out at a time when he just couldn't cope. I wish to God I could trade places with him right now." Behind me, my mother, herself weeping, was led from the courtroom.

That should have affected me. I should have noticed, maybe even been moved. My father, like most men of his generation, always saw emotion as weakness. He didn't think men should do things like cry. Even in private, I never heard or heard of him getting that upset. Now, here he was doing it, not just in open court, but in front of people who were going to spread his actions on front pages across the country. It should have mattered. I should have felt something.

But I didn't. I hardly moved. I was ice cold. Didn't respond at all. I'm not sure why. The world that psychosis had created for me was still a very comfortable place, so that had to do with it. I was still showing off my selfish side. This guy had done quite a bit for me, and I didn't appreciate it because I didn't have what I wanted. I was angry about that. I was looking for someone to blame, myself at the bottom of the list. So, for him to sit there and cry and talk about how responsible he felt, to me, it just came across as too little, too late.

That very day, I later learned, a group of local high-schoolers were observing the proceedings from the gallery. Apparently, a government teacher had offered some course credit if they showed up to watch. As much as I probably would have jumped at such an opportunity during my own schooling days, I wasn't happy when I learned that some teenagers were there to witness something like that.

Ironically, in a sad way, my emotions would kick all the way up a few hours later. For the first time, the jury got to hear from the object of my psychosis. Many of them had seen her play one character or another. I'm sure several had checked out *Taxi Driver*, both before and after the controversy I'd blasted around it. Now they got to hear what, up until then, only I and the lawyers had heard: a message from Jodie Foster herself.

Together, we all watched the same work that had triggered me in ways nothing else had since the shooting itself. The jury saw this lovely young scholarly lady, clad in the type of red glasses you would expect to see on someone between Yale exams, talking about the letters and phone calls she'd received. Then came the question that had sent me into a rage back at the deposition.

I don't know what I expected. I guess maybe, my psychosis screaming, I thought the video would be different. Maybe I'd been hallucinating or dreaming back at the deposition. Maybe she'd come back and re-taped the testimony without me knowing about it. Maybe anything.

I was sure that, even though she'd denied it, we still had a relationship, or certainly would very soon. Maybe that very day.

But no. Once again, she emphatically stated that she, in fact, didn't have the type of relationship I was certain we'd made together.

And again, it was too much for me. I didn't stand up and start yelling again. I didn't threaten anyone.

I stood up. I'm sure the lawyers were having flashbacks to my deposition blowup. I'm sure the bailiffs had one hand on their weapons, ready to take me down by any means necessary.

But I just waved my arms, like I could make the TV image vanish or change. Then I turned and ran for the back of the courtroom. Four marshals walked me out and took me to another room. Judge Parker held the court in recess for a few minutes, and things got started again. I stayed out until the tape was done, then returned.

Now it was time to get into the deepest part of the trial. Character witnesses would be on hold. My friends and family would be off the stand. Now the jury would get its first preview of those paid to research and sneak out the question that would determine my fate and future.

I'd been a son, a brother, though the definition of the family black sheep. I'd been an athlete, not for long. I'd been a student, not much of one. I'd been a musician, more in a future I could dream of.

But was I a psychopath? A sociopath? Completely insane? Was John Hinckley Jr. so different from others as to be judged differently by our legal system? Was I really so far from the normal society?

Who the hell was I, in that sense?

The next few witnesses would answer that question. It would become obvious why this trial quickly became known as "the battle of the shrinks."

33. SPEAKING ON MY MIND

"[I am] now known as the most infamous person in the world, [with] the feeling of superhuman stature, not good, but bad."

From my psychiatrist interviews

It was like watching my own movie, only without a screen to see, popcorn to eat, credits to roll, anything like that.

I was listening to a conversation. People had said it was me on the tape. I had trouble believing it. I couldn't believe I'd done this.

Not that I was ashamed. I still considered it a pretty courageous act. I'd known what, or who, I wanted, and gone after it. When others would have been afraid to take a step into unexplored, even dangerous territory, I'd roared straight at it. And I hadn't quite succeeded, but I'd come closer than even I'd expected or dreamed of, at least, back at the start.

For the first time, the jury was hearing my voice. Not just a word here or there, but complete sentences. Reciprocating in a full conversation.

I wasn't going to testify, and I hadn't taped my own deposition, so my phone calls with Jodie would be the jury's deepest trip into my personality, my psyche.

"I'm not dangerous, believe me," I assured Jodie over the phone in our Yale chats.

"You understand why I can't, you know, carry on these conversations with people I don't know," she responded. "You understand that it is dangerous and it's just not done, and it's not fair, and it's rude."

"You sound thrilled," I told her in our second conversation.

"I know," she answered. "I am thrilled, believe me." Over the phone, I couldn't tell if she was being sarcastic. My psychosis had long assured me that she wasn't, that she was actually overjoyed and honored to hear the voice of her biggest fan.

Would the jury be able to tell the difference between what she said and what she actually meant? That really wasn't important. What mattered was whether they could grasp my then-viewpoint that the thrills in her voice were the real thing.

That would end up applying to almost all of the next few days' testimony. Once the tapes were done, the mental doctors would battle it out.

I'd spent much of the past year being put through the mental wringer with one psychiatrist after another, and now my interviewers would tell the jury what I was about, why I did what I did, if I knew right from wrong, etc., etc., etc.

After 44 hours in over 20 interviews in eight months of deep discussions between him and me, Dr. William Carpenter started things off for my squad, explaining to the jury that I was afflicted with process schizophrenia, meaning that my illness had set in over time, slowing poisoning my mind with delusions. For the first time, the jury heard all about my aborted attempt to shoot Ted Kennedy, to go on a shooting spree near the White House, to kill Jodie, and everything else.

"There were two possible outcomes," explained Carpenter, the University of Maryland's Medical School Psychiatric Research Center director, "the assassination attempt and the termination of his freedom, or to proceed to New Haven to kill himself or Jodie Foster and himself... his primary purpose in this is to terminate his own existence." Reagan smiling and waving at me, he went on, gave me, "a sense of something highly personal."

When it came to both the legal and moral wrongfulness of the act, I couldn't comprehend either, he continued.

"In his mental state, the effect on the president and other victims was trivial," Carpenter asserted. "In his mental state, they were bit players.... His mind was filled with thoughts of homicide, suicide, death, and the end of the world."

Dr. David Bear had journeyed from teaching psychiatry at Harvard to agree that I was somewhere on the schizophrenia spectrum, my insomnia and antidepressants not helping much.

"There was no ability to plan," Bear said. "There was no ability to premeditate. Do I conclude he was logical and planning? My God, my sense of justice says absolutely not.... Option means a choice available to a man with a clear, rational mind. He was a man on a roller coaster, with jumping thoughts."

I appreciated that. It was nice to have someone who believed. But a few later, moments of his testimony sent me out of the room, literally.

Discussing my phone calls with Jodie, the doctor flatly stated that she'd told me, "The message is 'Drop dead. Go away.'"

I got up and slunk out.

I came back but left again about an hour later, when he told the jury how different I actually was from my film role model Travis Bickle. I couldn't hear that sort of insult.

It wasn't as big a spectacle as when I'd stormed out in the middle of Jodie's deposition, but now even the judge was getting pissed at me.

"He is not going to have that door as a revolving door," Parker tersely instructed my legal team. "He either stays or he doesn't stay. [He cannot] come and go according to his whims." They informed him, and me, that I wouldn't be leaving again.

Sadly, a later doctor seemed to heap on the inner trauma I was feeling, even though he was on our team.

"What he cannot countenance is the fact that he did not have a relationship with her," said Harvard graduate Dr. Thomas Goldman, who called me "pathetic" throughout his testimony. "In many ways, [Hinckley] perceives himself still as an errant child who's done something bad—not terrible, not unspeakably awful—for which he is sorry now and feels he ought to be forgiven... not as a competent, mature adult, but like a little boy with a gun."

Of course, he pulled out the old reliable when it comes to men using the insanity defense: mommy issues. Has there ever been a lengthy trial based on mental illness when someone didn't mention either Freud's Oedipus or Jung's Electra complex? Does every defendant pleading insanity have some sort of parental connection trouble?

Jodie had been a "mother figure," Goldman proclaimed, because my "infantile experiences of being mothered…[whose] primary motive force is the intensely dependent infantile wish to be loved and nourished." Hearing that twisted my stomach into a tornado. I don't recall if my mother was there that day, but if so, I'm betting it was about 10 times worse on her.

Pulling out my "Son of a Gun Collector" writing from my college years, he referred to it as a cry for help, me knowing that I couldn't turn things around on my own and shouting for someone to come help me do it before it was too late.

As I desperately tried to keep from breaking the judge's order about getting up and walking out in the midst of testimony, Goldman went on about the time I wanted to spend with Jodie.

"[Hinckley] has a strong conviction that he did indeed impress her," he said. "He was pretty sure somebody would have to die unless she showed she cared in some way… he didn't particularly care about killing anyone in particular. He wanted to be united with Ms. Foster, and [the other victims] were intermediaries." Concerned about a potential outburst on my own part, I stayed "home" the next day, watching the proceedings from a TV in my cell.

"Two self-assured psychiatrists and a psychologist," observed the Associated Press, "confidently describe [Hinckley] as a walking smorgasbord of mental diseases." The prosecution kept trying to undermine my defense by making it sound like I was trying to lie and act to get myself out of trouble, implying that I'd researched mental illness and just "happened" to start exhibiting the symptoms afterward.

Considering that I'd put Yale University in the news for all the wrong reasons over the past year, I was surprised that the school would allow one of its psychology professors to testify on my behalf. I'm not sure if the school could have legally prevented him from doing it, but Dr. Ernst Prelinger could easily have told my team to go fly a kite when we asked for his assistance.

But he didn't. He must have believed in me and my plight, if not the actions behind it.

"Here is a person who hates himself," said Prelinger, who ran a few psychological tests on me, claiming they showed not only schizophrenia, but extreme depression, "does not believe in himself, can see no future for himself, and has no motivations of his own. He is a person who has no sense of himself, but can only cling to somebody else. If he has nobody else to cling to, he becomes very desperate… dictated by a set of fantasies that had been there for a long time and were ready to spring."

Even as our presentation wound down, even as Vince and his team went to the mat on my behalf, so hard for so long, even as our witnesses handed over their time to testify for a guy who'd shot the president, I didn't feel much for them. They were much more worried than I was about, well, *whether I would ever see freedom again*!

I was just thinking about Jodie. How horrible the things that had been said about her, about us, had been. How much I'd affected her career and her life, so much for the better, and how we would be together soon. This trial thing was just something I was doing for now. It would be over soon, and I would be out, and we would have that relationship—and one of the first things I would do was assure her that I'd *never* wanted her to be a second mother! I was pretty sure I would be found guilty, but even so, I didn't think I would be away. Jodie would get me out. The judge and jury would see how moral my act had been and use that sympathy to override the law. Yeah, I was nuts enough to believe that a judge would sacrifice his own position—hell, his entire legacy—to help out a guy who'd just shot the president! Shows one more example of how crazy I was.

Vince made a few arguments about introducing some new evidence, but Judge Parker turned him down. As impressive as our witnesses had been (we hoped the jury agreed there), Vince had hoped for some more diversity in his evidence. Parker felt that the testimony had been enough.

"They've heard all of our witnesses now," a downcast Vince informed my father, "and I'm afraid the jury's not convinced."

And then it was over….

But wait!

44. SEEING *TAXI DRIVER*

The next day, Friday, I charged into the courtroom full of energy. This was going to be a great time for me, for my team, for the jury, for everyone. My legal team had fought for a treat for the jury, a thanks for the time they were putting in on everyone's behalf.

We were all going to watch *Taxi Driver*!

Vince had been trying to get the film in front of the jury for a while, claiming that it was relevant to see the flick that had, if not started my psychosis, certain kicked it a few levels higher. The defense had fought back, claiming that just discussing the film and the effects it had on me were enough for the jury to see the film's role.

Maybe they were afraid that some men on the jury might follow me into Travis's world or develop the same Iris fixation I had. I'd told my doctors that, just as Travis is barely stopped from shooting a politician in the movie, I would have been prevented from shooting one. Maybe the jury would buy that, or maybe they wouldn't.

Heck, I didn't care. It would be the next time in over a dozen that I would get to sit through one of my favorite flicks! Maybe the judge was allowing it as a present for my 27th birthday the next day.

Ridiculous. Vince had a much sadder, albeit more realistic reason for the film being shown.

"The prosecution thinks we've lost too," he told my parents. "That's the only reason they've withdrawn their objection."

Sitting in front of several TVs and speakers, I, the jury, and everyone else watched the *Taxi* tale. It must have been surreal for many of them to see a movie in this format; VCRs were just taking off, and I'm not sure how often *Taxi Driver* had been shown on TV at that point, if at all.

Sitting in the back, my parents watched my cinematic pseudo-biography for the first time. Never fans of films with too much violence and cussing, they probably wouldn't have watched *Taxi Driver* on their own, and my father found the end, when Travis kills people and tries to kill others and ends up a hero anyway, to be detestable.

Many reporters who observed the viewing noted how many people were said to look incredibly bored; others often turned their heads away from the screen, sometimes at the violent parts and some not.

Me? I wasn't watching them. I hoped they would pick up the film's context in what I'd done on their own. I was as fixated then as I'd been during the first 15 or so times I'd sat through this. My eyes stayed on the screen like they were literally glued there. My fists were clenched. It was like I was back in a theater, left to my own world to think about how Jodie and I would build a life together. I'm sure I probably was smiling throughout.

Except for a few times. I dropped my face when Betsy erupts on Travis for trying to take her to a porno film. I dropped it even farther, took off my glasses, and covered my face when Iris and her pimp engage in some mutual, though not pleasurable, dancing and caressing. I'm sure the jury, and the marshals standing behind me, expected me to get up and run out, but I didn't.

As the final credits rolled, Vince informed Judge Parker and the rest that he was done. Officially, the prosecutors would get their turn without the jury hearing from me.

And *then* it was finally over…

But wait!

While I'd celebrated my birthday in the wonderful world of jail, everyone else had been out celebrating Memorial Day, culminating in an extra day off before the prosecution got started on Tuesday. Maybe all that relaxation lulled Judge Parker into a jovial mood. As Vince and the rest of us showed up to go on the cross-examination offensive on June 1, Parker threw us another bone.

A few days ago, he'd handed us a hard defeat, ruling that the CAT scans and other procedures I'd undergone over the previous months couldn't be admitted, saying that the proof they offered wasn't specific enough. But that Tuesday, he reversed himself, saying he would allow it.

After flying down from her post up at Harvard Medical School that very day, my guardian angel arrived in the form of Dr. Marjorie LeMay. With a few short hours to prepare to testify in one of the biggest trials in American history, LeMay turned into a college professor, leading the jury through a huge diagram of my brain.

The wavy lines they saw weren't unheard of, but they were abnormal, she explained. They were folds called sulci, which rarely appear, to the size in these visuals, in people my age. I had more than most people. That, and my brain had shrunken in the previous years.

Again, not noticeably rare, as the prosecution pointed out. Roger Adelman took a certain pleasure in reminding LeMay that these symptoms happen in almost one-fifth of the population, and that brain shrinkage in and of itself isn't abnormal. But LeMay was ready.

Only 1% of people in their 20s showed them to this degree. Moreover, it came out later and, as rare as these issues were, they occurred in nearly a third of the schizophrenic population.

Okay, *now* it was done for the defense. Finally over.

Yes, for real this time. But although the burden was on the prosecution to disprove my insanity, many on both sides figured it wouldn't be too hard. Even my own experts were saying that I'd felt at least some remorse for my actions. Around me, Vince was always pretty optimistic. When I wasn't around, like when he was with my parents and, I'm sure, his teammates, that was probably a different story. It was tough to believe that a Hollywood film and some testimony about some *possible* abnormalities in my brain had made that much of a difference.

I was probably going down for good. Per usual, I would be the last to figure it out.

35. DEFENSE PRESENTATION

For John Jr. was and is a wimp, the runt of the Hinckley litter, a gutless little failure at everything he attempted, outclassed and outperformed by his brother and sister, an embarrassment and a heartbreak to his parents, a freeloader, a nerd. Yet, look at him now, smirking in the courtroom…. Everywhere he goes, he is guarded by marshals and police…. His dumb little poems reach an audience that would be the envy of a Robert Frost. His love for Jodie, the stuff of conversation, will soon be the stuff of legend. The attention of the nation is riveted.

Nationwide columnist and future presidential candidate Patrick Buchanan

I really appreciated what my opponents were saying.

I'd spent much of the past week royally ticked off and not being able to do anything about it. I felt ashamed for getting up and storming out before, and I vowed I would stay there and face the music, and the testimony, unless I got sick, which did happen a few days later.

I'd heard my own supporters whine about how pathetic I was, what a delusional loser, a mentally ill wacko with nothing going on but a deranged mind that was torturing me as much as anything else. That the Jodie I adored so much and still envisioned myself with was never coming around.

I wasn't necessarily surprised. It was part of our insanity defense. Vince had informed me of what I was about to hear. Technically, the doctors weren't saying anything I hadn't held forth in our interviews. But I still didn't much enjoy hearing those on my side make me look like an outsider far from society, a concept I myself hadn't accepted yet.

But while I would grow to dislike Dr. Park Dietz, I agreed with the first part of his testimony.

Basically, that I was normal. That there was nothing wrong with me. That I was just a fan who'd worked and tried too hard. I wasn't that far from anyone else in society.

Granted, such a statement was specifically designed to destroy my case. If the jury agreed with him as much as I did, they would be sending me to jail for the rest of my life.

Just as it had during its opening case, the prosecution began its rebuttal by buzzing through a series of witnesses. A doctor who'd examined me right after the shooting called me coherent, said that my blood pressure and pulse were fine, and that my only concerns were who was winning in the NCAA basketball tournament and what I could get for lunch. A detective claimed I'd laughed and joked my way through the first interrogation.

An agent said I was more worried about the Oscars being pre-empted and what my parents would think of me than about maybe killing a few people. A maid from a hotel I'd stayed at in Colorado told the jury about the conversations she and I'd had, mainly music-based, and how clean I kept my room.

Then things got a little technical. Dr. David Davis, a George Washington University radiologist, claimed that the X-rays that Dr. LeMay had linked to my psychosis didn't show any signs of brain disease, that the discrepancies "have no relationship to clinical situations. They have no relationship to disease," and that "most radiologists who read these scans read them as normal." (He mentioned that four of his colleagues who had seen the scans had the same opinion.)

Now came Dr. Park Elliott Dietz. On a temporary hiatus from teaching alongside Dr. David Bear at Harvard Medical School, he'd testified in over 100 trials.

He didn't waste much time. I was cool with him at first, as he discussed how normal I was. But then he started going a little deeper, and his shots got a little cheaper. I was sad. I was lazy. I was narcissistic. I was antisocial. I couldn't live up to my family's expectations and accomplishments. But nowhere near the level that my psychosis would be shattered to the extent that I didn't know murder was wrong.

Hinckley, he contended, "has his eye on becoming famous... to leave a mark on the world... not a man who is wild, but a man who chooses the opportunity that is best."

I wasn't psychotic or delusional. Rather, I was a spoiled brat full of "notions of achieving success and fame in a way that would not require a great deal of effort." Apparently, he wasn't aware that I'd been planning to bump off a president for years.

Then he crossed the line. He told the jury that not only had Jodie and I never had a relationship... but that I was aware of that myself. I was faking my feelings for a woman who had been my whole *life* for years? This guy was the one who was crazy. How the hell could anyone buy that? My mind, in all its garbled glory, couldn't even conceive of such a notion.

"He recognized throughout that the relationship was one-sided," quipped this ignoramus. "His love for her was not reciprocated."

That was his opinion. I knew he was wrong. Jodie had talked to me on the phone. She'd given me campus directions. She'd been polite enough to keep me from killing her when I slipped over the edge to go up for our murder-suicide. Yes, these thoughts were filling up my mind.

Not reciprocated? Just not yet! Any day now, she would burst through the courthouse doors and whisk me away!

Vince battled on my behalf, pointing out that I'd been in psychiatric care before, and that I'd claimed to be out of control then too. I also hadn't had a true friend since grade school. He also showed that Dietz himself had helped author a report saying that my actions "are not the antics of a completely rational man."

He displayed page after page of poetry I'd written, including the darkest of the dark. I was so proud. More and more people would see, and hopefully respect, my creative side. If they couldn't hear my music, they could read my words.

"A writer's writings are not that useful in determining the mental state of a writer," Dietz claimed. If poetry showed a true mental state, he continued, "our mental hospitals would be filled with some of the most distinguished poets in history."

He was right about that, but I'm not sure it helped his case. Maybe the jury would get the feeling of how tough mental illness is to diagnose, and how many people, many famous people, were actually mentally ill, even if no doctor was around to say so.

My writings, claimed defense attorney Vince Fuller, "reveal some of the most confused thinking one can imagine, from idolizing Jodie Foster as a godlike figure to maggots crawling in his brain."

The more I listened to Dietz testify, the less I liked him. Of course I didn't like what he was saying. I expected that. He was with the prosecution, so he wasn't going to sing my praises. He just kept coming across like he'd started with the mindset of, "This guy's going to be sane, no matter what I find!" The pains he took to get me convicted seemed to me like he hadn't approached this case with an impartial, open mind. I hoped the jury would feel the same way.

I was actually glad to see Dr. Sally Johnson again. As she walked to the witness stand, I waved and started to stand up. From the stand, she waved back. Her baby was with her, and I wished they would let me see it. I knew she wasn't on my side, but I'd enjoyed our sessions together.

Like with Dr. Dietz, she used my case as a jumping-off point to some of America's most visible trials. My case may have been Dietz's most visible to that point, but in the 1990s, he would help destroy the mental illness defenses of Jeffrey Dahmer and the Menendez brothers. Herself eventually Butner's chief psychiatrist, Johnson would later examine the Unabomber, Ted Kaczynski, then put together a report that many credit with convincing him to plead guilty to his crimes.

But as with Dietz, Johnson's testimony against me went south fast. She followed him up by claiming that any mental disorders I had were normal for general society.

"John was never so disturbed or distraught that he was ever unaware of what he was doing or why he was doing it," she asserted. "John wanted to prove to himself that he could do something of this magnitude, and it was a way to get back at all those people he felt had let him down, including his family." My fantasies about Jodie weren't my new, created reality, but merely "daydreaming." My hunger strike and "Little Miss Innocent letters" had all been for drama.

I couldn't believe this. My lawyers had reminded me a thousand times that she wasn't our ally, not going to help us, but she and I had established as friendly a relationship as two people in such a position could. We'd talked about my life, of course, but I'd asked her about hers, the status of her pregnancy, what she had planned when motherhood arrived, all sorts of things. Now here she was, tossing me under the bus like Dietz had. I guess I truly thought that she'd been so charmed with me and sympathetic to my plight that she would get up there, proclaim loudly that she was wrong, that I was insane and couldn't be convicted! But she let me down.

"I think he was ripe to idolize an actress or someone important like [Jodie] in a kind of superfan fashion," she continued. "I don't think John wanted to be seen as Travis Bickle. I think he wanted to have some attention or fame that was John Hinckley. He realized having some kind of intimate relationship with her was a very slim possibility. I don't believe he specifically wanted to win her love."

"You're wrong!" blurted through the courtroom. I glanced around. Had a juror landed on my side? Was there a surprise witness, here to battle on my behalf? Had my lawyer gotten a bit overexcited?

No. Moments later, I realized it had come from me. My brain, my mouth—neither was functioning very well at this point. I would add to my embarrassment later in the day, mouthing, "Go to hell," and "I hate you, bitch," right in front of the jury.

"Since the psychiatrists don't know what they are talking about any more than we do," trumpeted Syracuse's *Post-Standard*, "we offer the opinion that the hired witnesses for the defense are full of the baloney they see in Hinckley, and we vote for the prosecution's hires. At least a prosecution victory may result in Hinckley being kept off the streets where he might decide to take a potshot at someone else."

All the mental health issues started get very repetitive. Very overly technical. Basically, two teams were taking days to all say the exact same thing. My team's doctors were using all sorts of near-Harvard-level terminology to tell the jury that I wasn't liable for my actions. The prosecution's squad was saying that I undoubtedly was. But it was all about who the jurors would believe, and I wasn't sure they had the wherewithal, or were willing to take the time, to decide on that. Most of these people had hardly graduated high school. How could they establish enough of a criterion to decide which side to side with?

And even if they could, they still might put me away for the sins of others. In 1964, California teenager Edmund Kemper had killed his paternal grandparents, and a jury had acquitted him for insanity. Four years after Kemper's 1969 release, the SOB had killed eight innocent women, including his mother. After beating a man to death in Alaska in 1973, Charles Meach had also been acquitted for insanity. On May 3, 1982—literally the day before my trial began—he'd shot four teenagers to death.

How could they know I wouldn't follow in their footsteps?

I didn't think they could comprehend all this highfalutin stuff the doctors were talking about. I know I couldn't, not always. It was one more reason for this cloud of pessimism hovering over my team and me, getting darker every day.

Everyone expected the battle to continue, at least until the next week. Dietz had spent five days on the stand, longer than any other trial testifier. We had four witnesses; surely they would tie or better that number. We'd heard all along that they would put on as many witnesses as us. Five more, six more, 10 more? We didn't know. We just did all we could to be ready.

Then the prosecution did something that no one expected. Not me, not my team, not Judge Parker, and I'm sure not the jury.

Nothing. Nothing else.

They rested. They were done. They figured that, even with half the witnesses and far less time, they'd proven their case. That the thrust of Dietz, in all his professional glory, and Johnson, whose Butner connection might have given her some sort of special qualification, would be enough to override our efforts. That all the planning they could show I'd put into my action, my attempted stalking of Carter, and, of course, getting to see my actions up close and personal, would be enough for the jury to deem me sane—and therefore guilty.

I knew they would. They'd wanted to from the start, and now they were ready to rush back there and find some books to throw at me.

I wondered if the prosecution would even make a closing statement. They'd clearly had this one put away since the openings.

36. CLOSING ARGUMENTS

In the midst of a jammed courtroom, along with millions who would be reading his words across the globe that very night in newspaper evening editions, Roger Adelman started off one of the most (in)famous summations in the history of the law.

But not with speech. Adelman held up the very reason we were there that day. In his hand, he held the gun with which I'd almost killed the president. He was going to make for damn sure this jury knew what they were looking at, what had been done by it, and what they could do about it.

This was the weapon that had nearly killed the president and permanently damaged one of his aides, whose suffering, although we couldn't know it at the time, would last for the rest of his life.

"As John Hinckley held this," he surmised, "he must have been thinking, 'I'll never have a better opportunity.' When did he say that? As he stood there with a gun in his hand."

As I'd loaded the .22 with exploding Devastator bullets, "[Hinckley] looked at them," Adelman told the 12 jury members. "He probably looked at everyone. The word 'kill' went through his mind." All the time and effort I'd put in to chase Reagan across the country showed pretty good in favor of premeditation and, therefore, stability.

All the personality disorders I'd been diagnosed with were hardly serious enough to matter, as Adelman ascribed them to the same human flaws that affect millions of others. I was little more than a "fifth wheel," stuck behind two successful parents and siblings.

On the afternoon of March 30, 1981, Adelman raged at the jurors, Hinckley's thoughts were, "'Get the president! Get the president! Get the president!' The time has come for John Hinckley Jr. for the first time in his life, to take responsibility for what he's done! He can't avoid responsibility for shooting President Reagan, and, goodness knows, he can't avoid responsibility for shooting Jim Brady in the head." Probably figuring that his evidence had long convinced the jury, Adelman decided to put a little emotion into the hearing, to get everyone a bit aroused.

Now it was up to Vince Fuller to find a way back, to rehabilitate the image of me that had been created and implanted (by force, when Adelman was around), to convince the jury that, as horrible as my actions had been, people in my position needed some help, maybe even a little compassion, not hardcore punishment.

"I urge you in your deliberation," he urged them in his deliberation, "to free your mind of bias, anger, or passion, because of the damage inflicted upon these innocent victims. [Hinckley] is not aware of the humanity of these victims. They play a very minor role. They are merely a means to an end, to win the love and affection and to establish a relationship with Jodie Foster.... In his own mind, the defendant had two compelling reasons to do what he did, to terminate his own existence and to accomplish his ideal union with Jodie Foster, whether in this world or the next.... It is delusion to think you can assassinate the president of the United States and gain the love of a woman. Delusional thinking, pure and simple. It's pathetic."

With all the badmouthing that Adelman did to me early on, I just sat back and watched it. (I may have been sedated, but I don't recall.) But when Fuller got up and started addressing the jury, it all fell apart for me. When he started calling me "pathetic" in the same way that my doctors had, for the same reason of unrequited love, I lost it.

As in, I put my head down on the table with it buried in my arms and started bawling. Everything he was saying about how I was mentally ill, how I'd ruined my life, in so much detail, it hit as hard as anything I'd ever been through.

I couldn't control it. Couldn't stop crying. This time, I actually needed help to get *out* of the courtroom. I was okay in a few minutes, but Judge Parker decided to adjourn for the day.

The next morning, Fuller was back in character.

"He was in such a deluded state," he said of his client, "he was not aware of the humanity of those victims. They play a very minor role. Tragic as it may be, they were bit players to this defendant. They're not bit players to us, but to the defendant, in his delusional state, they were... he was a prisoner of himself for at least seven years before this tragedy... a psychotic who had a fear he was sick and was afraid to disclose it."

Following the law, Judge Parker gave the prosecution one last chance, one last word to the jury.

"John Hinckley was a hunter and stalker before March 30, 1981," Adelman said. "Hunting and stalking is what John Hinckley was about six months beforehand. I defy him, I defy anyone to look at the families of the victims and say, 'Forget about Devastator bullets.'"

He was finished. Vince was done. Now only one person was left to address the courtroom: Parker himself.

For nearly two hours, he instructed the jury about every little question to ask and answer, what to do when (or if) a verdict came about.

He warned them to, "Deliberate with fairness, impartiality, and objectivity, and not with sympathy, pity, or compassion."

Per usual in an insanity case, especially one of this magnitude, he walked the jury through just about every effect of mental illness, and how or if they should consider it, informing them that if they truly felt I couldn't follow the law, or, "lack substantial capacity to appreciate the wrongfulness of his conduct," then they needed to vote not guilty. Interestingly, he even took the time to address the verdict's potential effects, letting them know that, while a guilty verdict might put me in jail for the rest of my life, finding me not guilty by reason of insanity would send me to a local mental hospital, not let me go free.

Finally, just before 4:00 p.m. on June 18, 1982, it was over. For the defense, for the prosecution, for me, for my family, for everyone. Now it was all up to the jury.

A year and a half before, these people had seen their country thrown into chaos. A few months before, they'd been chosen, from so many prospective jurors, to straighten it out for millions of people, to decide how, or if, the guy behind it all should be punished. No more arguments. No more evidence. No more marathon sessions with one shrink after another on my part.

As the jury left the room to start their deliberations, my heart went out to them. I knew they had a tough job. But I wasn't inspired. Vince and his team had done a great job defending me from so many attacks, but I was pretty sure that even that much effort wouldn't be enough to overcome the strikes against us. After seeing doctors get on the witness stand and say these horrible things about me, why would the jury not believe them? I was just some directionless loser who couldn't be bothered to even finish college. These people were going to see me as more credible than a doctor who taught at Harvard?

I was dead in the water and had been for a long time. I was ready to go away, as much as anyone could be. I didn't feel much remorse for what I'd done, but I was starting to. Those jurors were going to step out, probably be back in about 10 minutes, declare me guilty as hell, and send the courtroom into a celebration, one that would spread through the nation's capital and maybe even farther.

37. THE VERDICT

I wasn't the only one who felt that way. Hell, there were people on my side who felt even more strongly on the matter than I did. While the jury deliberated on the following Saturday—Judge Parker allowed this rarity, based on the magnitude of the trial— my father was banging out a press release.

"Obviously, we are terribly disappointed by the guilty verdict for our troubled son, John," it read. "Our family knew from the state that we had two strikes against us because of the extraordinary media coverage of the shooting and unfavorable past precedents in insanity cases." On and on it went, but the tone never changed. That was the only document they created.

That's how sure they were that I would be found guilty. They didn't even prepare an announcement for a not guilty verdict.

Okay, neither did I. I'd already written out a speech based around asking for fair sentencing, though still including a dig that the trial had been fair, "despite the prosecution's cheap shots all the time." I'd also penned a piece called "The Conviction" that I hoped the media would enjoy.

Along with that, Judge Parker *happened* to decide to publicly release all of the jurors' names and ages. Not just the 12 serving on the jury itself, but even the six alternates. We'd been in trial for this long, and him randomly choosing to do this in the midst of deliberations, to me, was suspicious. Maybe he was trying to spread their information to the general public, to scare the jurors. To say, "You better convict this SOB, or certain people *might* take their own idea of retribution."

Still, as the days went on, we were puzzled, and not in a bad way. If the jury had been as convinced as we were convinced they would be, they would have come right back. Saturday went into Sunday—again, the judge wanted this thing done with—and then into Monday. My parents were in and out. I spent most of my time in my pseudo-solitary cell down in the basement, reading, hoping they would give me something more stimulating to occupy my time when I did go to prison.

The jury was putting in some heavy work. I'm not sure if the judge had ordered that, if it was by choice, or something else. Maybe even a bit of both. But they were at it until about 7:30 each evening, and all too anxious to come back the following morning.

Then, on Monday evening, with about an hour left in their self-made work day, a deputy came to get me. My parents' hotel phone rang.

The decision had been made. Twelve people had agreed.

Over the next hour, everyone seemed to be in robot mode. People were just getting where they needed to be. No one knew what to expect. Not me, not my lawyers, not the prosecution, not my family, not the reporters, not anyone who spent that evening jammed into that court like prisoners at an overcrowded jail. It must have been almost terrifying for the jurors, knowing that, for that brief period, they were the only 12 people who knew the world's biggest secret.

I was brought into the jammed courtroom. The last ones to enter were the jurors, looking like they hadn't slept since they'd started deliberating the case.

I was asked to rise. By the time I sat back down, decades of my future would be written.

The foreman, a Black man who looked like he spent serious time in the gym, and five years younger than me, the youngest juror, stood up, opened a huge brown envelope, removed some papers, and handed them to the clerk. Flipping through them, Judge Parker couldn't seem to take his eyes off the words. He kept flipping back and forth, like he didn't believe what he'd read, like a poker player who shuffles his card mid-hand in the hopes that they might change.

Then it finally came.

"As to Count One..." Parker intoned.

Then it began, and on and on.

I don't think I breathed for the entire reading. I just remember leaning back and closing my eyes. I've been told I was shaking, sweating, crying, covering my face, and it's probably true, but I hardly recall.

My mother was crying. I think my father was too. My lawyers were talking to each other and me, but I didn't comprehend any of it. I was shaking and crying myself, but it was like someone or something else was in control. Because on the inside, I felt nothing. I'm sure someone could have slugged me at that point, and I'm sure many wanted to, but I wouldn't have felt it.

Before he was finished, the judge's voice began to crack. It was like he was shocked and sad himself to be the messenger of bad, and very unexpected, news.

Finally, it was over. He'd repeated the exact same thing 13 times. In less than three minutes, the justice system had been handed a tsunami.

Not guilty. Not guilty by reason of insanity. On everything. Trying to assassinate the president. Assaulting three others with intent to kill. Even carrying a concealed weapon without a license. Nothing stuck for the prosecution.

Finally, someone was siding with me, even if I personally still didn't think I was off my rocker.

All around me, the courtroom was erupting. People were gasping, reacting, even crying, I'm sure. My lawyers sat back and grinned. Just about everyone in that room, including, I believe, Judge Parker, had both truly wanted me committed and honestly felt I would be, and now everyone was shocked, and almost everyone was heartbroken.

The courtroom kept erupting. Reporters ran, some staggering in shock, out the door for the pay phones in the hallway. All the while, I just stood there, although I'm sure I was swaying back and forth. I somehow managed to stay on my feet until he finished, but I couldn't take my eyes off the judge. Even when he polled the jury, I was stuck off in my own little world.

It was our shortest court outing of the trial—less than 10 minutes had passed between when I'd entered the courtroom and when I was escorted back all the way downstairs to my own personal cell. After eight weeks, millions of dollars spent (much of which came from my own family's cotters), a ton of arguments, witnesses everywhere, expensive doctors battling over my sanity, things were over in the time it'll take you to read this chapter. Yet, the world would never be the same.

Down in the basement, my parents showed up. We hugged and prayed. They told me they were working on a new press release to hand the media, celebrating my acquittal. We quickly learned that I would be sent back to Fort Meade, then to DC's St. Elizabeth's Mental Hospital.

"We've known all along from the very beginning that John was not responsible for his actions," my brother-in-law Stephen Sims informed the press, "and we're just extremely grateful that the jury also realized this… We're hopeful that he will receive some professional psychiatric care and can correct this." The prosecution, Delahanty, McCarthy, Brady, and, of course, President Reagan, didn't talk to the media.

Soon after, I went outside, got into a helicopter, and flew off. For the first time in years, I was looking forward to a future that seemed bright, that for first the first time in forever, gave me reason to hope.

"Unbelievable."

First Lady Nancy Reagan on the verdict

38. "THE CONFESSION"

"My actions of March 30, 1981 have given special meaning to my life and no amount of imprisonment or hospitalization can tarnish my historical deed. The shooting outside the Washington Hilton hotel was the greatest love offering in the history of the world. I sacrificed myself and committed the ultimate crime in hopes of winning the heart of a girl. It was an unprecedented demonstration of love. But does the American public appreciate what I've done? Does Jodie Foster appreciate what I've done?

There are many times when I wonder why the world is still revolving. Doesn't anyone understand the meaning of March 30? Jodie tries to carry on with her life as if nothing out of the ordinary has happened to her. She still keeps her distance from me and torments me with her silence. I gave my life for Jodie and she couldn't care less. I can't believe her heart. Yes, Jodie Foster knows who I am, just like the entire civilized world knows who I am. But does it matter now? I wanted Jodie's love, not eternal infamy.

Jodie has hurt me more than I've hurt her. She killed me first. For the past 15 months I've died a little each day and I'm sure the future will be no easier. But once again, I must state that I wouldn't trade places with anyone in this courtroom. It was my fate that I shot the President and it is my fate that I pay the price for my deed.

Jodie Foster may continue to outwardly ignore me for the rest of her life but I have made an impression on that young lady that will never fade from her mind. I am with Jodie spiritually every day and every night. I have made her one of the most famous actresses in the world. Everybody but everybody knows about

John and Jodie. We are a historical couple, whether Jodie likes it or not.

At one time Miss Foster was a star and I was the insignificant fan. Now everything is changed. I am Napoleon and she is Josephine. I am Romeo and she is Juliet. I am John Hinckley Jr. and she is Jodie Foster. The world can't touch us. Society can't bring us down. Jodie can't ignore history.

She will never escape me. I may be in prison and she may be making a movie in Paris or Hollywood but Jodie and I will always be together, in life and in death.

God does indeed work in mysterious ways. My life has become a melodrama. My past has been studied and analyzed not only by psychiatrists but by a large part of the general public. I am now a household name. It has to be pure and simple fate that these things have happened to me.

From the start, all I wanted was for someone to love me. I desperately wanted to be loved but I never could give appropriate love in return. I seem to have a need to hurt those people that I love the most. This is true in relation to my family and to Jodie Foster. I love them so much but I have this compulsion to destroy them.

On March 30, 1981 I was asking to be loved. I was asking my family to take me back and I was asking Jodie Foster to hold me in her heart. My assassination attempt was an act of love. I'm sorry love has to be so painful."

**By John Hinckley, intended to be read
in court after a guilty verdict**

39. HEARING FROM THE JURORS

"She said they relied on the psychiatrists' testimony. All the
testimony showed that he was insane, not in his right mind.
All of the evidence showed he was mentally disturbed."

Allen Smith, whose 61-year-old wife
Virginia was on the Hinckley jury

As it turned out, the jury had gone to my side sooner than I—or
my lawyers or family—could have guessed or hoped.

They'd started off with a few secret ballots on Friday, and no
one wanted to express much of an opinion. After being barraged
by loads of scientific testimony, these people were being asked
to sit there and decide which team of doctors (along with their
degrees, accomplishments, and whatever other background
information they heard) was more credible.

Was I sane? They had to decide. And where the hell to begin?
All that evidence to sift through, those names, theories, opinions,
all kinds of stuff. On one side, they didn't have to make many
decisions; the facts weren't in question. All they had to do was
choose which team had the right justification for my actions.

Twelve normal, unexceptional people had been yanked out
of their lives and now had to debate this? Few of them had even
gotten past high school, and now they had to say to one side or
the other, "Even with all of your backgrounds, your degrees,
your writings, your teachings, your treatments of others, your

accomplishments and success in the field, we feel that they're more believable than you!"

"If these psychiatrists they had, making a big pile of money," queried juror Maryland Copelin, "if they couldn't find whether he was sane or insane, how do you think a layman could do it? This guy isn't crazy. He's a genius. He manipulated his parents, and now he's manipulating us. He's not insane. This boy wants attention."

And not only that, but they would have to do so with the world watching, waiting, all but salivating. They couldn't know how people would react.

Saturday's rounds of debates ended about the same. Back and forth, ballots cast everywhere, no clear direction. But by Sunday, the numbers were shifting toward not guilty.

And emotions were getting higher and higher. Things almost got physical a few times.

"There was a lot of healthy arguing and shouting," said Lawrence Coffey, the very foreman who'd handed over my verdict. "It was worse in the middle part. People got mad, and then realized they had to come back and talk things out."

As Monday's debates went on, he and the rest of the group could feel, see, and probably hear the momentum switching my way. Dozens of ballots were passed around, and the numbers were slowly increasing in favor of the defense.

"[Hinckley's writings] to me, were those of a person who was confused," Coffey remarked. "His behavior seemed strange to me, dashing all over the country, here and there. From what I've seen in the evidence, he just couldn't achieve anything. I've never heard of anybody with no friends for seven years. He's not normal at all."

That evening, as much of the world and myself waited nervously to see where they would land, the jurors went out to dinner. When they came back, another secret written ballot was taken. This time, everyone went the "not" way.

"Hinckley had a mixed personality," explained juror Woodrow Johnson. "We tried to stick to the facts of the case, and not the emotions. We tried to make everybody understand that we were dealing with the documented facts."

Through the trial, I already respected him and the rest of the jury. These people had been going about their daily lives, only to get hauled into a courtroom and off to near full sequestration, their every word, and ultimately their names and addresses, becoming known to the world, almost up to the minute. These people probably felt as much like prisoners as I did.

Even if they'd convicted me, I still would have appreciated the time and effort they put in together. But I certainly respected them now a lot for just saying, "To hell with what the public said. We're finding him not guilty because the facts and evidence show it's the right thing to do."

Even before the verdict came down, the legal world was already debating my case's ramifications on the insanity defense. It was rarely tried, even less commonly successful, and my verdict was obviously the extreme exception to the rule. Even before I was acquitted, people were talking about changing, or even removing, the insanity defense from the court system.

A few days after they'd rendered me insane, five jurors were in front of the Senate Judiciary Subcommittee to try to get the insanity laws tightened. Not surprisingly, all of them claimed to have wanted me convicted but couldn't because of this reason or that.

"Put yourself in our place," Maryland Copelin told the committee. "You're shut off from family, friends, and any correspondence. We were more prisoners than the prisoners. The final turning point is when [the other jurors] said, 'Show us proof.' I said, 'I could go through every piece of paper here, and I can't show you proof.'"

She went on to discuss the "guilty but mentally ill" concept that had been introduced by Michigan in 1982 and would eventually be taken up by 20 states, although not by Washington, DC.

"If we could have explained," Copelin claimed, "Mr. Hinckley would not have been out on the street. [Other jurors]) were basing [the verdict]) on this mental disorder. If we could have gotten him on the mental disorder and, after they nursed him back to health, he could have served [jail time]."

Nathalia Brown discussed how she'd gallantly battled on behalf of the prosecution until there was just no weaponry available.

"Till the day I die," Brown remembered, "I'll believe he's guilty. But trying to fight ten other people was hard. My nerves were so bad, I just gave up. How could I stay and persuade these ten people to come across with me?"

As it turned out, the case would single-handedly change the insanity defense. In my opinion, not in a good way.

40. HARMING THE INSANITY DEFENSE

"I don't think he'll get out. It would just cause too much controversy, and they would have to change the whole law regarding the insanity plea."

Jodie Foster, 1984

They couldn't let someone else get away with this sort of thing. They weren't even going to let that person try.

Reeling from seeing me commit the crime of all time and get away with it—or as so many liked to phrase it—the legal system had to step in to save face. No one could comprehend that a defense as rarely tried and even more rarely successful as the insanity plea could render a not guilty verdict my way.

Steps needed to be taken. Changes needed to be made. The system was going to show those who believed in it that this wouldn't happen again. One way or another, certain people needed to save face, and if they couldn't do it in the sense that they'd hoped my jury would, they were going to get into the public eye and put on a show.

But how? Increase resources for the mentally ill? Strengthen testing methods to perhaps catch people like me before we went over the high side? Reexamine the methods already being used in mental hospitals and psychiatrists' office across the globe?

No! Better! They were going to… kill the insanity defense!

Yes, that would solve the problem, wouldn't it? After all, if people couldn't *plead* insanity, that obviously meant that it didn't exist, right? They would remove, or heal, insanity by simply removing it from the courts!

That seemed to be the thought process, and it didn't take long to go into action. The American Medical Association, of all groups, wanted the defense removed entirely. Iowa, Kansas, Montana, and Utah did away with it. Two years after his attempted murderer was acquitted, President Reagan signed the Insanity Defense Reform Act of 1984.

"Mental disease or defect does not otherwise constitute a defense," it proclaimed. "It is an affirmative defense to a prosecution under any federal statute that, at the time of the commission of the acts constituting the offense, the defendant as a result of a severe mental disease or defect, was unable to appreciate the nature and quality or the wrongfulness of his acts."

See that? They made for damn sure to include the adjective "severe." Basically, if you're just a little bit mentally ill, you're going down. But hey, if you happen to be drooling in a corner, eyes pointed in two different directions, smearing mud and feces on yourself as you preach the Bhagavad Gita in Pig Latin, you might just get away with counseling!

Several states went there at high speed, establishing the "guilty but mentally ill" verdict possibility. Right along with the Act, it gave jurors the ability to claim that a mentally ill person should still go to jail forever, sometimes because the person just wasn't strong enough to overcome it. Some states passed laws restricting, if not removing entirely, the use of expert witnesses in insanity trials. People like the ones who had worked so hard and faced so much fury for fighting on my side now would be unable to help others get the same due process.

Soon, the cracks in that foundation began to show. After playing drums alongside everyone from Joan Baez to John Lennon to Cher to Alice Cooper, not to mention winning a Grammy for helping Eric Clapton write "Layla," Jim Gordon's mind couldn't overcome the damning effects of years of undiagnosed schizophrenia. Taking orders from the voices in his head, Gordon stabbed his 71-year-old mother Osa Marie to death on June 3, 1983.

Ironically, if he'd done so a few years earlier, he might have gotten the same verdict I did. But the Act took away Gordon's right to plead insanity, and he would never see the light of day again, dying in prison in March 2023.

During my trial, Judge Parker had the discretion to decide whose job it was to prove my sanity, or lack thereof. This isn't the same as telling the difference between guilty and not guilty. There, the prosecution has to prove its case beyond a reasonable doubt, and the defense doesn't have to so much as blink. As we all know, and have for a long time, juries say, "Not guilty," instead of "Innocent." Innocent means that the person didn't commit the act, like with me. Not guilty means the prosecutors didn't have enough to go beyond a doubt.

But it used to be that the judge could decide to whom to hand the tough job. I got lucky when Parker placed the burden on the prosecution. They had to prove I was sane, rather than the defense showing otherwise. I'm sure that Parker did so because he felt my opponents had more than enough to show a jury I needed to go away for life. But as great a lawyer as Vince Fuller was, I'm not sure he could have beaten the prosecution at their own game if the judge had forced him to. Vince put forth one hell of an argument to get the prosecution to carry the load, and if he hadn't, I might not have been acquitted. If the jury had learned that I myself didn't believe I was insane, they would have found me guilty without leaving the courtroom.

Today, that's rarely even an option. Many states, including the District of Columbia, automatically place the burden on the defense. Some are charitable enough to go by a preponderance of the evidence, i.e., that a person is *probably* (more likely than not to be) insane. Others go so far as to demand proof of lack of sanity beyond any reasonable doubt. Many defense attorneys are fighting an uphill battle before opening statements.

All of this because a defense worked in one case in which an overwhelming majority wanted a conviction.

Personally, I thought it was overstepping and completely unfair. Whether I myself was mentally sound, enough so that I should have been found guilty, was irrelevant to this. There were, just as there always have been and still are today, people whose minds are so warped that they're not at all responsible for their actions. Even when I was at my worst, there were plenty of people who were lower than me, and plenty of them would never spend a day locked up in either a prison or a hospital.

But suppose one such person were to go too far? To see his mind go so far down that his actions got out of control? There are defendants who absolutely deserve to be found not guilty by reason of insanity. Now their ability to put up a completely valid defense was being taken away, or at least severely lessened, because of my verdict.

Ridiculous. Many people who would benefit most from psychiatric counseling, just as I eventually would, were paying the price for my actions and my jury's decision. Totally unfair to them. People attacked and in some cases ruined a legal defense simply because it had worked in a case they disagreed with. I'm fairly certain that if I'd been found guilty, none of this would have occurred.

> "[I'm in pain] a lot, and all the time. I thought an
> ice pick was being driven right in over my eye with
> a ballpeen hammer. I don't ever want to hear from
> [Hinckley]. I'm trying my best to forget that day."

James Brady, June 1994

Another movement that I inadvertently caused, however, I ended up supporting. Still do today.

Many people, with James Brady's wife Sarah right at the forefront, shouted from the rooftops about stronger gun control. Make people wait before buying guns! Create a national database!

While the Brady Handgun Violence Prevention Act, commonly known as the Brady Bill, was making its final move up through Congress in 1993, an argument that kept ringing out, usually by Brady's friends and family, was that, had it been in effect way back when, it might have stopped me. It's part of the reason why over 90% of America supported the bill. It might have saved Brady's life.

Absolutely right. This can never be discussed in anything but hypotheticals, but if the shop I walked into to grab that gun had been legally required—clearly, they were able—to say, "No, not yet," to me, who knows what might *not* have happened? If enough obstacles had been tossed in my way on my trail toward the assassination, maybe I would have given up. It's highly unlikely, as long as I had the plans in motion, but you never really know. We never will.

"Each day I live with the consequences of that easy gun sale," Brady said in August 1990. "This cooling-off period would prevent the John Hinckleys of the world from easily buying handguns over the counter."

But I absolutely agree with the Brady Bill. It has almost certainly saved lives, both the people who *didn't* get killed because their hopeful assassins were forced to chill out for the few days, and the shooters themselves, who *didn't* end up spending the rest of their lives in prison or even getting the death penalty because of the crimes the Bill prevented them from committing.

"Guns don't cause crime any more than flies cause garbage."

**Sign at Rocky's Pawn Shop, where I
bought the gun that killed Brady**

41. ARRIVING AT ST. ELIZABETH'S

"I don't think I would go stalking after [Foster]. If we were in the same room, there might be some problem. I just wanted at that point to just turn Jodie Foster's life upside down. I mean, just turn it upside down. It's just a problem I have with hurting the people I love the most. I didn't really care if I died in the shooting. I was at the peak of this madness I had been on for months and months."

Me, to *The Washington Post*, a few days after the verdict

I can't lie about it. I was enjoying this.

My chopper landed in the yard at St. Elizabeth's. As soon as I was escorted off, I heard a roar. A loud roar.

The patients were cheering me. Some of them crowded against windows, calling out to me. Others were already outside, cheering and applauding. Congratulating me, welcoming me, giving me some serious hero treatment.

As I walked through the hospital hallways, others residents stopped what they were doing to look at me. I saw groups of them crowded up against large windows of their rooms and group session classes, there to get a glimpse of me.

They knew who I was. They knew what I'd done. I don't know if they'd been informed in advance that I was coming there, but I'm sure word spread pretty fast once it got out.

I was as close to a celebrity as such a place could ever get. Not because I'd been a famous person beforehand who had done something horrible, like O.J. Simpson did over a decade later. Just because I'd committed the most prominent crimes in their lives, and now, as far as they were concerned, I'd gotten away with it. My ante was sky-high in their eyes. Of the roughly 1600 patients at St. Elizabeth's, it took me mere seconds to become the most well-known.

They admired me. I was famous. Not loved, but certainly familiar. These people couldn't believe it was me. The man. The sad myth. John Hinckley Jr. The guy who'd shot the president. It wasn't a distinction I wanted, but it certainly won me some favor at the hospital.

I would be waiting in line for something, and suddenly everyone would move out of the way to let me go up front. People argued over who got to battle me in cards or at the ping-pong table. I would go into the TV room and be asked what I wanted to see. They called me "Mr. Hinckley." When I started talking in group sessions, everybody shut up and listened—fast. I got a private room right next to the main offices. I was really excited that I would get to wear my own clothes around the grounds— until I learned that everyone had that option.

Then the mail started arriving. Every day, dozens of letters appeared with my name on them. Who knew what these letters said?

Well, all kinds of things. Honestly, most people wanted to ask the same question that had been pondered from the start: why? Why had I done what I did? I'd answered that before, but I don't think they bought it. Killing a president to impress an actress still sounded ridiculous to them, and they were sure there was more to it than that. They wanted a deeper explanation, more detail. I guess they figured that even after the media had put me and mine under a magnifying glass for over a year, there was still more to me than the public had learned.

Some, very few, even congratulated me. A few because they, for reasons much darker and more personal than anything in my mind, hated Reagan, what he represented as a politician, the government in general, or whatever else. Others didn't support my individual act, but they praised me for going to such lengths to chase my dreams.

And yes, many were threats. The hospital did a good job catching most of the people who informed me of their intentions to do worse to me than I'd done to Reagan, but I don't think they'd expected this volume of communication to crash down on St. Elizabeth's and, at first, they didn't have the manpower to handle it. They ended up having to bring in a few extra people to check over my mail, and my loads shrank significantly after that. But I still spent much of my first few years hunched over a table in my room, sharing back my thoughts and hopes with my new fans.

Yes, it was great to be the king on campus. At least for a while. I knew they would get used to me, and I would be just another guy in the hall. Some might even try to mess with me. It would certainly earn strong bragging rights to be able to say you knocked the hell out of the guy who almost killed the president. But I enjoyed it while I could.

Another aspect of my institutionalization made things even more awkward, if such a thing was possible. I think there might have been one or two other White people in the entire hospital. Everyone else was Black.

It was different than anywhere I'd ever lived, as though the streets of Colorado could ever compare to a mental hospital. But it helped me learn to let a few things go as well.

I was still holding onto the racist beliefs I'd had for a long time, though not nearly as strongly as when I'd almost made it my life's work. I would see a Black person and immediately go on the defense, if only on the inside. Just having one in my presence made me uncomfortable.

But I learned to let that go. I had to remember that several Black people, whom I'd never met or even seen before and who probably didn't have a high opinion of me, had put their minds together and sided with me in court, knowing they were pissing off the country in the process. Those same people could have heard all about what I'd done and the ridiculous racist beliefs I'd been holding, and made me pay for everything. No one would have had a problem. Many people would have praised and thanked them. But they'd done what was right instead of what was easy, and I couldn't forget that.

No reason why the people I was meeting here wouldn't be just as open and accommodating. It was time for me to leave that childish aspect of my life behind.

My first few weeks at St. Elizabeth's were pretty lax. They didn't want to thrust me right into the process, but let me adjust. I would go to more and more group sessions. I spent most of my time in my room alone. They even gave me my guitar and let me play on in, which I couldn't thank them for enough. Nothing cleared my mind faster than some sudden strumming. Others would stand at the door to my room and in the hall and listen, the most attentive audience of my music career.

But right off the bat, I ran into some controversy. Ever since the closing moments of the trial—I think it started right before closing arguments—the media was warning that this monster could be right back to his dirty work soon. Judge Parker had been the first I'd heard to openly announce this, but I'm sure he only did it because the law required him to. It was him saying to everyone else, "Hey, I gave this guy due process, just like I was supposed to."

"If Hinckley's deemed no longer a threat to society," became the collective expression, "he could be released from St. Elizabeth's in as little as *thirty days!*" I guess some people were preparing themselves if the verdict went the right way for me, and the wrong way for basically the rest of America. When Parker, and everyone else, even breached the possibility that I would be out by the end of the summer 1982, a new tidal wave of panic shot through America.

And, through my own immaturity and ego, I fed it a bit, blithering to a Denver TV station that, "When I get out, I want to be an astronaut or a psychiatrist. Possibly a Denver Bronco or a bodyguard," and bragging to *The Washington Post* that, "I'm going to walk out that door whether the public likes it or not."

There was never any chance of that. Many people made sure of that. Even my lawyers made it crystal clear that I wouldn't be out and about any time soon, just as much for my own physical safety as for what a danger I still presented to society.

After being deluged with enough mail (hate and otherwise) to sink an island, Judge Parker ruled that I was staying away for as long as it took to make good, but I could ask for release every six months, just like the other patients.

Oh, I still got fair treatment. As my first few months wound down, I had some private discussions. The doctors ran some tests. I got my "parole" hearing. A representative from the hospital informed me of the decision.

South Carolina Senator Strom Thurmond wondered, in what I felt was a cheap shot, "how Miss Jodie Foster feels right now, knowing that this man may be on the streets in just fifty days."

No way under the sun. I was going to be there for a while. And not only that—I was going to be alone. My friends at the hospital were of the Fairweather type. They would only like me until my celebrity status wore away. I had no friends to come visit. My family could only get there every once in a while. Huge swarths of the country still hated me.

Then, just before my first Christmas at St. Elizabeth's, I received my own personal coup de grace. Right in front of the entire country, Jodie handed me one last knockout punch, one that showed me what a waste the time and effort I'd made for her truly was. She insulted me, embarrassed me, tore my heart right out. Enough that I was almost forced back into the cold, hard world of reality, empty of morals, empty of happiness, devoid of real love. Enough that it convinced me to take one final trip out.

Just before that, however, someone else had shown up for me. Someone who, it took me far too long to realize, would make more of a difference, at least in the best way, in my life than anyone who ever had or since has. One quick interaction would set a new tone in my life, finally show me that things could be turned around, and should be.

Every day for most of the 1980s, I would kick myself for not realizing sooner how special Leslie DeVeau would be. Mainly because, tragically, I didn't comprehend it until it was almost too late.

42. MEETING LESLIE

It wasn't the doctors, the counselors, anyone else on staff at St. Elizabeth, who ended up making the biggest difference in my life. Who helped me turn around. Who helped me complete a long journey to stability. Who is the main reason I'm on the outside today.

Oh, they helped. Of course they did. But it wasn't their degrees, their treatments, or medical science in general that helped me step away, step up and away, from the deranged monster that had tried to take human life.

It was love. It was acceptance. It was another resident, someone there for reasons that many saw as even darker than my own.

Right off the bat, I learned that being judgmental with the staff and fellow patients was going to get me absolutely nowhere. I knew I was about to hear some sad stories and learn some horrible facts, but I also knew that if I looked down on the others for a second, I would have a very lonely time at St. Elizabeth's. The celebrity status I'd enjoyed could disappear in a second and, by the following October, it was already starting to.

I was around the rest of the people for the same amount as anyone else. People knew me, learned more about me. I didn't have the airy aura of a guy who'd committed the crime of the century. As people spent time with me in the halls, the group meetings, the card table, the lunch table, the pool table, everywhere, they learned more and more about me.

And they told me more and more about themselves. People didn't feel the need to hide or downplay the acts that had put them in St. Elizabeth's. It wasn't like prison, where everyone made themselves out to be a victim, whined at the screw job the government had pulled on them, pissed and moaned about getting cheated by those they thought they could trust.

I guess they figured that St. Elizabeth's was different from prison, at least in that there was little chance an innocent, perfectly straightforward person could wind up there. Many, like me, were there because of juror verdicts they'd fought for. Others were there voluntarily or, at least, without a big argument. There was no reason to make yourself out to be an innocent victim. Admit what you did, and know that the people next to you had probably done just as bad or worse.

Like, that I wasn't that different from them. What I'd done was extremely visual and made me so as well around the world, but that mantra wore off fast. Once people hung out with me, knew me, my newness went away, and I was just another person who was there for horrible reasons. That didn't make them disrespect me or anything, but that reverence, kid-glove treatment that I'd gotten upon arrival disappeared quickly.

And back to what I mentioned moments ago; I had no business putting myself on any kind of pedestal with these people. I'd shot four people who'd done nothing to me, and nothing wrong at all. That hardly gave me any kind of right to badmouth anyone else there. I spent time with killers, abusers, rapists, pedophiles, everyone who'd done the worst things ever, and I tried to show them as much respect as they did me. If a person gets a reputation as an egomaniac in a place like St. Elizabeth's, many will go out of their way to make their life a living hell (and I'm sure it's much worse in prison). I'm talking staff, guards, and especially other patients.

Remember, I would be there for as long as certain people wanted me there. It wasn't like I'd been sentenced to five years with an early chance for parole. Good behavior wouldn't cut my time like it might have if I were in the slammer. I would get the same chances for release, the same scheduled conferences with the people who decided who stayed and who went, but there was no way I was getting out for a good while, although many others, like my family and legal team, figured this out before I did.

Forget my self-imposed upper class. These people would have destroyed me if I'd given them reason to, and one quick way to do so was to come across like I was any better, or even different, than them.

A few months after I arrived, Halloween came along. As they always did for the patients, the staff tried to create a festive atmosphere. We would all get together, hang out, share some candy, get to spend some time together. Basically, if only for a few hours, we could forget where we were.

As I stood off to the side of the room, wondering what to do or to whom to speak, I saw a thin brunette reaching up to remove a silver mask from her face. Then she got it off, and I was struck.

First, sadly, might have been because of her skin. She and I were the only White people there, and that was still awkward. But when I got a good look at her, I wasn't sure why everyone didn't suddenly stop to gaze into her lovely eyes.

As she turned to me, I noticed that she was wearing a huge sweater that covered her entire upper body in layers. Didn't think much of it. Figured it was part of her costume, the best she could do living in a mental hospital.

She smiled. It might have been my own race. Who knew? She later informed me that she had no idea who I was when were first met, so it might have been my skin, my smile, my handsomeness, my natural aura, whatever. The concept of having any type of female relationship was still almost foreign to me, but now I'd met a lady who looked like she might care for me, not just trying to be nice. She wasn't Jodie, looked nothing like her, certainly acted nothing like Iris, but this was alluring without being too awkward.

We got to chatting. By this point, I'd heard enough sad, violent stories from my fellow patients that I wasn't going to respond visibly at someone else's mistakes, but it was obvious that many people had done so at Leslie's expense upon learning what she'd done. Just as they had, and still would, with me.

I hardly reacted when she told me how far she'd fallen, what she'd lost. Not long before, she'd been among the highest circles of DC's social life. She had rich friends, and a lot of them. Her husband had introduced her to the upper class. She'd been a social worker and a teacher.

And a mother. That was her proudest accomplishment, so it made the next part of her story as heartbreaking as anything I'd heard there, before or since.

Honestly, that was one aspect I'd never really considered. I'd gotten the typical, "When are you going to settle down, marry, have kids?" as often as anyone, particularly as both the youngest in a family and the only one without a spouse or offspring. But it always went in one ear and out the other. First had always been marrying Jodie. Whether we would have kids of our own, I figured, was a discussion we would be having soon after walking the aisle.

But Leslie had been there. And now she was in the worst way.

Her husband had been awful to her. Depression, as it had for her entire life, enveloped her and just got worse and worse. Life seemed like one round of torture after another. She couldn't handle it, couldn't face that this was the rest of her life. Not for her, and not for her daughter Erin.

Early on March 18, 1982, Leslie stole her husband's Remington shotgun. With Erin sound asleep in her bed, Leslie pressed the gun up against her daughter's back and pulled the trigger.

Now, all that was left for her was to join her daughter. Leslie sat on her own bed, aimed the gun right at her heart, and fired.

That sounded strange. If she had any kind of aim with such a huge gun, no way should she be here with me right now. No way should she be walking and talking.

Because the gun had jumped, and she'd missed. Instead of blasting out her own heart, Leslie had taken her left arm. Adjusting her sweater, she showed me the remaining stump after doctors had removed her limb.

Again, I just nodded along, as if she was describing her favorite restaurant or choice in music. This was the way people talked in there. It was commonplace for residents to get into some pitch-black games of one-upmanship. "My crime was worse than yours!" "Oh, yeah? Guess what I did to my victim!"

That didn't happen with us. She hardly flinched when I informed her of myself. I'm sure she'd heard of me but, as I later learned, she'd had more than her share of trouble to deal with when I'd jumped right into infamy. She wasn't paying much attention to society outside her life, even so close by, when that had happened.

She was one of the few people who heard my name and didn't react at all, neither with disgust nor lionization. I'd experienced both, and to have someone take the "None of the Above" option was a little strange. But I didn't give her any grief about what she'd done either, and she really appreciated that.

At the outset, and to those lucky enough to be on the outside looking in, her crimes seemed unimaginable. As many people had wanted her dead as had me. But just as had happened with me, Leslie had been acquitted (by a judge, not a jury) on insanity grounds.

Also, just I had since I'd arrived at St. Elizabeth's, Leslie had found a certain amount of acceptance, an escape from the dark judgment that everyday society had dumped on her while calling for her head.

And I was going to be next.

"I'd ask you to dance," I remarked to her, "if I danced." Instead, we spent the past two hours passing information back and forth.

"He was still operating under the delusion that it made sense, what he did," DeVeau recalled. "That he was supposed to do this to prove his love for Jodie Foster."

That very day, we even got to make out a little bit before the party ended. It was the most affectionate experience I'd had in over a decade.

Even through all of that, though, I still just had one woman on my mind. One illusion. One version of the truth that still resulted in my getting my own happy ending with Jodie. Leslie, for her part, was always very understanding, even supportive, in my quest for Jodie's love, encouraging me that I was doing right, assuring me that Jodie would see the same good in me that Leslie herself had enjoyed.

But then something happened. Jodie did something to me, even worse that when she'd insulted me while she was testifying. Now, she was embarrassing me in front of the entire country. She tore my heart out one more time.

And now, more than ever, I was sure I didn't want it started again.

43. ADJUSTING

Institutionalization in a place like St. Elizabeth's isn't nearly as oppressive as the hardcore prison I would have been locked away in had I been found guilty, but there are some parallels. You earn your privileges through obedience to the rules. You keep your head down and your mouth shut as much as possible. You show that you're there to adapt and improve.

Now, of course, for my first few years, I didn't actually think I should work on those things. I thought I was fine the way I was. Knowing Leslie was helping me more and more. But I had to earn the trust of others, just like everyone else.

I'm sure the rest of the staff had as many issues and reservations toward me as anyone else. These people were only human, and I'm sure they resented having to wait on a guy who'd become one of the most hated humans in world history.

But they were good. They were fair. They looked at me as an individual resident, not someone who'd committed a horrible crime. Or at least, not just like that. They gave me my assignments, told me the rules, and made it quite clear that I would face serious discipline if I gave them any grief. Some members were given leeway when it came to punishing those who screwed up, and I figured that I would get the worst they could give me if I messed up.

So I stayed focused. I smiled and nodded. "Yes, ma'am," and "Yes, sir," became the majority of my vocabulary. And every single day, I went out and worked like I was getting paid for it. The freedom I would earn from showing this could win me more favor than a couple of dollars.

As much effort as I showed, I kept my head down and my mouth shut. That's how you stay out of trouble, especially when everyone's watching you. I went to my therapy sessions, group and individual. Ironically, few people mentioned their actual actions—as in, what had gotten them thrown in there to begin with—but more about what was going on in their daily lives. Same with my individual chats—about 90% of my conversations in there was about Leslie.

I sat in my room and played my guitar. I never gave anybody any trouble, even when a fellow resident started issues with me or when I was pissed at a member of the staff. I was the new guy, and I'd carried in quite a rep, so I was pretty sure no one, staff or resident, was going to believe me over the older, more established folk.

Eventually, I earned a bit of freedom. Once they realized that I wasn't there to make their jobs harder, I got to play my guitar a lot, and I was even gifted some recording equipment. Strangely, the staff allowed me to play and record, but not to send out, let alone sell, my music to the outside. That would probably have been considered me profiting from my crimes, and the outside outrage, still heavy against me, would have only blown up if anyone had found out I was cashing in on my notoriety.

Along with that, I got some good work. Good in the sense that it was more suited for a guy who preferred offices to becoming a janitor or something else physically challenging. I was working in the finance department doing data entry. It took some time, but the staff started trusting me more and more. I would show up, work all day, whatever they wanted, then head out. They started treating me with more respect; not really an equal in the workplace sense, just an employee who was there to work, not just take up time and space, per often in the confined world. I became a regular part of the department, chatting with the staff, discussing our plans for the day's work, everything. It was nice for a few hours, being able to forget that this wasn't my regular spot to live. If I'd found such a job on the outside, I might have thrived in it enough to avoid crime.

And then, per usual for me, came another backstabbing—and this one almost took me out permanently.

44. ONE MORE FAREWELL

It was the epitome of irony. Dark, pitch black, good, bad, however you want to look at it, my life almost ended right before Valentine's Day 1983.

That was also the moment it started turning around. This time, for good.

Jodie had betrayed me yet again. All I'd done for her, the sacrifices I'd made, everything was a waste. I didn't want to believe it.

The St. Elizabeth's staff was surprisingly good about leaving at least some sort of communication between its residents and the outside. Everywhere I went, there was a TV on, and it was almost always on the news section. I was still being discussed there once in a while, so I stayed out of it.

We also got to read newspapers and magazines. Here's why my heart was torn nearly out. As I sat there with the December 1982 edition of *Esquire Magazine*, I couldn't believe what I was seeing or reading.

"A man can buy a poster, pin it on his locker, and imagine the most minute details about a slinky starlet," Jodie claimed in an article ironically titled "Why Me?" "He'll know her through and through. He'll possess her external reality. So *of course* Hinckley 'knew' me. That woman on the screen was digging in her bag of tricks and representing herself for everyone to assess, to get to know, to take home. The most intriguing actors are those who hold back and keep something—whatever that may be—for themselves. They are at once tangible and intangible, accessible and inaccessible, readable and mysterious, friends and strangers. And people are both attracted and extremely angered by something they can't quite 'have,' whether it be a piece of chocolate cake, a multimillion-dollar corporation, or an aloof young actress."

It wasn't exactly a secret who she was talking about here. Intended or otherwise, Jodie only made three movies from 1981 to 1986.

"I guess you'd call it playing hard to get," she continued. "I guess that's what actors do. I guess that's why other people often 'love' them and sometimes feel obsessed by them." By now, people were strolling up to her everywhere—forget that anonymity she'd longed for as a college student—and making smartass comments like, "Ain't you the girl that shot the president?" It's sad how far people will go to needlessly harm each other.

"Love should be sacred," she went on. "It should be uttered in a soft breath, on misty mornings, in secret hideaways. Love does not exist without reciprocation, hugging that person and feeling the meeting of two minds, two hearts, two souls, two bodies. Obsession is pain and a longing for something that does not exist. John Hinckley's greatest crime was the confusion of love and obsession. The trivialization of love is something I will never forgive him. His ignorance only prods me to say that he's missing a great deal. Love is blissful. Obsession is pitiful, self-indulgent. This is a lesson I've learned. I'll always be wary of people who proclaim their love for me."

So there it was. Not only did she not care for me, never had, but now she was making it sound like her whole life had been ruined, and that what I'd done would harm her forever. Forget those Oscars she would win, the movies she would make and direct; everything was gone. Maybe she would quit. Edward Richardson had shown his willingness to follow in my bloody footsteps; she couldn't know if someone else would, and if their tactics would prove more successful.

Basically, there was nothing there for us. There never had been or would be. Never. That word kept racing through my mind. Nothing that I'd thought about Jodie had ever been real. No feedback. No relationship. No love whatsoever. I was the bad guy and always had been.

I didn't want to accept that. Who would? Realizing that someone and something that had been at the head of your psyche for years had been a mirage all along… Who could possibly deal with that? Who could put it all aside in a second and move on?

I couldn't. This burden couldn't be carried, and being asked to, in my mind, was just one more betrayal. And this from a society so gleeful about punishing a man who'd acted out of love.

Now, all I could see was a time at St. Elizabeth's that would never end, the friends and family I would never have, the career I would never accomplish, so many prices I would be paying for the rest of my life. Before my 30th birthday, I'd already screwed everything up behind repair. Getting up another day, let alone for my full time there, was unthinkable. Selfishly enough, I didn't even consider how Leslie might feel about what I was about to do. I figured that, even in the best-case scenario, she might pretend to like me long enough to get a new angle, a new story, then run to the papers to blow it all up, getting her name out there by stabbing me in the back, just like I felt Jodie had done.

I wouldn't have that. If she did so, I wouldn't be around to see it. I'd been humiliated enough in front of the planet for almost two years, and I didn't want it again.

For the next few weeks after that article came out, I stockpiled my antidepressant medication. I was hoping, believing, that I could demonstrate just how dangerous too much of a good thing can be. I still smiled at everyone, didn't start trouble, was friendly to all, behaved in my sessions, but I knew all along I had a finish line. This illness was terminal, if only I knew so.

I made it through the 1982 holiday season, still collecting my meds, never letting on to anyone that anything was wrong. Over the next month, I put together a pile large enough to take me all the way out.

One evening, I sat on my bed, all the pills there in front of me. I accepted that this was right. I knew this was the last thing I would ever see or do, and I was okay with it. The alternative seemed so much worse. Every other outcome, I felt, was torture compared to this. All I had to do was toss them all back, swallow quickly, and I would be out of there for good. Let the press and Jodie and everyone else find someone else to embarrass, once they finished dancing on my grave.

Time to get started. Handful after handful went down. Then I sat back and waited to fall asleep for eternity.

And that's how they found me on the floor the next morning, covered in puke, my blood pressure at a whopping 60/0.

And that's when reality—stability would be a better world—reached out, did everything but backhand me, and scream, "Hey, idiot! Get your head out of this cloudy sky it's been stuck in for so long and live in the right, in the now! You're not even thirty years old. You've got time to make someone great happen, but you've got to step up and take the right steps, the first of which being to ditch this stupid obsession with Jodie and focus on maybe finding one of the other few *billion* women that might give a damn about you!"

One already had.

As she'd been in the midst of a church service, someone had come in and disrupted it with a special prayer request. It was about me, Leslie had been horrified to learn. I'd been hauled off to the infirmary, and no one knew if I'd taken too many pills to be saved.

She knew about my past attempts, but I'd assured her they were a part of something that would never happen again. I don't think that was a lie. I'd meant it then, but I was probably still so crazy about Jodie that I didn't think I would have to. I still knew she would show. When she didn't, especially so publicly, I went deeper than I ever had before. That might have actually been my lowest point, mind-wise.

This wasn't like the aftermath of my previous attempts. I'd made it through them, then somehow convinced myself that Jodie was still out there for me, still waiting to be found, still worth trying for. But the moment my faculties came back after this attempt, I finally realized that everyone had been right all along. Jodie, my friends and family, the staff, Leslie, and yes, even a truth I'd just been scared to admit for so long.

But once I made it out of that—fortunately, my last attempt—everything seemed a little bit clearer. The day I came back to St. Elizabeth's, Leslie was waiting there for me, herself still crazy with remorse for what she'd done to her daughter. For the next six months, the staff ground up my medication, poured it into my applesauce, and stood there lording over me while I ate it.

"It takes a long time to really realize that what happened was a delusion," she said. "As you're coming out of that, you realize that it was all awful, because there's nothing, and you're alive, but you don't want to be and you're not supposed to be." We weren't allowed to talk to each other, so we learned sign language to communicate and kept taping notes under tables and everything.

I didn't get right out of my delusion with Jodie. People don't just suddenly heal up from insanity. It's a step-by-step journey that's longer for some than others. Sometimes, you don't know where to put your shoe for that first step.

If I didn't realize it at that moment, I certainly did very, very soon. Now, for the first time, I openly admitted how sick I was, but also how much I wanted to get better. I could be a part of society. I could do some great things. I couldn't do it alone. I don't think anyone can.

But now I had someone. Someone real. Someone who wasn't there pretending to be someone else. Someone who, unlike Iris, would be the same person tomorrow, next week, next year, for the rest of time, not just pretending to be someone else until the final cut.

45. KNOWING LESLIE MORE

In the weeks and months after that incident, Leslie and I did as much to make our relationship work as anyone in such a situation ever could. I lost a lot of privileges. I was confined to my room, forced to take my medicines in bowls of applesauce. Escorted to and from therapy sessions, I didn't have much interaction with the other residents. I could still play my guitar, but no more recordings.

It was actually kind of exciting, romantic. I was confined to my room, up on the fourth floor, but Leslie eventually won the right to wander around outside. I would see her on the grounds, the walkways, run up to my window and yank it open, and start a conversation from dozens of feet up there.

And they would last for hours at a time. We would chat about our pasts, what we were up to that day and had been recently, things coming up soon, etc. Nothing abnormal about two folks having a discussion, albeit one that required shouting for a lengthy while.

"We'd shout," deVeau remembered. "He could hear me, and so probably could the rest of the world, but we weren't aware of anybody... I think what we both realized was that we couldn't stop talking. It was as if we'd both had this core of loneliness for a hundred years. I'd go out on the grounds at nine o'clock in the morning, and we would spend the whole day talking. There was this worn spot where I stood."

I could tell there was strong remorse in her voice. I'm sure it had always been there, even if people didn't want to consider that she was sorry for her deeds. But seeing her sorrow made me feel more of my own. I hadn't regretted what I'd done before, nowhere near this extent. But she was obviously taking the pain she'd caused herself, very willingly. I guess I deserved to feel some as well.

We taped notes under tables for each other to read. When we did get to meet, like for holidays, we would still kiss and hug. She started signing her notes to me, "Love, Leslie." We learned sign language to talk to each other; residents weren't always allowed to speak to each other. I would notice that she would be wearing some extra makeup, jewelry, ribbons in her hair, everything.

For my birthday in March 1983, I decided to give a gift instead. Hopefully, one she would cherish forever.

We'd reached the point where we didn't really dance at the social meetups, as rare as they were. I don't consider myself a particularly bright person, but I'd at least finished high school and spent some time in college. That's not to say I was smarter than those who hadn't, like almost all of the rest of the hospital, but the formal education I'd had gave me some background on subjects beyond what was going on then and there or even yesterday. Leslie and I could sit around and chat for hours at a time, stimulating the hell out of each other's minds in ways that neither of us could find with our roommates.

We were sitting and talking. About what, I don't even remember. But suddenly, I took a shot in the low-lit area.

"Will you marry me?" I asked, as earnest as I'd been since we'd met.

She agreed immediately. She was hardly shocked. Maybe because we knew the staff, and those above the staff, probably wouldn't let two residents marry. I'm pretty sure that was against the rules. But just to make it a little more "official," I presented her with a token of our love the following summer: a ring made of a red bread bag twist-tie, and damned if she didn't wear it.

"We joke about it now," deVeau says. "'Yes, I'll marry you. By the way, what did you say your name was?' It wasn't totally real. It was all about having something to hold onto. There was somebody that loved me in all my ugliness."

The staff probably took us, and our relationship, with a grain of salt. I think they figured we would create some sort of puppy-love type relationship, vow to be there for each other forever, and forget one another as soon as one of us was released. For whatever reason, they didn't have a problem with our relationship. They informed us in advance when we would see each other. We would send messages back and forth through the staff. Both of us had lived very detached, secluded lives—mine by choice, hers because of a marriage that had shoved her into a trophy wife situation, a piece of arm candy for her husband to show off in the social circles, then take home to be a wife and mom while he searched for glory.

And that release in question came sooner than many, including Leslie and I, expected.

46. MORE FREEDOM

1984 was a pretty eventful year, if not for me, then for the ones close to me.

My parents handed me a pretty large surprise. They weren't just closing their business. They weren't just retiring from the oil world. They were moving—and this time, even farther than their jump from Texas to Colorado a few years before.

They were coming all the way over to Virginia, where they would live out the rest of their lives. Both of them were getting seriously into golf, and Williamsburg, Virginia is full of scenic, historical courses.

Of course, they would also get to see me more. I actually felt pretty selfish about that. Like these two hadn't done enough for me. All the money they'd wasted on my college education, and then on my legal defense. All the time they'd spent worrying about me. All the time hanging out with their other kids and eventual grandkids they'd given up.

Now this. I didn't want them to do it, but I let myself believe that their golf game and retirement were the main reasons for their move.

The next thing set off something of a chain reaction in Leslie's and my relationship. She'd been fighting to get outside the hospital for about a year. Considering her crime, she had some pretty strong opposition from the government and legal system. But that October, she finally landed a once-a-week freedom, and she spent her first outing making her first visit to her daughter's grave.

As soon as she scored that, everyone was convinced that I would be following her out soon. I'd stayed out of trouble, worked hard, mostly kept my mind off Jodie, and established a new relationship. As Leslie's freedom privileges grew, she started hanging out with my parents more, keeping our relationship strong even if we couldn't make contact.

However, it wouldn't be long for that either. By the middle of 1985, Leslie was released, although she still had to stay in touch with the hospital. She managed to get an administrative job there, and we started seeing each other almost every day.

Some people, both in and out of the hospital, were upset when she was released, calling her time at St. Elizabeth's far too short. But the average stay time at the hospital was only about five years. My nearly four decades at the place were the extreme exception.

By this point, the heat from my suicide attempt had cooled. I was given some ground work—no better place for it than a Washington autumn afternoon—and a little more freedom to go along with it. Leslie would bring up my guitar and recording equipment, and we would go out on the hospital grounds and wander.

And do much more than that. St. Elizabeth's had a recreation yard of over 350 acres, over half a square mile. I spent many wonderful moments in a particular spot.

It's called The Point. You could go there and literally look over the entire city of Washington, DC. There isn't a better place in the world for a picnic, or to just sit there and relax. I spent many days and evenings there, sometimes with other residents, just hanging out. Sometimes with my family. Sometimes with Leslie.

You see, an area that wide can't really be supervised, especially in the mid-1980s, years before much in the areas of drones, internet cameras, or even electronic surveillance. It may not have been commonplace for residents to sneak off with their visitors for some serious alone time, but it was hardly unheard of.

Basically, we were free, and the higher-ups felt that two people, one nice enough to be released and the other stable enough to pick up some freedoms, could be trusted not to start trouble or run away, as though I wouldn't have been arrested in about two seconds.

We sat. We had a picnic. I played my guitar. I could tell she was wowed. We snuck off behind the bleachers of the baseball diamond.

And then it happened. For the first time since my dalliances with New York prostitutes several years before, I was able to make love. It was one of the most meaningful moments of my life. It meant more than any such experience in my life.

For those few minutes—and the repeat performances we would enjoy in the future!—it was like everything went away. All the horrible acts I'd committed, all the hate I'd faced because of it, everything I'd ever done wrong. I didn't have to think about them anymore. I didn't have anything wrong in my life. Yes, I was locked away and would be for a while, but I believed that most people would have traded places with me in those few minutes. Getting to gaze on that amazing view of our nation's capital, then engaging in the most passionate and meaningful experience, and even getting to look back over that nearby neighborhood afterward, I felt like there wasn't anything else in the world that anyone could need or want.

Yes, soon after, the sun went down, the guards came out to look for us, she had to go, and I had to head back inside. But for those few moments, I was as free as I'd ever been. And because of Leslie's devotion, I would get to enjoy it more and more in the future.

47. TALENT SHOW

So this was what it felt like. This was what it meant to have the feeling of a full audience waiting for you. Staring at you. All but demanding you get out there and entertain them.

All with the unfamiliar, if not entirely unwelcome, visitor of stage fright.

Right in the midst of it all, one of my dreams re-emerged, in the very last place I ever thought it would.

I'd recently learned of the hospital's annual talent show. Once a year, for a few minutes, residents could show their creative sides. No rules, no regulations, no formality, just a bit of expression that could only come from within.

And one thought raced straight into my mind. Now was a new chance to experience that musical thrill I'd always chased. For all I knew, it might be my last or only chance. Maybe the hospital would suddenly decide to do away with the show. Maybe my guitar would get confiscated forever. You never knew when I might run into a resident having a full psychotic break, or a staff member on some kind of one-man (or one-woman) avenging crew, smashing my instrument into a million pieces on President Reagan's behalf.

You can bet I wasn't going to miss this. I never even considered skipping it. I felt like I didn't even have a choice. Per usual, Leslie all but manhandled me onto the stage herself, encouraging me in ways few others had.

After playing in one empty room after another—from my folks' home to St. Elizabeth's—and dreaming of actually scoring a gig somewhere, now I actually had one. A real one. Almost everyone at the hospital, staff and residents, had heard at least a snippet of my guitar playing, mainly from my room. They seemed to like it. Now they were going to get more.

Day and night, every free moment I had, I rehearsed. This wasn't my personal concert, just a chance to play a few songs. Over and over, I was working on those tunes like crazy.

Then came the night of the event. Rows and rows of attendees filled up the John Howard Pavilion, a huge auditorium. Staff members, visitors, and well-behaved residents were there for the show. Now was my chance to really make my own musical mark, which the outside society never allowed.

Some inmates sang, danced, juggled, all sorts of displays you would expect at such a show. Then it came my turn.

I could hardly move. Part of me was ice cold. Part was numb. Part was feeling a near-electrocution current of fear rushing through me.

I wobbled onto the stage. Most of the audience sat silently. Others shone out mocking grins. More and more clapped and cheered me on. I never realized how important that would feel, and how helpful.

So much so that I got down to singing work.

"Yes," I answered before they could even wonder, "and how many years can some people exist before they're allowed to be free?" It was a question many of them probably asked themselves every day… even if Bob Dylan had been querying it for two decades.

"Yes," I continued in a personally dark tone of irony, "and how many deaths will it take till he knows that too many people have died?" The answer, of course, my friends, was blowing in the wind.

As I went, I saw some of them singing along. Others were moving and grooving to my words.

Now I was feeling it. I was confident. I represented a window back to American pop culture that we couldn't really enjoy as long as we were confined. Bob's lyrics had entertained others for years, but this was a new kind of freedom to preach. If not by him directly, then with his message.

And I have to tell you, I think I may have even sounded better than he did. As outstanding a lyricist as Bob Dylan is, he has never really been known for having an outstanding voice.

As I asked and answered every question Dylan queries in his song, the crowd started rocking even more. When the song came to an end, the building blasted with applause. For the first time, I felt as close to seeing my dreams come true as I ever had.

Only one thing was missing: hardly anyone had ever heard anything I'd put together myself. The pages and pages of songs I'd knocked out had only reached my own ears, and occasionally Leslie's.

It took a while to make it back, mainly for a few reasons that will be discussed shortly. But a few years later, I stepped back onto the Pavilion stages. This time, I had my own creation and mantra that I was sure would resonate through the place.

"Freedom!" I roared, emitting both the title and opening lyric of my song. "Freedom, yeah, it's such a beautiful word! Freedom! Freedom, sweetest word I ever heard." My guitar in my enthusiastic hands, I was walking everyone toward a hopeful future with words I'd personally created. On an individual level, this work meant even more to me than my Dylan performance. Because I wasn't a hopeful wannabe version of someone else. I was my own person. I was John Hinckley Jr. singing a John Hinckley Jr. song.

And the crowd appreciated it just as much. Most of them were already aware of my dreams of making it in music and, for many, this was their first taste of my original talent. They couldn't sing along, having never heard it before, but they moved along to it as best they could. They gave me a hell of an ovation once it was over. For those short, touching moments, from the first strumming of my guitar to the last clap of the applause, my dreams of music stardom had become reality.

48. HOME FOR THE HOLIDAYS

Santa Claus never delivered me such a welcome present: My hard work at the hospital. Leslie's championing of me. A feeling that, after a while, the national hatred of me was starting to lessen just a bit.

I could finally see a payoff. Right before Christmas of 1986, I learned that I would get to spend it outside! Not just out on the grounds, either; miles away. I was going home for the holidays!

Well, with some limitations. I wasn't actually going home, but to the DeMoss House, a training center for prison volunteers in Reston, about 20 miles from the hospital. It wouldn't be on Christmas, but on Dec. 28. I wouldn't even get to spend the night; I would be leaving in the morning and returning after sundown.

But who cared? This was a taste of freedom. I hadn't had anything close to it in years, and I was going to enjoy it.

There was a federal law that allowed St. Elizabeth's to release its residents for a short while without a court's permission or even notification. More on that later. But after denying me any new freedoms only the previous March, they decided to give me a one-day breather.

It may have been my best Christmas ever. Surrounded by friends and family, I got to sit down and relax, open presents, eat some food that was slightly above the hospital's in quality. The staff had decorated a small area for my family and me, and we enjoyed every single second.

Especially the time Leslie and I got alone together. Per the law, we were accompanied by a hospital staff member. But let's just say that he wasn't the most attentive. Maybe he figured that even I wouldn't be stupid enough to try to escape or harm anybody.

Maybe anything. But enough that Leslie and I were able to sneak off to a basement and exchange more than just presents.

Strangely, my parents were quite aware of that act, maybe even during it. They didn't really mind. As long as I'd found a potential soulmate who wanted to be there for me in ways few ladies every had.

As downcast as I was to have to go back to the hospital, it was a magical day, and I was on a serious high. I was already looking toward the future.

The visit had served its purpose. I'd been handed the burden of proving I could behave myself on the outside. Away from most of the rules, the sessions, everything else. All on my own, I'd done everything right—and what I'd done outside of the rules, Leslie and I had hidden! I hoped this was the first step toward more freedom. More time outside. More time with my family. More time with Leslie, with us free to spend it as we wished.

That, however, would prove to be the most wishful of thinking. As I stated before, I'd been allowed to slip in and out of the hospital without a court's permission. Once the local court system found out what had happened, everyone had a collective cerebral attack.

The government bugled about how I had no business out there, and how it would have overridden the hell out of the decision to let me out, if it could have. The Secret Service went out of its way to mention what I threat I still presented to the outside. You would have thought that they'd done everything but put a machine gun in my hands and point out President Reagan's up-to-the-second whereabouts. Fortunately, he was in California at the time. That may have been a factor in them letting me out.

At the end of the day (literally, from the day it came out I'd been in and out), the courts made it quite clear that I wasn't so much as looking out the door at St. Elizabeth's without their permission, and that wouldn't come without the most thorough of court hearings, which would be happening every single time I ever thought about asking to step out. It wouldn't be long before I learned how serious this was.

49. NOT GETTING OUT

Walking into my 1987 hearing, I felt hopeful. I'd stayed out of trouble, been a model patient. I'd gotten along well with everybody. I'd shown an ability and a desire to get along with everyone I'd met. I'd worked very hard for the St. Elizabeth's community, in the library, out on the grounds, everywhere. Prisoners don't get paid much, so I'd been working very hard for my fellow patients as much for my benefit as for theirs.

My personality, my work ethic, my clean disciplinary record... maybe I deserved a little more freedom. I'd been going outside alone, or at least unsupervised, for years. Maybe I could go a little farther and use these skills on the outside as well.

I knew I wouldn't get fully released, and I was fine with that. It wasn't time. But maybe I would get to venture out into society for a few hours, even days at a time. Maybe I'd progressed to that point.

Stepping into court, I saw the worst of omens. Sarah Brady, wife of the brave man named James whose life I'd nearly ended, was sitting right there in the courtroom. Who could find it in themselves to go easy on the guy who'd so selfishly and needlessly ruined her family while she sat right there?

For a while, though, things seemed to be going our way. Staff members testified about my work ethic. They talked about how easy I was to handle, how much of a subordinate I could be. I felt better and better. How had Washington, DC, seen as the centerpiece of America for years, changed since I'd been away. Reagan was still the president, so I wondered how much of his work had paid off. I wanted to see my folks' new home and spend time there.

I was almost sure I would be getting out. Not out, out, not in the same sense Leslie had, but just outside for a while. Maybe a full day. Maybe overnight. I knew they wouldn't just turn me loose, and they shouldn't. People as deep into the darkness as I was shouldn't be tossed out the door, but slowly eased out instead.

You know, that might heal or at least help our recidivism problem. The world changes at high speed. What is normal today will be almost unthinkable in about a month. How many changes does America, let alone the globe, go through in a period of a few years, even decades?

And yet, we expect criminals who have basically lived in a box for such a period of time to walk out the door and readjust to a time and place that's light years away from when we went in. It's a terrifying premise. Where to go? What to do? Who to ask for help? Too much to comprehend at once, and little to offer in the way of guidance.

Criminals get scared and intimidated, so they go back to the easy way out. Not the career field, which is, of course, not what it was when they first went in—and those who run it, once they see a conviction on the record, are all too eager to say, "We're not going to help you." It's a cold, angry place, and many go back just because prison life hardly changes at all.

So that's what should be done with those in prison. Not the institutionalized, like me, but those who are doing heavy time. Social passes. Daily passes, under supervision, of course. Ease these people back out, one day, one outing, one experience at a time, not all at once.

Yes, this should *not* apply to everyone. Pedophiles, rapists, serial killers, people who have no value in society should be locked up with the key to their cell melted down and disintegrated. But we need to look this over as an option, because it certainly helped me, and many others who were involuntarily committed, a chance to make my way back.

Now it was just a matter of someone, a few people, saying "Okay, he can go." But just as things started to truly brighten, my own doctor took the stand.

And she nearly dropped some atomic bombs into the hearing.

"Psychiatry is a guessing game," I'd written in a journal she'd read, "and I do my best to keep the fools guessing about me. They will never know the true John Hinckley. Only I fully understand myself." That may have been wishful thinking on my part.

First, it came out that I'd been caught with a stack of photos of Jodie. I'd written to a guy in Japan who had a book about her, then cut out all the pictures and hidden them. That didn't sound the slightest bit suspicious, did it?

But if that was a jab, the knockout punches were about to fly.

Forget the angry letter I'd written to Edward Richardson in the summer of 1982, bitching about and threatening Jodie. With all the letters I'd written to all my impromptu pen pals, I'm sure I'd expressed similar, maybe even worse thoughts about her in other letters during my time at St. Elizabeth's. That letter was mentioned, as was the correspondence I'd shared with Penny Lynn Bailey, who'd offered to take out Jodie on my behalf. They talked about the writings I'd shared with fellow St. Elizabeth's resident James Snyder, who'd beaten a murder rap with an insanity plea, then escaped and killed another woman. He may even have eaten her. But I'd only been asking for assistance with getting out of there, legitimately or otherwise.

But that wasn't nearly as horrible as what came out next. If these had been the only letters I'd written, it would have been enough to keep me inside for a long time. If this guy had been my only pen pal, near-solitary imprisonment would have been sufficient for me.

My correspondent? Ted Bundy. Yes, that Ted Bundy.

About a year before, I'd read an article about him in *The Washington Post*. His execution date was coming up, so I decided to write him. Ironically, he wrote back very fast.

We didn't talk much, only about three or four times. And when we did talk, it was always pretty mundane. We talked about our daily activities, what we had planned, etc. We didn't talk about the crimes we'd committed, just about everyday life, as much as we had to discuss.

I'd informed my doctor about this. I guess I didn't consider that any doctor-patient privileges don't always extend to the parole hearings—especially when someone, like me, is demonstrating a future danger to society. Corresponding with a serial killer, even just to say hello, doesn't exactly send a reassuring message.

There's actually a sense of irony behind this story too. I'd almost chatted with another pitch-black name in American crime.

Since before I'd even gone to trial, I'd gotten some letters from Squeaky Fromme. I didn't mind it. She was nice enough. But then more and more of her friends and family members started trying to get in touch with me. And as anyone who's reading this has probably figured out, her "family" was that of a man named Charles Manson.

Others who supported their legendary leader were now throwing their weight behind me, and I saw it as another burden. I didn't need anyone, particularly those who would be deciding my future, to think I had any connection to them.

I didn't respond. But the letters still came, including one from Charlie himself.

Yes, he knew of me. Apparently, he even liked me, saw me as something of a kindred spirit. His letter salutation was "John Boy," with a nice little swastika right in the middle of it.

I decided to contact him personally, to ask that he call off his men and women. As someone who'd been getting blasted by the media for years, I can't believe I hardly even considered the effect that someone like me trying to communicate with someone like him would have if it became public knowledge.

What a mistake that would have been. If I'd even tried to contact him, I might not have even gotten another hearing for years. Fortunately, I never sent him any letters. However, in my infinite wisdom, I'd mentioned to some other folk that he was a "great prophet" and a "good guy." These were more pieces of information that I'd believed would stay between myself and the listener.

But that revelation ended my hearing almost at that very second. It also killed my chances of release. That mistake reached right out and yanked me back. I know a lot of people—the staff, Leslie, everybody, including me—felt that I'd let them down. I had. They'd worked hard getting my head out of my illusion, and they had, but nowhere near the extent they'd hoped.

For almost two years, I pretty much lost everything: my office job, solo ground privileges, everything. I was right back at maximum security, where every resident begins until they earn otherwise. I could still watch TV and read newspapers, and I even got to spend time with Leslie, but now we could only talk in the office.

50. FINALLY GOING RIGHT

Toeing the line. Toeing the living hell out of the line.

That was it. That was all I thought about for years. For a very long time afterward, I did everything to turn myself into a machine.

I didn't do a damn thing that anyone could even invent a problem with. Forget breaking the rules. I didn't even come near them. Didn't try to even test them.

I got up in the morning, did just what I was supposed to, and went to bed. Routine, routine, routine.

I was starting over. I'd spent the past few years building up some trust and goodwill with the staff, and my chances for, if not release, certainly more freedom, and it had worked, hence why I got out for Christmas. But now I was back at the starting line. Now I had to overcome not just the notoriety of my name and crime, but the label of troublemaker right there at St. Elizabeth's.

Clearly, I had some work to do. First off, I told the staff to ditch whatever little "fan mail" I was still getting.

I cut off contact with everyone. Obviously, that wasn't an issue with Ted Bundy, who had long since gone under Florida's electric chair, and eventually its crematorium, but I'm not just talking about him, Manson, and whatever others of the worst of the worst who were writing to me.

Everyone.

I wasn't talking to anybody but the staff, my fellow residents, my family, and, of course, Leslie. I never knew what I might say or write that might be seen or misconstrued by the wrong people. It was better to go silent and say nothing. I'd rather tick off some of my pen pals than get into more trouble. I had to remind myself that the people I'd been writing with, even those who'd sent me all sorts of gushing letters, would never actually be there for me in person the way that Leslie would.

One day after another, the same thing again and again. And I was okay with that. I had to keep believing that I might get another shot at freedom.

And in the midst of it all, one day someone said something about Jodie. I don't recall when or why. Probably about her latest movie.

But for the first time in as long as I could remember, I didn't really react. It got my attention, but I didn't drop everything I was doing and go into a near-catatonic fixation, like might have happened in the past. The name was noticeable, but not particularly special. Not anymore.

And that hit me even harder than hearing her name itself. I realized, then and there, that I couldn't even remember the last time I'd thought about her. It might have been days. It might have been a few weeks. Maybe longer. Certainly, the longest amount of time I'd gone straight through since before I'd seen *Taxi Driver*.

I was accepting a new reality. Or maybe my mind had tricked me into subtly affecting it a while back, and I just hadn't realized it. I wasn't over Jodie, but I was farther than ever before.

And it wasn't so bad. Not being around her, not even thinking about her, had seemed ridiculous for years. Now I'd taken a few steps away without even realizing.

That was mainly due to Leslie. It was in part from the St. Elizabeth's staff. And, in a tiny way, it was my mind, my own maturity, finally moving forward. Finally finding a foothold in my psyche and clearing it out. Shoving me toward reality—the clean, unscarred reality untouched by my psychosis—that still existed. I'd lived in my own little world for so long that I didn't know anything else. Didn't want to know anything else.

I saw the world the way I saw the world, and I liked it, even with the obsession, the violence, the hate, everything else. But if I was ever going to get back outside these walls, especially for a lengthy period of time, I had to change. I had to adapt. And it wouldn't be such a horrible thing to do so. There was more to the world than Jodie, than Reagan, than St. Elizabeth's. Even more out there than Leslie. She always told me about how nice it was to be outside. The people she met. The work she did, and the people she worked for. Not really her bosses, but her clientele. I could tell she felt she was making a difference in this world. Like me, she could never fully make up for what she'd done to get in trouble to begin with, but she could do something, some sort of contrition.

I wanted that. I wanted to do more than hear about the world from her. More than see it in the newspapers and on TV. I wanted to get back out there and do something, and the first step there was admitting that my world wasn't the Utopia that I'd long believed it was. It wasn't even that nice, mainly because it wasn't possible. But there was a world out there that might be just as good, if I could only step outside and back into it.

Yes, all of that sounded nice to say to Leslie. It was pleasing to think about. It was intimidating, knowing that I still had a ways to go. But now I felt as sure as ever that I could make it. When I realized that my mind had already pushed me on my way with me realizing, I could only hope it would keep doing so.

Jodie kept straying further and further from my mind. I still thought about her once in a while. I still heard about her a lot. She was a public figure whose movies were always a big deal, so it's not like I could just mute her existence.

But as to her publicity, I felt, still feel today, that I was a major career boost for her. When she finally won the Best Actress Oscar for 1988's *The Accused*, playing a young woman who finds the courage to help prosecute the scumbags who raped her, I think that was due in part to the sympathy she received from my actions.

As further proof that I was moving away from her, I only saw *The Accused* once. I don't think I've ever seen *Silence of the Lambs*, despite how legendary that film became, with her work up next to Anthony Hopkins's fellow Oscar-winning work.

For years, that was my reality. One day after another, eventually one year after another, the same things happened. And that was fine with me. Routines. Repetition. Rule-following. Respect. Nodding, obeying, limiting my vocabulary to, "Yes, ma'am," and "No, sir," for months at a time.

I was going to become a model resident.

And I did. Year after year, the staff would examine my records. And they found absolutely nothing. No disciplinary black marks. No writeups. No writings about issues with staff, other residents, whoever. I even asked permission to be in the talent show again, to ensure I wouldn't get in trouble.

If there was a group meeting, I was the first one there and the last one out. I held forth all kinds of details with my therapists. I took my medicine without so much as a grimace, let alone a complaint. I knew I could never fade into obscurity at St. Elizabeth's, but I could sure as hell keep my record clean, and that's the sort of thing that might just get me a little more freedom, someday.

And Leslie was there every step of the way. Almost every day, she showed up to have lunch, to hang out, to be with me. Like about everyone else, she'd seen through my Jodie-based delusions a hell of a lot sooner than I had and, in her own subtle way, she helped me ease away from them. She knew what it was like to have insanity grab us in its evil grasp and make us do horrible things, and she'd found a way to get better. Now she was helping me out.

I was making progress. Becoming more and more receptive to the counselors. Participating more in the group events. No one recovers from psychosis, especially as deep as mine, overnight, or even over the course of years, but it's possible.

At least, I hoped it was. At this point, hope was all I really had. It was always going to be up to other people as to how healthy my mind was, how close I was to being ready for more freedom. Many people still wanted me punished for personal reasons. But if I could take away the ability of staff, and ultimately the judge who would be making the decisions, any way to find a problem in my background, eventually they would have to give due process to even the guy who tried to kill the president.

Or would they? If they couldn't find a legitimate reason to keep me away, they created one.

One of my closest friends was a pharmacist at St. Elizabeth's. We chatted about our tastes in books and music. She was always so glad to see me, upbeat as she was with most people. We talked all the time for about two years, and she never seemed at all uncomfortable around me.

Until someone forced her hand. I was stepping in for another shot at freedom in 1997. And one of the first witnesses was none other than her. I was fine at first. I was sure she was there to talk about what a social fellow with all sorts of diverse interests I truly was.

No. As my heart sank faster and faster, she told a sob tale about how uncomfortable she found me. How I couldn't keep myself away from her. My habits of sitting there entranced whenever she was within eyesight.

It was all an act. The government had gotten to her and "convinced" her to testify a certain way. It worked. I found out very quickly, and very bluntly, that I was going to stay on their version of restriction.

I'd been betrayed again. Still, as depressed as that made me, I'd gotten myself into a position where things like that didn't get me down for long. Nowhere near where I'd been. I was down for a few days, and then I went right back to the routine. It hadn't worked yet, but it still might.

At this point, and for a long time after, all I could do, all I could control, was to work, follow rules, and just keep hoping.

51. LOSING A FRIEND, MAKING NEW ONES

All the while, Leslie and I had been keeping up something of a façade. I referred to her as my wife. We told everyone we were closer than most married couples—probably true!—and how we would be getting married the day I was released. She still probably wore the makeshift ring I'd tied together with string and other objects.

As the millennium came to an end, though, I could see her getting tired of waiting. She wanted things to happen between us, and we couldn't control anything. She was as frustrated as me about my requests for freedom getting ignored and turned down—if I even got to ask.

We'd been stuck in a holding pattern, and we would be as long as I was confined to the hospital. That had worked for over a decade, but she eventually wanted more. She wanted a boyfriend, maybe a husband, who could come see her any time either of them wanted. One she could spend romantic dinners and other outings with and fall asleep next to. St. Elizabeth's certainly didn't offer much in the variety sense when it came to relationships, and many of my fellow residents envied me in the sense that I had a great enough lady to come see me as often as she did, but I could see it going in a bad way.

Her visits became less and less frequent. She didn't seem as attentive or affectionate when we would get our time alone.

In March 1999, *The New Yorker* published an article about us in which she admitted that we had a joint bank account—and knocked a floodgate open in the bargain.

The government subpoenaed her bank records. I guess they thought she was hoarding money for me, or stealing it from somewhere else. She'd moved out and moved on from St. Elizabeth's, and she was doing great. Leslie was inspecting halfway houses and outpatient homes across the nation's capital, and eventually moved up to monitoring them, sending others out from her office. Now, the very people she was serving were desperately searching for a way to stigmatize her, to expose some criminal activity that existed in their minds. They thought that if they followed a money trail far enough, they would eventually find some dirt.

But they didn't. She was clean. There was nothing to find, and there never had been. But after seeing how fast so many of them would react, or completely overreact, at the slightest provocation made her very iffy about even discussing, let along continuing, our relationship.

We tried to make it work. Once in a while, she would come by. It wouldn't be until 2005 that she decided, and I agreed, that we'd gone as far as we could, that we needed to end things, at least until I got out of confinement.

Which, at that point, no one knew when it might be. But we would end in one of the saddest tragedies of my life.

Without her around, I needed something else to occupy my time and mind. I didn't want to be seen blindly wandering all over the place with nothing to do. That might tend to get the staff talking and thinking the wrong way.

I made some new friends. Furry, four-legged friends.

Sometime in the fall of 1998, I noticed a feral cat sitting on a trash can, trying to search it for food. Forgetting any dangers about rabies or anything else, I snuck some grub out of the dining room and fed it.

Leslie wasn't optimistic. "If you start feeding one," she warned me, "more and more will just start coming around." I told her I certainly hoped so. One of my best friends during my college years was my parents' cat Twitter, and my new friends were bringing me back to a great, forgotten time.

Per usual, she was right. Apparently, my feline friend spread the word around the local area. More and more cats showed up almost every day. It got to the point that I would go out there and not be the slightest bit surprised if I saw a few dozen.

Leslie started bringing me, and them, tons of cat food. My resident friends handed over the remnants of their lunch and dinner. When I eventually won some freedom to get outside, I never came back to St. Elizabeth's without several cases full of food.

I started building them some shelters out of whatever wood I could find. Soon after, a lady who worked at the hospital arranged for them to be spayed and neutered for free. Then we gave them out to the locals.

But not all of them.

Between work shifts in the hospital, I spent all kinds of time with the cats. As Leslie drifted further and further away and eventually disappeared altogether, the cats became like confidants to me. Many people prefer the company of animals to humans, and when you're locked in a mental hospital for decades, that rings even more true. Even after Leslie, I considered looking for a relationship in or out of the place, but I always found myself drifting back to my cats.

Some at the hospital thought it was weird. Others saw it as pretty cool. But no one ever gave me any trouble in an official sense. I was showing more care to the local animal colonies than any other resident had before, and they respected that. Actions like this worked in my favor as I kept asking for more freedom. I'd shown the ability to care about and care for creatures that could never offer anything in the way of payback.

When I got out, the cats couldn't follow me, as much as I, and I hope and believe they, wished they could. But I've never been without a feline friend since. Whether I lived with my mother or on my own, I always had a cat. I tried very hard to get a job or even volunteer at a cat shelter on the outside, but such places were always too leery of me to hire me. I wished they would take about five seconds to learn about the time and effort I'd spent on these animals for over a decade.

Not long after I was living on my own, I started creating huge paintings of my cats. I didn't think I was too good at it, still don't, but selling them on the internet gave me a new source of income that still comes in today.

52. THINGS MOVE UP SLOWLY

There's no one set, perfectly, instantly gratifying technique or tool to cure what I had. No pill, no medicine, no technique can take someone as psychotic as I was and heal them right up.

It takes time. It takes effort, both from the patient and those treating him. Most people suffering from mental illness get better with age, as long as they're around the right people, getting the right treatment. I didn't have a place in everyday society in my 20s or 30s. I didn't belong. I needed to be set apart from the rest of the world to clean myself up. If I'd stayed out there, even if I hadn't shot President Reagan, I probably would have done something just as bad to someone else. Maybe to myself.

St. Elizabeth's became a healing haven. Everything was structured. Everything was controlled. Nothing, in the privilege sense, was ever just handed to you. You earned everything, and you went one small step at a time.

When I got there, that was just what I needed: someone to get in my face and let me know exactly what was going to happen and when. It wasn't safe for me to think for myself and make my own decisions. That had gotten innocent people hurt and me destroyed in front of the planet.

Little by little, I got better. There was no one moment of cleansing, of realization. I had an illness that took forever to treat. It was talked out, counseled out, medicated out with the help of those around me. I couldn't have done it myself. But I can't look back and say, "Hey, that's what made me better!" or "Here's the exact second I went from insane to sane!" Mental health treatment just doesn't work like that.

It took far too long, but my delusions went all the way away. My depression desperately hung on for years, but it slowly withered, far enough that it didn't consume me anymore.

Of course I was still ashamed. I'll always be ashamed. That's one thing that has stayed the same, though it's gone up and down at times. That's an aspect of my depression that will never go away, and no one expects it to.

When I look back at the guy who shot the president, he's like a stranger. I don't know him, certainly don't like him, wish I'd never been associated with him. I'm nowhere near the person I was back then.

By the time I got turned down in 1997, I'd been off medications for years. I'd stayed out of trouble. I think everyone basically admitted that I would have been out long ago had I just shot, even killed, a nobody somewhere in a crime that might get a brief mention in the local paper.

But I'd tried to kill the president. It was the system's job to let everyone know that I was going through the wringer. I was going to get as much as they could give me, and everyone needed to know and see that, on TV and in the papers. This had long gone from a legal issue to a personal one.

Like I said, everyone, except the few with authority, agreed that I was safe enough to be released by the late 1990s. By then, I was staying in because the public, the press, and the government, everyone on the outside looking in, wanted me to pay dearly.

Nothing to do about it now. A few years ago, the depression that tormented me for decades might have pushed me into another attempt to take my own life. But I was better by this point. Stronger. I could believe that things would improve if I just kept trying. That sooner or later, they wouldn't be able to say "no" anymore.

I could do that by adding to my chart. Or rather, not adding to it. No discipline issues, no rule breaking, nothing. They would lose the ability to say, "Here's why he needs to stay locked away!"

Yes, I know that sounds sad, considering why I was in the hospital to begin with. But I was entitled to due process, even after my violence. Despite the system's dismantling, or at least harming, the insanity defense after my crime, they would eventually have to apply the same considerations to me as to others who'd done just as bad or worse, albeit much less visibly.

The worst they could do was slow it up. And they did that to the highest levels of effectiveness.

Not until 1999 would I leave the hospital again, and that was under heavily supervised Secret Service guard, and only for a few hours at a time. I mainly just went to my parents' house and hung out there. (The hospital made sure I was far from Washington, DC, Richmond, or anywhere else that someone with certain extreme beliefs might take matters into their own hands.) I would leave in the morning and come right back.

And I didn't complain. I didn't act out. I followed all the rules, smiled and nodded a lot, and did exactly as I was supposed to. It took a few very long years but, just as had happened during the 1986 holiday season, I got a wonderful Christmas gift in 2003: the chance to spend the night outside the hospital. The courts decided that I'd earned it.

"Without doubt," proclaimed Barry Levine, who'd taken over representing me in court from Vince Fuller in 1992, "he is the least dangerous person on the planet." That sounded like hyperbole to the extreme and still does, but it worked.

Finally, the wheels started to turn. I'd kept up my end of the bargain, doing everything I could to improve, and the system was starting to respond and show its appreciation.

But then a very sad event broke the nation's heart and gave that very system, and the people who ran it, a new reason to say no.

53. MORE LOSSES

On June 5, 2004, Ronald Reagan died. It was hardly a surprise; the man was 93 years old (a record for longest-living president, though it has since been broken), and had been battling Alezheimer's disease for years, but it was still a sad day in America.

Not surprisingly, though, one of the first issues the public raised—or re-raised, as it had been on the backburner for years—was how courageous he was to come back from my attempt on his life. Newspaper and web sites everywhere were publishing "Where are they now?" stories detailing the lives of everyone involved in the near quarter century since my crime.

Including, of course, me. My freedoms, or even my attempts at them, had been in the newspapers every time I walked into court, but this was bigger. Millions of people learned about everything I'd been through since the crime, and they weren't happy. Several who hadn't talked about me for years, or at all, were suddenly trying to burn me at the stake, still angry that I'd gotten away (as if decades of institutionalization could be considered lenient), and wanting me hurt again.

But my family, Barry Levine, and myself decided that I should shut up and fade away for a while. No attempts at freedom. No more asking for privileges for a while. Emotions against me that had lain dormant for years were suddenly at high velocity again. Those in the system might very well turn me away for reasons far from the law. I'd never had any trouble with anyone on the outside, but with my name and face suddenly right back out there, people were more likely to notice and respond with unfavorable force.

It would be almost another year before I would even ask for any sort of modification to my release. But by late 2005, I'd won regular overnight visits with my folks. The next year, I was given four-day visits with them. I was able to visit Washington, under Secret Service monitoring. Then the monitoring went away. Then I was allowed to venture all the way down to Williamsburg.

One small step after another. The process kept repeating itself. Barry, who really went to the mat for me all this time, would wait until the newness of my next privilege went away, then ask for more. The same things would keep happening. He would ask, the government would say no, and he would keep pointing to the same factors, like me staying clean in St. Elizabeth's and just as much so on the outside. I followed all the rules, left and returned when I was supposed to, did everything I should. Both before and after leaving the hotel, every single time, I had to sit down and discuss with the staff everything I was planning to do, everywhere I was going to go, and I'd damned well better stick to it. That list was always pretty short, and I didn't dare break it.

Of course I couldn't talk to the media. I'm sure some of them were looking for some scandalous tale or tell-all tabloid stuff ("The monster re-emerges!"), but it didn't happen. I didn't go near the hotel where the shooting had occurred. I didn't see any of the famous monuments all over either DC or Williamsburg, where I might have been recognized or accused of looking for trouble.

I was different than a prisoner being locked away from society for decades and decades, with no access to the modern world's offerings or knowledge of its happenings. We got to watch TV, to read news articles and, very, very slowly, peruse the internet as it came around. Stepping back out into the public wasn't an entirely new world for me. The world was different every time, but not so earth-shatteringly so that social reintegration was an issue for me. I would get out briefly, learn what was going on, hang out with a very small group of folk, then go back in. Society doesn't always do right by the incarcerated, when we say to them, "Okay, you've been living in a box for decades, but we expect you to, like *that*, automatically know what's going on in this new world and re-adapt yourself quickly and accordingly!"

Not fair, and not even remotely possible. If St. Elizabeth's had done that with me, I might have reoffended and this time gone to jail, not the hospital.

Back and forth, more and more. More time outside. Getting a driver's license. (First try, and no violations since! Not bad for a guy who'd spend so little time behind a wheel for so long!) Being allowed to step off the grounds once in a while to get food for my ever-present cat family.

In the midst of all that, though, my family had its own loss to suffer through.

Just as they had since literally the day I shot Reagan, my parents were there for me. Always were. They put everything aside for me and kept doing so. They moved across the country, gave up their friends, family, and, to an extent, their careers for me. Nothing else I could ask for. I'm sure they faced a great deal of anger from society for what I'd done. People wanted someone to blame for my acts, and if they couldn't get me, they badmouthed my family. But they always kept that private from me as well. As tough as I'd made things for myself and for them, they never tried to add to my mistakes.

As my visits grew, my father's health deteriorated. I'd noticed that he wasn't playing golf as much, then quit altogether. He wasn't as attentive in my visits. He'd always run things in and out of the house—he'd been born and raised in the South, and that's what a man's supposed to do, as far as he was raised—but my mother was subtly taking over. She had to. He was losing the ability to get around and care for himself. I couldn't imagine what she was going through.

Soon, it became clear that his mind was being destroyed by one of the medical world's most destructive enemies. This man, who'd raised a family, run several businesses, done everything, was becoming a shell of himself over something he had no control over.

By the time I got any kind of significant freedom, Alzheimer's had put him in a nursing home. I was home for a visit with my mother in 2008 when the phone rang. It was the home, telling us he wouldn't see another week.

I called St. Elizabeth's and begged to be able to stay long enough to see him off. They said no and ordered me back. Once there, I asked for an exception to go home again.

They said no again. Two days later, with me stuck at St. Elizabeth's, my dad passed. To give them a little credit, they did allow me to attend his funeral.

For one of the first times, I was glad I was at the hospital. My depression came back, but this time, I couldn't show it. Not there, not in public, not until I got back to St. Elizabeth's, where I could get a little help from the counselors and my resident friends who helped me out. I wasn't going to act out in front of my mother, who'd watched the man she'd built a life and family with slowly fade away and disappear.

Once I made it through the grieving process, or at least the worst of it, I found a new reason to try even harder for my freedom. My brother was planning to move over to Virginia to help our mom, and I was going to be there as well. If I couldn't be there every day and night for her, I sure as hell wanted to get there as often as I could.

But that didn't happen either, not that I should have expected it to. The court system wasn't going to cut me much slack just because of my losses. It took years for any further freedom.

54. HEALING, SUFFERING

Not until 2011 did my doctors go far enough as to state that my mental illness was in remission. Literally, that's what they said at my freedom hearings: remission.

That sounded like a strange word to use about my illness and me. When we think of remission, we tend to go straight to cancer or some other horrible ailment. Not depression, let alone insanity. The medication that I'd been using at St. Elizabeth's had been helpful, as had the counseling, but you can't radiate psychosis or use chemotherapy to get rid of what I had.

I guess it just meant that my treatments had worked to the highest extent they could. Like I've said and still believe, I would have been out long ago if I'd shot a nobody on the streets.

It didn't matter to me what they said. All that counted was that I was getting out and staying out for longer. Not all the way, but longer.

I was allowed to spend 10 days at a time at home. I took my mother to church. I would lie on the beach, go bowling, see museums, everything I'd missed. I found some cats to take care of and hang out with on the outside. I was required to carry a cell phone with a GPS monitor so they knew where I was, all the time.

But I almost ran into trouble. I was still being monitored, and someone saw a few things that could have landed me in scalding water.

One day in October 2011, I was strolling around a bookstore and happened by the biographical section. For all of about 15 seconds, I stopped to look at something.

Then I grabbed and purchased some tomes on Elvis and Bob Dylan and strolled out.

Soon after, someone, I'm not sure who, dropped me off to see a movie. I stood in front of the theater for a short while, then doubled back into another bookstore, where I stayed until they came and got me.

Those experiences in and of themselves nearly caused me to lose my freedom. At my next hearing, people who'd witnessed me got on the witness stand and talked about them.

First off, if I'd claimed to want to see the movie, only to change my mind, I was obviously being dishonest and manipulating everyone, right? Who knew what secret plans I had? Who could guess who I might lie to next, or what about.

Next was the first bookstore issue, described in all kinds of detail by an employee.

Here was the matter: when I'd stopped and stared, I'd actually been right in front of a piece on President McKinley's assassination. I didn't recall even seeing it, but that was what he claimed.

Petty? Yes, it seemed so to me, and probably would to most people. But with a guy who was still required to walk the straight and narrow after years of institutionalization, no one was taking any chances. I'd been a textbook case for healing, but no one could know what might trigger me again. I guess they thought that seeing up close and personal the story of another president who had been killed might do it.

Sitting there in court watching all of this, I couldn't believe it. I didn't comprehend, and this time not because of mental illness, how these issues could land me right back away. Maybe somewhere worse than St. Elizabeth's. Maybe even jail.

But they didn't. The courts ruled that my trek toward freedom could continue. Eventually, I made it to 17-day vacations.

Then another tragedy occurred, and it was all because of me.

Each time I ventured out, my victims' families were notified. Not surprisingly, Sarah Brady, James's wife, had always been outspoken about me getting anything when I'd cost her family so much.

James Brady's livelihood, and eventually his life, was stolen from him because he'd done what was right, what few others would ever have had the guts to. I know I wouldn't. A man who wasn't in the Secret Service, no kind of security or law enforcement at all, saved President Reagan's life and paid with his own.

My bullet took away his career as the press secretary. James Brady could hardly walk, talk, think, or function at all because of what I'd done. For decades, he fought on, becoming a face of American heroism and fighting to prevent others from going through what he had, to save them from people like me. The Brady Bill that he and his family helped pass undoubtedly did so.

After more than three decades of pain, James Brady died in August 2014. I told everyone, as I always had, that I'd never been more remorseful for his agony than anything in my life. I hadn't even known his name, and I'd taken his life. Every time I heard about him, and much more so when he died, I wished that I could have put the bullet that hit him through my own head.

But in a selfish way, I was a little nervous. I was concerned that I might face new charges. I'd been acquitted of attempted murder in his case, but now I was worried I might be charged with the murder itself. Many people certainly hoped I would be.

This would prove not to be the case. My insanity acquittal carried over in that I wouldn't be charged. If I was insane at the time of the shooting, they couldn't use my healing as a way to prosecute me. My lawyer informed me that this would be considered double jeopardy, in that a person, once acquitted, can't be tried again.

I was relieved, but not happy. I knew his family was still suffering, as I'm sure they are today. I'd robbed him of a chance to do some amazing things for the Reagan administration and them of the chance to be there and cheer for him as he did. He should have been standing next to his boss for all the great things he did over the course of his term, not being forced to watch in pain from a wheelchair because of me. I just hope James Brady is remembered for the guts he showed and the great things he did, more accomplishments than I ever will have in my life.

55. MY NEW "RELEASE"

Ironically enough, as I tried to get more freedom, the prosecution tried to use my lack of social extroversion against me. Basically, I was being too quiet for them. In 2014, I was required—not given as a privilege, but forced as a condition of release—to make eight trips to Williamsburg. Then the government tried to claim that I wasn't working hard enough to integrate myself into the Williamsburg community, claiming I kept revisiting the same stores and restaurants again and again.

I couldn't believe they had such a problem with my lack of diverse interests. They shouldn't have been surprised, as that had been a major factor during and after my trial. I guess they thought I would be so anxious to get out there that I would rush out and try to do everything at high speed.

Not happening. I was more concerned with staying out of trouble, and keeping my head down was an effective way of doing so.

Eventually, I was granted convalescent leave. I was on the way out all the way. This meant that I was out of there. No more visit limits. No more returning every other week.

I was going home for good, and damned if I would be back. I was on top of the world. I felt like, as horrible as my past action had been, I'd made up for it, paid my price, and proved everyone wrong. The outsiders who'd badmouthed me in the papers, the magazines, on TV, and eventually, the internet. The government and all its intelligent and expensive witnesses who had taken an oath to tell the truth and then gone to the ends of the earth to keep me away. Even the doctors, residents, and counselors who had badmouthed me at St. Elizabeth's. They were in the extreme minority, but they were there.

Years after I should have been, I was out of there. But remember, this was a convalescent release, meaning that there were still a few conditions.

I had to live at my mother's house, and I couldn't go outside of a 50-mile radius at any time. I had to keep erasing my internet browser history, and I couldn't look at any adult sites or news about my case at all. I couldn't have any overnight guests unless my mother was home. The Secret Service had my cell number and the make and model of my car, along with monitoring my phone and email address. I couldn't own any alcohol. Definitely couldn't touch a gun.

I certainly couldn't talk to the media. I couldn't contact the Reagan family or friends or family or any of my other victims. They made it quite clear that if I did so much as think about Jodie Foster, I would be going back in.

That was actually one of my easiest steps. I hadn't thought about her in years, read about her, seen any of her movies, nothing. I hardly remembered what she looked like.

Twice a month, I would have to drive back to St. Elizabeth's to chat with a social worker, psychiatrist, and therapist. Then it became once a month. Then every other month. Less and less as I showed I could follow the rules.

And I got right to work.

I got a job working at an antique mall kiosk, mainly selling old books, records, music, and movie posters, all kinds of things.

And I got right back to work on the music career I'd dreamed of. I started writing more and more songs. I got to recording them. I had a technique of knocking out the melody first, then filling in the lyrics. Sometimes I would do my own versions of other songs, like the old reliable "Blowing in the Wind."

I started posting some on the internet. I created a YouTube channel. At first, I wasn't sure how people would respond to it. I was worried that people from my generation would badmouth it, and people from the 'net-loving group wouldn't be interested in the actions of a guy who'd gone out of worldwide infamy since before they were born.

Fortunately, I was wrong. Tens of thousands of followers joined my page. I went on other social media sites and found just as much success. I was planning to do some concerts, open a media store, all kinds of things as soon as I could free myself from the clutches of institutionalization for the last time.

I was almost there. Almost free. *That* close to being all the way away from the rules and regulations that had governed my life for decades. Within a chance or two of the music stardom I'd long dreamed of.

And then, right out of nowhere, tragedy hit me like a wrecking ball.

56. MORE LOSSES

I stepped into St. Elizabeth's for my required monthly visit in the summer of 2017. As always, I sat down with a doctor to discuss my current state.

Same as it had been for years. No depression. No delusions. No urges to do anything even remotely illegal. It was the same very quick and easy conversation I'd had dozens of times, with her and others.

Then she looked up at me, a painful look on her face. I could tell she'd just remembered there was something she needed to tell me, and that it wouldn't be something I would want to hear. Maybe the Reagans or the Bradys had filed a new motion to put me back away for some reason. Maybe President Trump, in all of his self-righteousness and love for the spotlight, was going to punish me so he could go on TV and brag, "That SOB almost killed one of the greatest men in American history, and I—yes, I, no one else!—am going to fix him so he never can again! That's how much I—yes, I, no one else!—love this great nation!"

No. It was actually worse than that.

"You know that woman you used to hang out with here?" she asked, as emotional as if she was telling me tomorrow's weather forecast. "She died."

What?! What woman? I hadn't been in a relationship for a long time, not since Leslie and I had broken up over a decade before and…

Wait a minute. No. God no.

She couldn't have… please don't say… she wasn't talking about Leslie, right?

"Yes, Leslie something," she continued. "Leslie Devon, Devo, whatever her name was."

It was deVeau. This woman couldn't even remember, let along pronounce, the name of a woman who'd been my closest confidante and friend for years. Someone who had been as helpful in my triumph over mental illness as the St. Elizabeth's staff. Certainly, a better human being than this cold, heartless shell sitting across from me.

I could hardly move, let alone speak. I kept waiting for her to tell me it was a mistake, a bad joke, maybe a test to see if I would go over the edge again. Something. Anything but what it meant. Anything but reality.

That wasn't the case. She was ready to move on with our meeting.

I managed to look at her. I found a few words from within.

I asked when Leslie had died. How she'd died. When was her funeral, if it hadn't already happened. Whether she would be buried so I could go visit her grave, or cremated so I might get some of her ashes.

Her answers were all the same. She didn't know. Well, she *said* she didn't know. It was just something she'd heard. Whether any of that was true, I'll never really know for sure.

And that was it. That was all I would ever know about it. No one ever could answer a single question I had. I was never able to find an obituary, a notice about what was done with Leslie's body, or anything else. To this day, I still have no clue what happened at the end, or the last few years, of a woman I loved as much as I've ever loved another human being in my life, and who gave me more love and acceptance than anyone else. When I was the most hated man on earth, she was one of the few people who reached out to me and showed me that not everyone felt that way.

It broke my heart, and it'll never really heal. Leslie and I hadn't been in contact for a while, but the memories that we made, the love that we shared, meant as much to me as any relationship I'd ever had, and now I had nothing.

And I felt that way for a long time. I quit writing music for a while. I kept my job at the mall, but now I looked for something else.

I volunteered all over the place. I offered to work for free at a cat rescue shelter, a botanical garden, the Salvation Army, even the law offices at a college nearby. As soon as they saw my name, they didn't call back. No one wanted to take a shot with me because of my notoriety. If people weren't going to get in my face and tell me where to go, they sure didn't have to help me move up on the outside.

A local mental hospital finally gave me a chance with some volunteer work. For a long time, I worked in the library and cafeteria, watching others who had been where I was and hoping they would be okay. Some of them knew me, recognized me, and even wanted to talk to me, but nothing too in-depth about my crimes. I've noticed that those who have committed horrible acts like mine and Leslie's avoid discussing them, even with each other. I'm sure it's the same in prisons.

Yet, even when I found some solace, tragedy kept chasing me around.

Not long after my release, my case manager informed me about the National Alliance on Mental Illness (NAMI), which helps people across America still struggling with mental illness. I say "still" because it's an ailment you never really recover from. You just get to a point where you can function alongside the rest of those with some sort of mental defect (in other words, everyone). With usually a counselor or some other mental health professional at the head, you sit around, share your thoughts, your triumphs, your failures, and your hopes that there are other people in the same boat as you. I've never been to an Alcoholics or Narcotics Anonymous meeting, but I'm guessing there are some common threads between these groups.

I didn't have to worry about acceptance. Much like the majority of the staff and residents at St. Elizabeth's, these people had seen and sometimes done as bad as or worse than I had. They knew me, who I was, what I'd done, but like not enough people, they saw me as someone in need of help, not punishment. It's an outstanding feeling to work really hard to help another person and see them benefit from the work you did. I doubt there's a bigger ego boost than knowing you helped save the guy who convinced himself it was a good idea to shoot the president to attract a stranger!

One such person was a lovely lady named Laura. Like everyone else there, she welcomed me with open arms.

And, yes, like me and everyone else there, she had a past. There were sex criminals, murderers, everyone.

Including recovering drug addicts. Like her.

She'd abused substances long enough to permanently damage her mental health, and now she was looking for help to get a little bit of it back.

It was tough for us to understand each other at first. I'd never had drug issues. She'd never been violent. But soon we realized that we really didn't have to focus on why we'd made the mistakes we'd made. The point is, we had. We'd made different mistakes for the same reason—our minds being warped. Why that happened, whose fault it was, if anyone's, simply didn't matter. We were still sick, and we were there to help each other get better.

Laura became the highlight of my Tuesdays, and then even more often. She lived close to me, so we would go out. We spent all kinds of time together. We talked for hours.

Like everyone else who met her, I had trouble seeing any sort of mental illness, or any disabilities of all, in Laura. She was funny, she was smart, she could talk to you about anything. Week after week, month after month, we became each other's reliables.

In the summer of 2021, I got some great legal news. On June 15, I was informed that one of the doctors in my case would sign off on my full release, and that the judge would back him. Even the government, which had fought so hard and pulled one weapon after another to keep me locked up, said they would be okay with my release. If I could stay out of trouble for one more year, I would be free and clear for the first time in half a century.

Piece of cake. I'd never gotten into trouble during or after my time at St. Elizabeth's, so I knew this wouldn't be a problem. What would it be like, becoming a part of society with no strings left attached? From the day of the declaration, I was counting back from 365.

I was so happy, so optimistic for the future, that I didn't notice some things about Laura. Things that were getting worse and worse.

She didn't come over or return my calls like she used to. When we hung out, she was more and more quiet. So many times,

I would catch her staring off, a frightened look on her face, me having to do everything but scream to get her attention back. She started missing meetings.

However, I thought we'd turned a corner. She was at my house one afternoon, and we were chatting on the deck outside. She seemed happier, more upbeat, more like the old Laura, than I'd seen in a while. I figured she'd gone through a down phase, and Lord knows I could relate to those, and that she was back up and would stay there.

I stepped into the next NAMI meeting just as visitors were about to take their seats. I glanced around, looking for Laura. We always saved each other a nearby spot.

Then one of the organization officials came up to me. It appeared that his mood was battling between fury and deep sadness. People in his position aren't allowed to show much emotion at these meetings, so I knew something was going on.

It was. He told me that Laura had killed herself.

I couldn't believe it. First Leslie, now this? Was I some kind of human curse that destroyed everyone who dared to give a shit about me? Was everyone I cared for going to disappear?

It wasn't long after before I got another sad answer to that. My mother had been on a slow decline since breaking her hip in 2017. With my father gone and my siblings out of the area, I was her sole caregiver.

Not that I minded. It was the least I could do. She'd given up so much, been humiliated in the national public eye by my actions, even had some ignorant folk badmouth her and snidely claim, without a shred of evidence or credibility, that my parents were responsible for my actions or could have stopped them. If these comments hadn't pissed me off so much, I would have felt sorry for these fools. Some people just talk and write to hear their own voices for a few seconds.

She and my father had been each other's rocks. Actually, his death might have been the beginning of the end for her, although she hardly showed it.

Honestly, she didn't show it much even after her injury. She and I spent hours in front of the TV, debating the latest sitcoms and movies. Less and less, but still as often as possible, we tried out as many new restaurants as we could. I loved that, because it gave me an excuse to hide what a bad cook I was. I'm sure she knew, considering I made all her meals, but she never said anything.

Too sad to face the NAMI crowd, I stopped attending after Laura died. Over the next weeks, my mother headed downward mentally for the first time I could tell. She'd always been active until her injury, and that depressed and angered her as much as I'd ever seen. Her friends, also in their 80s and 90s, couldn't exactly get up to come see her, which I'm sure harmed her mental health even worse.

One day, in late July 2021, my mother fell asleep. The next morning, after 95 years on this planet, she didn't wake up.

Now I had no one. No one to talk to, to rely on, to rely on me. And I wasn't sure I wanted it. I'd lost the two most important women in my life in a short while. Maybe it was best that I stayed away. With all the red tape holding me down for years, I was legally unable to do anything on my own, to make something of myself, by myself. Now I wouldn't have a choice. I couldn't pack up and go live elsewhere; the hospital rules wouldn't allow it. If I were to go and live with someone else, they would have to approve that and, again, I was afraid to go near anyone for the time being.

But they were understanding. They told me that if I kept following the rules, kept coming up to see them, stayed away from the cops, I would be okay. I would still get my full freedom the next summer. It would be all I could do to stay focused on that calendar, every single day.

57. SEEN ON THE SCREEN AND STAGE

I've been depicted on stage and screens big and small a few times. I don't think I've seen a single one, at least not on my own initiative.

The *Family Guy* cartoon, which has spoofed just about everything under the sun a few times over since it came about a few decades ago, has made fun of me before. One episode had me papering the Sistine Chapel with photos of Jodie. In another, I fired the starter's pistol to a boat race, enticing Jodie to appear and declare she'd been wrong about me. But I didn't even see those clips until early 2025.

As early as November 1982, a few months after my trial, *Saturday Night Live* had Brad Hall playing me… in an asylum, much more secure and ancient than St. Elizabeth's… running for president!

"On March 30, 1981, I shot the president of the United States and three other people in order to impress a girl," Hall recalled as me. "I know that sounds like a terrible thing to do, but I'm completely crazy. I'm insane, and I can't be held responsible for my actions. Sending a John Hinckley like myself to an institution instead of some wretched prison is the American way. This reaffirmation of the American dream proves that our system works. But only a wacko can see how it works. I am that wacko, and to prove it I am today officially entering the race for the presidency of the United States of America. I winged Reagan in the streets. I'm gonna knock him dead in the polls, and then, my girlfriend Jodie can assume her rightful place as First Lady of this great and powerful nation." I'm sure that sketch was a serious case of "too much too soon," to many, and hit a little too close to home for others.

Early the next year, the same season, Buckwheat strolled out of a building up to a limo, then waved to his fans before being gunned down by crazed loner John David Stutts (both men played by Eddie Murphy), who himself was blasted down walking past a group of reports—in one sketch, the show managed to parody both my actions and Jack Ruby's killing of Lee Harvey Oswald! That's an accomplishment.

But of course, my dark moment has shown up in pop culture many times over, and all of them were meant to be frightening and incredibly sad.

Strangely, my first depiction, if one can even call it that, came on the Off-Broadway stages. I guess I was a little flattered that Stephen Sondheim, one of the pioneers of stage musicals, wanted me in one of his shows. From the guy who had already brought *West Side Story* to the stage and screen, it felt like somewhat of a step down.

His 1989 show *Assassins* started off with several title characters who had killed, or tried to kill, presidents from history, being handed a gun by the Proprietor, who promised that their problems would vanish if these acts were completed. Everyone from John Wilkes Booth to Giuseppe Zangara was there.

Soon, Lynette Fromme found me in my room, strumming a guitar and gazing at a photo of Jodie, pushing us into a duet of "Unworthy of Your Love," me singing to Jodie and her to Charles Manson. Eventually, all of us would wind up in the Texas Book Depository, pep-talking Lee Harvey Oswald into taking his frustrations out on President Kennedy. Welcomed into our ranks after acting out the act, he joined us all on stage as our final victims became the audience.

"The most interesting thing to me," explained actor Alexander Gemignani of prepping to play me in a 2004 performance in New York (my parents' book *Breaking Points* was a major boon to his getting ready), "is that his parents didn't have any idea. They were more shocked than anyone. They thought he was just shy and quiet. All the characters have a sympathetic side; you find part of you identifying with them, and you have to remind yourself you're not as troubled as these people are."

Let's hope not!

That play took creativity and a ton of guts, both of which Sondheim always had. It would take time, but the show would eventually get to Broadway and win five awards at the 2004 Tonys (theater's equivalent to the Oscars), including Michael Cerveris scoring one for playing John Wilkes Booth.

Especially when it comes to musicals, theater has a different burden (some say objective) than TV and movies. If someone tried to put a story like that on the screen, especially without the play coming first, it probably wouldn't happen. The ones I'm referring to come across as very different, but certainly, and sadly, much more real.

I think I may have seen one TV show or movie that depicted my act, but it has been so long that I don't remember which, assuming it existed at all. Why would I want to see that? I know Hollywood will turn me into some dark, brooding monster, some ominous creation that just *looks* like a guy who would kill a president! Movies have the ability to manipulate the truth, in action, appearance, everything, and of course, I'm going to look like a horrible villain in these shows.

I'm sure that every depiction of me, those that have been done and those that will be, follows about the same script: Reagan walks down the sidewalk to a round of cheers, waving and beaming. Suddenly, a guy who looks like an even creepier version of me on that day manages to step forward. As the motion slows and the eerie music rises, we hear gunshots, probably much slower than the ones I actually fired. People fall, Reagan is taken away, and the wannabe killer is tackled and beaten down.

Yeah, I've been there, up to a point. I lived it. Yes, I caused it. So why would I want to see that? Why would I watch someone else act out the most shameful moments of my life?

Part of it also had to do with being forbidden from everything but thinking about the Reagans. During my institutionalization, I obviously couldn't write to or read or watch anything about him and his family. These rules continued to apply after I was freed.

Even today, when I see Reagan or any of his family members, I change the channel, click off the web site, turn the page. That stuff sticks with you, and it's some strong paranoia. Even doing something like that unintentionally makes you feel like you're doing something wrong, and that you're going to get in trouble for it.

The TV movies *The Day Reagan Was Shot*, *Killing Reagan*, and *Without Warning: The James Brady Story* focused nearly all on my assassination attempt. The 2024 biopic *Reagan*, with Dennis Quaid in the main role, depicted the sad moment in theaters across America, although, sadly, Lauden Baker didn't even get credited for being me.

Lauden Baker: Before *Reagan*, I spent many years working in the budding Oklahoma film industry. When I learned that *Reagan* would be filming in Oklahoma and I saw the caliber of talent that was attached to the project, I knew I wanted to be involved. I originally auditioned for multiple other small parts in the film that I was not cast in. It would be nearly a year later that a casting notice was released for the portrayal of John Hinckley, Jr., and I submitted for the part after meeting all the requested size and age specifications.

There were only a few days between the time I was cast and the time we filmed. I also knew that we would be recreating an iconic moment in American history, and I wouldn't have any lines, so my eyes and physicality would have to tell the story. I watched as much footage as I could get my hands on, as well as listened to podcasts about the day of President Reagan's attempted assassination, trying to understand context and John Hinckley Jr.'s motive.

I specifically avoided watching articles or interviews from after the events of that day because I didn't want to be distracted by the results of the attempted assassination, but rather what led up to it. Even though my scene was only a few seconds long, I felt a responsibility to do what I could to serve the story.

We filmed my scene in the summer of 2021. The first time I saw any polished footage was while watching the official trailer in April of 2024. So much time had passed, and my personal life had changed so much in those three years, I found myself tearing up the first time I saw it. As an actor, I have worked on many projects where my scenes hit the cutting room floor. *Reagan* would be the first time my work was released into theaters, and it was a very special milestone in my creative career. I wouldn't see the scene in its entirety until the Oklahoma premiere in August of 2024. I felt a great sense of pride in collaborating on that film with so many of my friends and colleagues in the Oklahoma film community. I was particularly impressed with the editing in that scene that included multiple quick cuts from different angles, slow motion, and other special effects. It was truly surreal.

58. WINNING AND LOSING AT ONCE

It was supposed to be one of the happiest days of my life. It was supposed to be my final victory of redemption.

Maybe it was, up to an extent. But fate had one more dark trick to play on me.

The previous September, Judge Paul Friedman had publicly announced he would let me all the way out if I could stay out of trouble just a little bit more. I had—and on June 15, 2022, he proved himself a man of his word.

"This is the time to let John Hinckley move on with his life, so we will," Freidman said. "If he hadn't tried to kill a president, he would have been released unconditionally a long time ago."

No more monthly visits. No more hearings to hold. No more chances to take. No more rules to follow. I'd finally earned enough trust among the hospital, the courts, and everyone else to be known as "John Hinckley Jr., FORMER resident." I was free at last.

Now I was ready to rock and roll. Literally. I told my Twitter followers that very thing that very day. ("After 41 years 2 months and 15 days, FREEDOM AT LAST!!!") In less than a month, I was finally going to take my music career on the road.

About a month before, a music promotor in New York had contacted me. He'd been chatting with the owners of a hotel in Brooklyn about setting up a show with me.

This was supposed to be the first step toward something huge. This was going to be more than a one-shot deal. We would be kicking off the "John Hinckley Redemption Tour." Soon, venues across the America would be lining up to host my next event.

As soon as word got out, people responded. From the moment the event had been announced, before I was even all the way out of confinement, buyers bought. In three days, the hotel sold every ticket it had available.

My dream would come true. Then it would keep coming true, larger and larger, all across the nation. Soon, millions of people would hear my words and know my name for the reasons I'd always desperately wanted.

I'd been rehearsing for weeks. I knew everything I was going to sing, in what order, all the acts. I had some friends coming along to back me up. I was finally going to make it.

But almost to the moment that Judge Friedman delivered one of the most welcome messages of my life, another phone call knocked me right off balance.

The hotel was canceling out. They appreciated the success my show would have had, but security was a concern. Too much of a concern. Apparently, the place had been threatened online. Maybe some customers and business partners had threatened to walk away, even for good. Maybe anything. But I wasn't worth the chance they would be taking.

Literally, these things happened on the same day. Within a few minutes of my new life beginning, it came to a screeching halt.

The fellow in New York promised he would keep looking. He would keep trying to find me my debut gig. We were sure that this had simply been a misfire, that someone else would grab the hotel's missed opportunity.

But that didn't happen. A gig in New York City canceled on us. Then one in Connecticut. And another in Chicago. We would set things up, get a date, then get a message saying that the owners' minds had changed somehow.

We tried to double back, to start closer to home. But again, no one stepped up and stayed there. Concerts in Williamsburg, Richmond, and Newport News fell through. Over a dozen gigs said yes, then no.

I don't understand that. I didn't then and still don't. I can't figure out why no one, even after two-plus years, can give me a chance to get on a stage—which, as we've seen, would probably sell serious tickets—and give everyone something very special. All I ever wanted to do was entertain and inspire with my lyrics and melodies, and I know I can if I just get one try.

Still, at least one record company has. Right around the time I was supposed to be hitting the Brooklyn stages, Asbestos Records put out my debut album *Redemption*. It's the first of many. It's a message I'm going to try to keep sending.

The scariest thing that has happened to me since my release, by far, came about on the day Donald Trump was elected president in November 2024. That night, I was checking my social media.

And I was appalled.

"John, we're all very big fans of your early work," one person praised. My smile and ego grew, just knowing that the poster was talking about my music career. Then I found out how sadly wrong I was.

"You should definitely go back to that more than ever," the post continued. That's when I went dead cold. They were screaming for the head and the life of their president. Pictures of Trump with blood and bullet holes were all over the place. One person put a shot of Trump right after the assassination attempt on him the previous July and asked me to do a better job. Some people created fake images of me shooting Trump, standing over his body with a gun, the sickest things I'd ever seen. I literally had to turn off my computer and walk away, or maybe even run away. I thought I might throw up.

The stuff that people were posting there was obscene. One absolute piece of human trash even went so far as to entice me to, "Do it for Jodie Foster." That still twists my stomach when I think about it.

I couldn't believe people were saying this. I couldn't believe I actually had to go on X (or Twitter, or whatever it's called now) and point people right.

"I'm a man of peace now!" I claimed. "Please stop with all the negative comments!" I'd made similar comments after the horrible assassination attempt against Trump.

Think about that for a second. People needed a guy who had almost killed the president, and who did kill another innocent person at the same time, to instruct them not to want the new president dead. It's pathetic what some people need pointed out to them.

I don't care much for Trump, as a person or as a president. But I'm not important in that sense. These people were going out of their way to personally ask me to murder him. Sickening. I don't understand what makes people talk like that. I can only hope these people were just running off at the mouth, as those hiding behind social media tend to do, and not serious. I hope.

CONCLUSION

"I don't seem to have my father's gift for forgiveness—not yet anyway. Over the years my rage toward Hinckley has turned icy but hasn't diminished. I thought perhaps by looking into all aspects of his case, I could at least rid myself of some of the anger. But instead I've only proved what I already thought: he has worked the system; he's still working it; and he'll keep on until he's a free man. The legacy of violence is the rage it ignites in others. I wish I didn't feel it, but I do. And the worst of it is, that keeps him in my mind. He did, after all, crave attention. Sadly, he still has mine."

Patti Davis Reagan, April 2000

"I think that John Hinckley should not have been freed."

Future president Donald Trump (who actually called me David during the press conference), July 2016

If I'd had it my way, if everything had gone like I'd hoped and intended, everyone would know my name. People would be discussing me, talking about me for generations.

Well, they are. But I never wanted it to be like this. I wanted to be known. I thought I could be famous.

But not for why I'm known now. Certainly not.

Ever since that wonderful day when I first picked up a guitar, I wanted people to know me. But I wanted to be famous for my music career. I wanted to be known for headlining major concerts, for selling records—and then cassettes and then CDs and whatever else—and for having people lining up at ticket halls to see me, at record stores to meet me and get an autograph and photo. I wanted people to see me and think of me and say, "Yeah, his music is greatness!" I wanted them to like me, to see my name and smile, maybe start singing one of my personal tunes.

And as crazy as it sounds, that's all I wanted them to say. I never wanted to have my name linked with Lee Harvey Oswald or Sirhan Sirhan or John Wilkes Booth or any of the others from history that people think of and immediately feel a dark cloud rush through their mind.

No one will ever forget my name, for the worst reasons.

I'm not famous. I'm infamous. I'm known, but hardly loved, or even liked much. I've accepted that, and have for decades. There could never be any justification for what I did. I'm responsible for the death of one unbelievably brave man, and the near-death of three others. Nothing will ever make up for that. That's how it's always going to be.

I could say I'm sorry. I have many times in the past. I will always feel that way.

But that will never be enough and, to be frank, it shouldn't be. Not for everyone. Some people will accept it and forgive me, like President Reagan and his son seemed to. Others, like, Patti Davis and so many, many more, never will.

"Now Hinckley says he's sorry," Davis said in 2000, as I started getting more and more releases from St. Elizabeth's. "But is he sorry for what he did, or only sorry that he didn't succeed completely?" I'm sure she's one of millions who have asked that very question.

The answer is the first option. Of course I'm sorry for what I did. The president was almost killed. James Brady, an innocent and incredibly brave man, did something that wasn't even his job, taking a bullet for that president. Then, his political career over, he suffered for decades before dying.

And that's all my fault. I took a human life and tried to take more. I feel sick even writing that. I look back and can't believe I would ever do such a thing. What a ridiculous reason to do something so horrific! How can things seem so plausible at the time and unthinkable in the past?

It's obscene. And it's all very sad. To kill an innocent man? To shoot three other innocent men? To honestly believe that anyone, let alone a public figure like Jodie Foster, would ever be impressed by such a barbaric act. How could I have expected her to support what I did? Hell, how could she not have outwardly despised it? To even consider the possibility of that, let alone to the extent that I truly believed, is absurd, itself an understatement.

At the end of the day, this wasn't her fault. Of course not. It wasn't Reagan's fault, and it wasn't Brady's fault, and it wasn't Thomas Delahanty's fault, and it wasn't Tim McCarthy's fault, and it wasn't the people who made *Taxi Driver*'s fault, and it wasn't my family's fault, and it wasn't society's fault, and it wasn't anyone else's fault.

Just me. Just me and the warped mind that had taken control and turned me into someone who did the worst of the worst. Who did the epitome of evil.

But if my main target could forgive me, I felt that everyone else could and should as well. In 1983, I tried to write a note to the president, pouring my heart into how sorry I was. My reward was a visit from the Secret Service. But what I didn't know, and wouldn't for years, was that President Reagan had actually asked to meet with me himself, that very year.

Yes. Right in the middle of a trip on Air Force One, Reagan (who, as we've seen, made many expressions of sympathy toward both my family and me) asked his own physician about forgiving me face to face.

What I wouldn't have given to have that happen. Even up to the time he died, I dreamed of that moment.

Obviously, it never took place. But the president's son, inspired by his dad, said that he forgave me as well. I hope more and more have and will do so in the future.

"What was good enough for my father is good enough for me," Michael Reagan said shortly after my release. "When he asked God, the Father, to 'forgive us our trespasses as we forgive those who trespass against us,' he meant it. I'm not going to be angry for the rest of my life at a mentally disturbed guy who tried to take my father's life. My father didn't hate Hinckley. Why should I?"

"I found out he wasn't thinking on all cylinders. I added him to my prayers that if I wanted healing for myself, and maybe he should have some healing for himself."

Ronald Reagan, January 1990.

This book was never written for sympathy. It wasn't to justify what I did. Because I can't.

The name of John Hinckley Jr. will always have a huge black mark on it, long after I'm gone. American history stamped it there, and it's never going to go away. I think I just wanted to maybe rub a little bit of it off, as much as I ever could. It's about me very much wanting people to see and know more of me. Not as John Hinckley Jr., the crazed killer—or not *just* that, as that will always be ascribed to me—but as a guy who always wanted to be so much more than that. Who wanted so much better, even if he never truly achieved it.

It's still awkward for me today. I leave my house, go to McDonald's, food shop, whatever. I never know who might recognize me. People might walk past me in public and think, *That's the guy that tried to kill the president!* I worry about what they might do if they did. I'm all over social media, so my physical location around Williamsburg, Virginia isn't exactly a secret.

I try to keep a very low profile. I don't say much, even hello, all that often. I don't do eye contact if at all possible. I try to avoid having my name said when I'm out and about, by myself or others. You never know who might recognize it.

What are people going to say and think? What do I expect? I'm pretty sure they're not going to think of me and say, "Well, other than shooting the president, he's probably an okay guy!"

Actually, scratch that. As strange as it sounds, I do sort of hope they end up feeling like that, in a weird sort of way. It seems crazy to say it, to think, and now, here, to write it, but I hope people don't judge me all the way by one horrific act. They shouldn't forget it nor brush it aside, but just see that I'm not a bad guy in totality. I don't want them to see me as a horrible person, but one who was sick, sick enough to do what, again, to me, somehow seemed acceptable.

And it seems like more and more people are feeling that way. My daily routine isn't much different from anyone else's.

I get up. I go out and shop. I come home and play my guitar, write some songs, go on the internet to spread the word about my music, hoping someone with a venue and an empty stage one night might give me a chance. I grab an easel and some brushes and get rolling on my next cat painting, or put the latest one for sale on the 'net. I get on the phone every day and chat with my friends, some of whom I've stayed in touch with since we were fellow St. Elizabeth's residents.

Never having been anywhere close to an extrovert, I still keep a low profile. I don't go out of my way to start conversations with people. There's always a certain amount of concern that someone might see me and, even decades after the fact, still look for their own form of revenge, but that hasn't happened. People are more likely to walk up, shake my hand, ask for a photo. Some even compliment me for what I did or tell me that what I went through, and still do, is inspiring to them, which I think is frightening. I don't mind holding forth with strangers about certain issues, especially my music career, to an extent, but I try to exit the chat fast if people put a positive on what I did. I would never try to do that, and anyone who would really creeps me out. It was a different time, and the person I was back then is unrecognizable to me now. I wish he was so to everyone else, but if you're only known for one major event in your life, people are going to bring it up. I wish they wanted to know more about me besides my mistakes.

I actually get that quite often on my YouTube page. Even people who weren't around when I did what I did contact me to tell me I'm something of an inspiration. Not because of what I did, but because of what I did afterward. They talk about how I battled mental illness and came out okay. Many of them, and others they know, are in the same battles, and they see me as a symbol of someone who can do it. The world of the mentally ill is often senseless and terrifying. It's sad, for so long, knowing you won't fit in in the real world, at least not yet. But winning it isn't always a fully uplifting experience either. You're depressed that you missed out on so many wonderful things that life can offer because your focus was so jumbled elsewhere.

I think most people who know me, at least since I unscrambled my mind, would think the same way. I think people who meet me might be surprised to know just how far I've come in the past four decades. I learned to leave my judging ways outside when I was at St. Elizabeth's. I met some people who had done some horrific things—some I felt were so much worse than mine, if certainly far less visible—and I thought they were disgusting people at first. But over time, and interacting with them, I realized that wasn't true. I learned not to look down too far at people for the horrible mistakes they'd made.

I spent enough time around them to see more than just their horrible sins. Hell, if I'd felt that way, I never would have gone near Leslie! This woman killed her own child, and many people would have wanted her taken out about three seconds after they learned it. But she taught me a lot about acceptance. She showed me as much love as anyone I'd ever known. I hope I had some of the same effects on her. If I'd leaped as quickly to judgment as many did about her, and certainly had about me, I would have missed out on maybe the greatest experience of my life.

That was how things worked at St. Elizabeth's. It was how I learned to think. It was how I found a new willingness to know the people I was around. It was common for fellow patients to say to me, "Man, that guy did this!" or "She did that!" which almost always led to something horrific. That affected me up to a point for a while, but eventually it went away. I'd spent about 98% of my life living in my own world, my own head. Now was a chance to expand it, and spending time with these people gave me a way to do so.

Most of them weren't inherently evil human beings, not all the way. There was good in them if someone was willing to look for it. I hope people can figure that out toward me.

I'm not the same person I was back in the early 1980s. I wouldn't want to be. Even if I'd never been put away, I would still like to think that I would have changed over time. Anyone who's the same person after that many years has wasted far too much of their life. As much as anyone who did what I did ever could, I hope I've changed. No one will ever forget, or even put all the way behind them, my actions that tragic day, but I hope they can move past it. Move on and move up. That's what I've been trying to do, and it's not always easy. Of course, everyone always puts my name right next to that act, but when I think about it, it's hard for me to comprehend. Maybe it's because I don't like remembering my horrible act, but I think it's because I've turned a few corners. The guy who did that is nowhere close to who I am now, and I haven't been him for a very, very long time. I think I'd gotten away from him long before I was released from St. Elizabeth's.

I think that's more of why you're reading this right now. Again, not for sympathy. God knows I don't deserve that. I've done the whole self-pity thing before, for far too long, mainly because no one could understand me in this totally messed-up world. No one wanted to hear from me at all, which started long before I shot anyone. I was just tired of things not working out. I was tired of people desperately wanting to see me as some sort of monster, some sub-human creature who took a human life because he's just an evil SOB. I'm too old, and it has been too long, for me to go around begging people to forgive me. I know who I am. I know who I was. People like me or they don't. After seven decades, over four since I became the worst kind of household name, they're not going to change their mind either way.

I think it's just more for understanding. Understanding that yes, there's more to me than that. There was more to me, not all of it especially great, in the 25 years before I shot President Reagan, and there has been more in the decades since. This is about knowing all that and accepting it. Accepting me.

As of now, I have hope. I'm 70 years old, so I know I'm closer to the end than the beginning, but I wake up every day with a reason to keep looking forward. I still have a dream. I still hope that one day, in some way, my music career can happen. Not a day went by during my decades at St. Elizabeth's that I didn't at least think about hitting the stage. Now I don't have many chances left, but I have some.

We all have that, one way or another. That hope that one day, someone might give me a new chance. Someone might come up to me and say, "Despite what you did, we'll help you with that music career. Here's a gig. Here's a place to play and an audience. If only for a few hours, your music dreams can come true."

I hope people will give me a chance. I want them to know me as something else. I want them to understand that a lot can happen in almost 45 years. I don't think I was a bad person, just a sick one. I'm not an evil fellow turned good, just a sick person who healed.

I don't really have the depression anymore. Certainly not the delusions. Jodie Foster was never going to be my lady. We were never going to be a couple. It was tough for me to accept that, and I still get down about it every once in a while, but that's my fault. I still admire her today, but it's for different reasons, not the least of which was making it through the garbage I pulled and turning it around into a career that's pulled in two Oscars and lasted a half century. Anyone who can do that, let along with some psychopath stalking you, deserves all the respect.

But I don't think I see her today any differently that her average fan. After decades in the business and the public eye, there's people everywhere who love and respect her. Many do so much more than I do. I don't really watch her work. I don't read about her. Don't really think much about her. I've put enough, or wasted enough, time on that, so much that it cost me over half my life. I was hardly a part of her life at all. Now she's a part of my sad past.

I'm trying to redeem myself, trying to find a positive light. In less than two seconds, I covered America, and much of the world, with a thick, dark cloud, one that will never truly lighten. But I'm still trying to do something right, something positive. I'm trying to redeem myself, as much as society will let me, with my creativity. My music and my art. I hope I can offer something that people want to see and learn from and respond to—and, hopefully, enjoy very much.

Even over the past few years, things haven't worked for me there either, but they still could. I'm still playing my guitar. I'm still trying to put together some songs, albums, videos, everything else. I'm on the internet as much as an upcomer can be. I still have a dream of taking a stage somewhere, firing off on my trusty guitar, and having an audience sing along, chanting my name between sets. Not quite Ed Sullivan, but good enough for me.

That day could still come. It might be all I would really need. I don't expect to hit it big, to start touring, to become music's next heartthrob smash, but I don't really want that. I just want to get up on a stage, have a huge room of people cheering for me, chanting my name, singing along, having a great time. I'm still trying to find someone, maybe a few someones, who will give me a chance.

Most people know who I am. I'm just trying really hard and hoping that maybe more and more will want to know me a little bit better.

Not surprisingly, Jodie Foster has declined to comment for this book.

REFERENCES

2 "Holdouts" Bowed to Fatigue, Pressure. (1982, June 23). *The Star-Ledger*, p. 22.

2 Men in 60s Punched Hinckley. (1981, April 3). *Orlando Sentinel*, p. 14-A.

Another Psychiatrist Gives Expert Opinion of John Hinckley Jr. (1982, June 13). *The Sunday Rutland Herald and the Sunday Times Argus*, p. 2.

Another Threat is Made. (1981, May 14). *The Kansas City Star*, p. 2A.

Araz, Mark & Baylin, Lee. (1982, May 6). Loan For Hinckley to Redeem Self Cited. *Evening Sun*, pp. A-1, A-3.

Assassination Try Link Seen. (1981, April 25). *The Hanford Sentinel*, p. 2.

Asylum for John Hinckley. (1982, June 22). *Edmonton Journal*, p. A3.

The Awful Truth. (1982, June 30). *The Morning Call*, p. A16.

Baker, Lauden. Email interview. June 3, 2025.

Bamigboye, Baz. (2012, Dec. 20). Time for Tough Guys to Drop Their Guns, Says Robert DeNiro. *Daily Mail*. Retrieved March 16, 2025, from https://www.dailymail.co.uk/tvshowbiz/

article-2251360/Robert-De-Niro-Time-tough-guys-drop-guns.
html

Baylin, Lee. (1981, November 25). *The Evening Sun*. Hinckley is
Called Severely Suicidal. pp. A1, A3.

Beck, Marilyn. (1982, May 21). Hinckley's Movie Model Helps
Some Loners. *Ottawa Citizen*, p. 68.

Beck, Marilyn. (1981, April 20). Old Insecurities Bedevil Sly in
"Rocky III." *The Star-Ledger*, p. 25.

Bizarre Thoughts and Drugs Drove Hinckley, Doctor Says. (1982,
May 20). *The Columbian*, p. 3.

Brady, James. (1990, August 29). The Brady Bill. *Floyd County
Times*, p. A4.

Brady, James. (1994, June 26). In Step With: James Brady. *Parade
Magazine*, p. 18.

Buchanan, Patrick. (1982, June 9). Who's Crazy: Hinckley or
Public. *The Dothan Eagle*, p. 4-A.

Byrnes, Jesse. (2016, July 27). Trump: Hinckley Should Not Have
Been Freed. *The Hill*. Retrieved March 16, 2025, from https://
thehill.com/blogs/blog-briefing-room/news/289430-trump-
hinckley-should-not-have-been-freed/amp/

Cauvin, Henri E. (2004, June 12). Reagan Wanted to Forgive
Hinckley. *Seattle Times*. Retrieved July 1, 2025, from https://
archive.seattletimes.com/archive/20040612/hinckley12/reagan-
wanted-to-forgive-hinckley

Cimons, Marlene. (1982, June 23). 2 Thought Hinckley Guilty,
but Gave in to Other Jurors. *Akron Beacon Journal*, p. A10.

Closing Argument: Hinckley Not a Desperate Man. (1982, June
17). *Thousand Oaks Star*, p. 23.

Connelly, Christopher. (1981, Oct. 22). Inseparable Hall and
Oates Still Doing What They Want. *Post-Bulletin*, p. 20.

Courts Calls Actress in Hinckley Probe. (1982, March 31). *The Commercial Appeal*, p. B4.

Davis Reagan, Patti. (2000, April 10). Don't let Hinckley roam free. *Time Magazine*. Retrieved Feb. 27, 2025, from https://edition.cnn.com/ALLPOLITICS/time/2000/04/10/hinckley.html

Deal on Hinckley Proposed. (1981, May 25). *Edmonton Journal*, p. A11.

Detective Says John Hinckley Helped Cop Spell "Assassinate." (1981, Oct. 27). *Casper Star-Tribute*, p. A9.

Detective Testifies John Hinckley "Seemed Normal" After Shooting. (1982, June 3). *Del Rio News-Herald*, p. 9.

Did Hinckley Invent Story of Girlfriend? (1982, May 9). *Sunday Courier & Press*, p. 12-A.

Dietrich, Tamara. (2011, December 4). Hinckley Hasn't Earned Freedom. *Daily Press*, p. A2.

Doctor Claims Hinckley Doesn't Understand Crime. (1982, May 25). *Journal Tribune*, p. 2.

Doctor: Hinckley's Actions Not Product of Delusions. (1982, June 15). *Omaha World Herald*, p. 28.

Doctor Says Hinckley Did Not Want Infamy. (1982, June 11). *The Columbian*, p. 3.

Dooley, Kirk. (1981, April 5). Hinckley Remembered As Smiling Classmate. *St. Lous Post-Dispatch*, p. 1-8C.

Family Dissolution Blamed of Threats. (1981, April 11). *Desert Sun*, p. A4.

Few Jurors Favored Conviction. (1982, June 23). *Great Falls Tribune*, p. 7-D.

Finley, Ben. (2019, March 3). Hinckley Says He's "Happy as a Clam." *Daily Press*, p. A5.

For John Hinckley, Birthday No. 27 Was Just Another Day Behind Bars. (1982, May 30). *Miami Valley Sunday News*, p. 8.

Foster, Jodie. (1980, October). Has Jodie Foster Lost Her Mind? *Esquire Magazine*, p. 40.

Foster, Jodie. (1982, December). Why Me? *Esquire Magazine*, pp. 101-8.

Gallagher, Maria & Freeman, Mike. Suspect's Link to Hinckley "Cosmic." *Philadelphia Daily News*. pp. 3, 18.

Gamperlein, Joyce. (1982, May 25). Hinckley Views Himself as a Child, Psychiatrist Says. *Philadelphia Inquirer*, p. 5-A.

Gamperlein, Joyce. (1982, June 5). Maid Says Hinckley Was Normal, "All-American." *The Philadelphia Inquirer*, p. 12-B.

Goldman, John. (1981, April 2). Notes Persistent, Actress Recalls. *Fort Worth Star-Telegram*, p. 3A.

Gordon, Gregory. (1982, May 27). Freudian Elements Emerge in Hohn Hinckley Trial. *The Herald*, p. 21.

Green, Blake. (2004, April 25). Tales of the Gun. *The Morning Call*, p. E3.

Gresko, Jessica. (2022, June 2). Full Freedom Granted to Reagan Shooter. *The Republican*, p. A9.

Hagstrom, Andres. (2022, June 15). Attempted Reagan assassin John Hinckley fully released after 41 years. *Fox News*. Retrieved Aug. 8, 2025, from https://www.foxnews.com/politics/attempted-reagan-assassin-john-hinckley-released-41-years?msockid=1171089da08a68ac21c31caea1136985

Hall, Dan. (1981, July). Conn. Man Pleads Guilty to Threat Against the President. *Lewiston Daily Sun*, p. 6.

Hall, Margaret. (1982, April 2). Targeted For Death. *Daily Mirror*, p. 5.

Hasson, Judi. (1981, Oct. 20). Guard Admits Reading John Hinckley's Papers. *Rutland Daily Herald*, p. 3.

Hasson, Judi. (1982, May 29). Hinckley Jury Sees "Taxi Driver": Defense Rests. *The State*, 2-A.

Hasson, Judi. (1982, June 19). Jury Still Deliberates on Sanity of Hinckley. *Telegraph-Forum*, p. 3.

"He's Not Crazy, He's a Genius," Jurors Claim. (1982, June 23). *The Spectator*, p. 5.

Here are transcripts of two telephone conversations between John... (1982, May 13). *United Press International*. Retrieved April 13, 2025, from https://www.upi.com/Archives/1982/05/13/Here-are-transcripts-of-two-telephone-conversations-between-John/4651390110400/

Hijack Note, Card to Jodie Foster Found in Hinckley's Room. (1982, May 6). *Wichita Eagle-Beacon*, p. 5A.

Hinckley: 20 Unexpected Answers. (1981, Oct. 4). *The State*, p. 1-A.

Hinckley Called "Exhibitionist." (1982, June 11). *The Indianapolis Star*, p. 7

Hinckley Defense Presents Closing Argument. (1982, June 18). *Abilene Reporter-News*, p. 12-A.

Hinckley Defense Rests After Viewing "Taxi." (1982, May 29). *The Daily News*, p. 12.

Hinckley Depression Halted by Shooting. (1982, May 25). *Austin American-Statesman*, p. A5.

Hinckley Enters Plea: Innocent in Shooting. (1981, Aug. 29). *The Sentinel Star*, pp. 1-A, 9-A.

Hinckley Fantasy Described. (1982, May 25). *The Kansas City Star*, p. 2A.

Hinckley Felt He Had No Other Choice: Doctor. (1982, May 19). *Indianapolis News*, p. 3.

Hinckley, Jack and Jo Ann. (1986). *Breaking Points*. Berkley Books: New York.

Hinckley, John. (2020, March 25). John Hinckley, Incredible Letter: "I detoured to Wash. D.C. and shot Reagan" and about Jodie Foster: "One day I love her, the next day I want to kill her." *University Archives*. Retrieved May 20, 2025, from https://www.universityarchives.com/auction-lot/john-hinckley-incredible-letter-i-detoured-to_679474DA69

Hinckley Jury Views Film. (1982, May 28). *Lincoln Journal Star*, p. 5.

Hinckley Lauds Reagan. (1981, Oct. 5). *Daily Sentinel*, p. 1.

Hinckley Mentioned in Yale Bomb Threat. (1981, April 7). *La Crosse Tribune*, p. 7.

Hinckley "Not Guilty" on all Counts. (1982, June 22). *The Home News*, p. 25.

Hinckley Planned Assassination: Psychiatrist. (1982, June 8). *Cleveland Press*, p. A7.

Hinckley Pleads Innocent in Shooting Reagan. (1981, Aug. 29). *Des Moines Register*, p. 6A.

Hinckley Profile. (1982, May 5). *The Baltimore Sun*, p. A11.

Hinckley Seeks Forgiveness, Claims He is Sorry. (1982, May 15). *Flint Journal*, p. D4.

Hinckley Suicide was Feared: Official. (1981, Oct. 21). *The Gazette*, p. 11a.

Hinckley to Jodie: "I'm Not Dangerous." (1981, Sept. 30). *The Morning Telegraph*, p. 1.

Hinckley to Use Insanity. (1981, Sept. 29). *The Indianapolis News*, p. 3.

Hinckley Trial Enters 5th Week. (1982, May 23). *The Anniston Star*, p. 12A.

Hinckley Use of "Honesty" Called Tipoff He's Lying. (1982, June 9). *The Indianapolis News*, p. 3.

Hinckley Weeps as Counsel Describes Him as "Pathetic." (1982, June 18). *Record-Journal*, p. 7.

Hinckley's Brain on Trial. (1982, June 10). *The Post-Standard*, p. A-10.

Hinckley's Condition Rebutted. (1982, June 5). *Bismarck Times*, p. 18.

Hinckley's Fantasies Revealed in Writings. (1982, May 6). *Transcript-Telegram*, p. 2.

Hinckley's Fate in Hands of Jurors. (1982, June 19). *Sidney Daily News*, p. 1.

Hinckley Found Innocent, Bound for Hospital. (1982, June 22). *Potomac News*, p. A2.

Hinckley's Mother Tells More Troubles. (1982, May 7). *News Chronicle*, p. 9.

Hinckley's Mother Testifies for 4 Hours. (1982, May 7). *Star-Tribune*, p. A-4.

Hinckley's Parents: Son "is a Sick Boy." (1981, April 5). *Grand Forks Herald*, p. 4D.

Hinckley's Parents Talked out of Committing Son. (1982, May 8). *Duluth News-Tribune*, p. 7B.

Hinckley's Poems Tell of Love & Life. (1982, May 6). *Daily Sentinel-Tribune*, p. 3.

Honderich, John. (1982, June 6). Thoughts Make Me Edgy, Hinckley Tells Trial Judge. *Toronto Star*, p. B4.

Hooker, Brenda. (1981, April 7). Fresh Perspectives. *Mesquite Daily News*, p. 3.

Is He Crazy About Her? (1981, Oct. 12). *Time*. Retrieved May 28, 2025, from https://time.com/archive/6858773/is-he-crazy-about-her/

Jackson, Robert L. (1982, May 15). Psychiatrist Gives Testimony Saying Hinckley Mentally Ill. *Flint Journal*, p. A5.

Jodie's Set for "O'Hara" Film. (1981, April 11). *News-Pilot*, p. B5.

John W. Hinckley Jr.: Inside the Mind of Ronald Reagan's Would-Be Assassin. (2016, August 1). *Newsweek*. Retrieved Aug. 1, 2025, from https://www.newsweek.com/john-hinckley-profile-ronald-reagan-assassination-484720

John Hinckley Achieved Peace at Last After Shooting Reagan: Psychiatrist. (1982, May 21). *Gazette*, p. D14.

John Hinckley Goes on Trial. (1982, April 28). *The Palm Beach Post*, p. A3.

John Hinckley Sued for $12 Million. (1981, Jan. 31). *The Paducah Sun*, p. A-7.

John Hinckley's Conduct Angers Judge. (1982, June 16). *Shreveport Journal*, p. 12A.

Johnson, Sandy. (1987, April 14). Hinckley Wrote Letter to Bundy. *The Island Packet*, p. 7-A.

Johnston, Steve. (1981, April 7). The Horror of Reagan Shooting Was Not Lost on Our Children. *Charlotte News*, p. 5.

Judge Warns Attorneys About Hinckley's Behavior. (1982, May 22). *Mount Vernon Argus*, p. A5.

Jurors Say Letter of Law Forced Vote for Innocent. (1982, June 23). *Chronical Tribune*, pp. 1, 8.

Jurors Study Tape of Assassination Try. (1982, May 5). *The Daily Herald*, p. 2A.

Jury Hears of Hinckley Obsession With Actress. (1982, May 13). *Salina Journal*, pp. 1, 3.

Kiernan, Laura. (1982, June 29). Hinckley: I Thought For Sure I'd be Convicted. *Minneapolis Star and Tribune*, p. 1A, 9A.

Kiernan, Laura. (1981, Sept. 20). Hinckley Pens Note to Explain Travels. *Greensboro News & Record*, p. A2.

Kiernan, Laura A. (1982, June 16). Hinckley Prosecution to End Today. *The Charlotte Observer*, p. 18A.

Kiernan, Laura. (1981, Oct. 21). John Hinckley Alleges Conspiracy. *Evening Journal*, p. A7.

Kiernan, Laura A. (1982, June 29). John Hinckley Calling. *The Greenville News*, p. 2C.

Lack of Sleep, Medication Tied to Hinckley Illness. (1982, May 18). *Evansville Press*, p. 18.

Local Citizens Stunned by Reagan Shooting. (1981, March 30). *Shreveport Journal*, p. 1B.

"Lovesick" Hinckley Upset Actress Not Showing Interest. (1981, Oct. 5). *Columbus Record*, p. 3-A.

Lewthwaite, Gilbert A. (1982, May 9). Hinckley Had Mystery Girlfriend. *Tampa Tribune*, p. 8-A.

Lewthwaite, Gilbert A. (1982, May 26). Hinckley Said to Feel He Impressed Foster. *The Sun*, p. A3.

Lewthwaite, Gilbert A. (1982, May 1). Networks Denied Foster Testimony. *The Baltimore Sun*, A7.

Margasak, Larry. (1982, June 15). Doctor: Hinckley was Daydreamer. *The Huntsville Times*, p. A-7.

Margasak, Larry. (1982, May 18). John Hinckley Weeps During Trials Final Arguments. *The Herald Palladium*, p. 15.

Margasak, Larry. (1982, April 29). Jury Selection Resumes in John Hinckley Trial. *The Paducah Sun*, p. A-5.

Margasak, Larry. (1982, May 6). Move to Dismiss Hinckley Trial Denied. *The Paducah Sun*, p. A-3.

Margasak, Larry. (1982, May 21). Psychologist Concedes He Saw Hinckley Only Twice. *Huntsville Times*, p. A-7.

McCarthy, Delahanty Testify in Trial. (1982, May 5). *The Belleville News-Democrat*, p. 2A.

McGrory, Mary (1982, May 22). Hinckley, Psychiatry in the Dark. *The Post*, p. 2D.

Mengden Opposes Insanity Plea. (1982, April 7). *The Longview Daily News*, p. 9-A.

Murdock, Deroy. (2003, November 21). The Case for Guilty-But-Insane. *Salina Journal*, p. A7.

News in a Nutshell. (1982, March 1). *Standard-Freeholder*, p. 2.

One Year That, Hinckley Still Awaits Trial. (1982, March 30). *Syracuse Post-Standard*, p. A-2.

Parents Split Over Handling Hinckley. (1982, May 10). *The Daily Dispatch*, p. 3.

People in the News. (1981, April 11). *The Sun*, p. A3.

Prosecutor: Hinckley Not Insane. (1982, June 7). *Columbus Ledger*, p. A-3.

Psychiatrist: Hinckley Knew He Was "Twerp." (1982, June 6). *San Francisco Examiner*, p. A6.

Psychiatrist Plays Down Role of Hinckley Writings. (1982, June 10). *The Post-Standard*, p. A-4.

Psychiatrist Tells Hinckley Play for Murdering Actress, Killing Himself. (1982, May 14). *Bremerton Sun*, p. 7.

Quiet Surrounds John Hinckley. (1981, May 15). *Valley News*, p. 15.

Readers' Opinions. (1982, April 7). *Birmingham News*, p. 12A.

Reagan Forgives Hinckley. (1990, January 12). *Public Opinion*, p. 7A

Reagan Gunman Reacts to Requests to Assassinate Trump. (2024, November 9). *The Day*, p. A5.

Reagan, Michael. (2021, October 4). I'm Sticking With my Father—He Forgave John Hinckley Jr. So do I: Michael Reagan. *New Jersey Herald*. Retrieved July 2, 2025, from https://www.njherald.com/story/opinion/2021/10/04/michael-reagan-forgive-john-hinckley/5990270001/

Renier, Mark. (1981, June 27). Your Opinions. *Florida Today*, p. 10.

Rosenthal, Harry F. (1982, May 19). Harvard Psychiatrist Testifies. *Jonesboro Sun*, p. 8B.

Rosenthal, Harry F. (1982, June 13). Hinckley Functioned Too Well to be Insane, Witness Says. *Sunday Herald-Leader*, p. A2.

Rosenthal, Harry F. (1982, May 13). Hinckley Runs Out of Courtroom. *Jonesboro Sun*, p. 13B.

Rosenthal, Harry F. (1982, Feb. 14). John Hinckley's Real Target Was Himself, Says Psychiatrist. *Santa Barbara News Press*, p. A-8.

Rosenthal, Harry F. (1982, June 19). Jury Deciding Fate of Man Who Shot President Reagan. *The Rapid City Journal*, p. 18.

Sargent, Wayne. (1982, January 24). Editor's Perspective. *San Bernardino County Sun*, p. AA-2.

Shapiro, David. (1981, June 14). John Hinckley: Subject of Intense FBI Investigation. *El Paso Times*, p. 1-C.

Shaw, Gaylord. (1981, March 1) Reagan Recovers Strongly; Suspect Had Mental Woes. *Buffalo News*, pp. 1, 16.

Scars Haven't Healed From Attempt on Reagan's Life. (1986, March 30). *The Enterprise*, p. 10.

Siskel, Gene. (1981, Nov. 8). Breaking Silence: Scorsese on Films and Violence. *Chicago Tribune*, p. 24-6.

Snaps, Scraps, & Scribbles. (1981, April 21). *Daily American Republic*, p. 8.

Some Evidence Barred From Hinckley's Trial. (1982, Feb. 23). *Kansas City Star*, pp. 1A, 6A.

Some Hinkley Jurors Disillusioned by Law. (1982, June 23). *Johnson City Press-Chronicle*, p. 18.

Suspect in Attack May Plead Insanity. (1981, April 3). *Orlando Sentinel*, p. 14-A.

Taylor, Stuart. (1982, July 9). Hinckley Hails "Historical" Shooting to Win Love. *New York Times*, p. 10.

Taylor, Stuart. (1982, June 19). Jury Opens Deliberations in Trial of John Hinckley Jr. *The Spokesman-Review*, p. 5.

Taylor, Stuart. (1982, May 6). Prosecutions Present John Hinckley's Writings. *Anniston Star*, p. 1D, 2D.

Tears Shed as Mother of Hinckley Testifies. (1982, May 7). *The Kansas City Times*, p. A-3.

Telephone Tapes Show Jodi Foster Talked to John Hinckley Jr. Twice. (1981, Sept. 30). *The Evening News*, p. 36.

Thornton, Mary. (1982, June 25). Some Jurors in John Hinckley Trial Say They Have Misgivings on Verdict. *The Muskegon Chronicle*, p. 3A.

Time is a Key Element in John Hinckley Case. (1981, May 29). *Hattiesburg American*, p. 6.

Van Riper, Frank. (1982, May 14). Court Hears Hinckley Tapes. *Daily Press*, p. 3.

Van Piper, Frank. (1982, June 3). Hinckley Calm, Talkative After Shooting, Witness Says. *Austin American-Statesman*, p. A4.

"Verdict Was Unjust": 2 Jurors. (1982, June 23). *Chicago Tribune*, p. 1, 6.

Weiss, Philip. (1981, April 9). The Street Was His Pulpit. *Philadelphia Daily News*, p. 18.

What Happened to Hinckley's Victims? (1982, June 23). *Chronicle-Tribune*, p. 21.

What People Are Saying. (1984, January 3). *Goldsboro News-Argus*, p. 4.

Wilbur, Del Quentin. (2011, December 11). Improving, or Still a Danger? *Lexington Herald-Leader*, p. A3.

Wilber, Del Quentin. (2011). *Rawhide Down: The Near Assassination of Ronald Reagan*. Henry Holt and Company.

Williams, Betty Anne. (1982, June 23). "Guilty" Never in Running. *Detroit Free Press*, pp. 1A, 8A.

Witness Says Hinckley Was Able to Map Plan. (1982, June 8). *The Greenville News*, p. 5A.

Your Opinions. (1981, April 13). *Florida Today*, p. 12A.

For More News About John Hinckley Jr. and Jason Norman, Signup For Our Newsletter:

http://wbp.bz/newsletter

Word-of-mouth is critical to an author's long-term success. If you appreciated this book please leave a review on the Amazon sales page:

https://wbp.bz/johnhinckleyjrr